P9-CRX-652

"In frightening times like these, what is desperately needed is an informed and wise voice that speaks clearly and with conviction about the situation we are in, and what can be done. Henry Giroux is one of the great public intellectuals of our times, and *American Nightmare* is exactly the book for people grappling with how to understand the Trump era and how to proceed. This is precisely the book that needs to be shared with friends and acquaintances. It will provoke hard thinking, bring clarity, and stimulate much-needed conversation and action."

—Robert W. McChesney, co-author of *People Get Ready: The Fight Against a Jobless Economy and a Citizenless Democracy*

"At a moment when the news cycle presents the dangers of Trumpian authoritarianism through disjointed and discrete hottakes, Giroux's wide-reaching analysis accounts for our current American nightmare with necessary historical context, and in so doing creates an aperture for resistance more meaningful than a hashtag."

—Natasha Lennard, contributing writer for *The Intercept*, co-editor of *Violence: Humans in Dark Times*

"We have no greater chronicler of these dystopian times. Giroux's critique cuts to the crux of today's authoritarian crisis, yet his voice remains one of hope that the people may collectively regain control. Even while living though systemic efforts to privatize hope, Giroux's critique enacts the sort of shared resistance that can effectively challenge authoritarianism. *American Nightmare* demonstrates how we can resist the normalization of hate, authoritarianism and alienation in Trump's America. He shows us that not only are we not alone, but we are among a majority who oppose the cruelties of American social policies."

—David H. Price, author of *Cold War Anthropology: The CIA and the Growth of Dual Use Anthropology*

"In this passionately argued volume, Henry Giroux, long known for his critical commentaries on the de-democratization of the U.S.A., on its rising inequ(al)ity and neoliberal excesses, reflects very thoughtfully on the specter of Trump's America: on its violence, cruelty, and incivility, its burgeoning authoritarianism, its inexorable edging toward a Grave Neo World: in short, a rising specter that demands to be countered at all cost if the U.S. is to be rescued from itself."

—John Comaroff, Professor of African and African American Studies and of Anthropology, Harvard University

"It is all but impossible to do justice to the value of this tapestry of explication and insight, essential elements to a broadened and deepened awareness of the horrific political and economic developments that are unfolding in America and elsewhere."

—*Chicago Life Magazine* (distributed by the *New York Times*)

"In this current era of corporate media misdirection and misinformation, *America at War with Itself* is a must-read for all Americans, especially young people. Henry Giroux is one of the few great political voices of today, with powerful insight into the truth. Dr. Giroux is defiantly explaining, against the grain, what's REALLY going on right now, and doing so quite undeniably. Simply put, the ideas he brings forth are a beacon that need to be seen and heard and understood in order for the world to progress."

—Julian Casablancas

"This cogent and hard-hitting book puts on display the many factors that are eating away at democracy in the United States as the public embraces a new brand of toxic authoritarianism. . . . The snappiest section in *America at War with Itself* contains a detailed and thought-provoking profile of Donald Trump and his vision of America animated by guns, walls, surveillance, prisons, media, wars, racism, and xenophobia. . . . Whether he is pondering the racism of police in Ferguson or the pursuit of revenge by ISIS, the author always brings us home to what this all means for us today. In this regard, he concludes: 'Violence has become America's national sport and its chief mode of entertainment.'"

—*Spirituality & Practice*

"Henry Giroux has become the Left's most articulate and insightful critic of America's distorted political life, highlighting its authoritarian turn and the political illiteracy that our culture fosters and that the media help channel into racism, the worship of money and power, and an ethos of survival-of-the-fittest that produces the foundation for renewed fascistic movements. The alternative is a critical pedagogy linked to an ongoing project of democratization and 'the defense of public spheres capable of producing thoughtful citizens, critically engaged communities, and an ethically and socially responsible society.' Giroux manages to link together almost every dysfunctional aspect of American society in a cohesive account that is really important to read!"

—*Tikkun Magazine*

"Giroux, a public intellectual, academic, and prolific author, sounds a wake-up call about growing threats to democracy. He observes that cutthroat capitalism nurtures intolerant viewpoints that muzzle opposition and label swaths of society as undesirable outsiders. Popular media and hyper consumerism emphasize celebrity culture and material distractions over civic engagement, creating social passivity. Education focuses on technical skills and multiple-choice tests, rather than helping students see how knowledge can lead to an effective life. Time and money are being shaped by nonstop markets and a get-rich mania, not by long-term investment in the public good. Giroux prescribes ways to teach critical thinking. . . . His argument for active citizenship is important and stimulating."

—*Booklist*

AMERICAN NIGHTMARE

Facing the Challenge of Fascism

Henry A. Giroux

Foreword by George Yancy

City Lights Books | Open Media Series

Open Media Series Editor: Greg Ruggiero

ISBN: 978-0-87286-753-6

Cover photograph: Roger Ballen

Library of Congress Data
Names: Giroux, Henry A., author.
Title: American nightmare : facing the challenge of facism / Henry A. Giroux
  ; foreword by George Yancy.
Description: San Francisco : City Lights Books, [2018] | Includes index.
Identifiers: LCCN 2017058312 (print) | LCCN 2018012428 (ebook) |
ISBN
  9780872867796 | ISBN 9780872867536
Subjects: LCSH: United States—Politics and government—2016- | Trump,
  Donald, 1946- | Authoritarianism—United States. | Political
  culture—United States.
Classification: LCC E912 (ebook) | LCC E912 .G569 2018 (print) | DDC
  320.0973—dc23
LC record available at https://lccn.loc.gov/2017058312

City Lights books are published at the City Lights Bookstore
261 Columbus Avenue, San Francisco, CA 94133
www.citylights.com

CONTENTS

To Julian and Sam for their talents and courage

To the memory of Zygmunt Bauman

To Simona and a future filled with hope

To Susan for everything

To Robin D.G. Kelley for his brilliance, compassion, and courage

"It is far easier to act under conditions of tyranny than it is to think."

—Hannah Arendt

"The strategic adversary is fascism . . . the fascism in us all, in our heads and in our everyday behavior, the fascism that causes us to love power, to desire the very thing that dominates and exploits us."

—Michel Foucault

fascism | ˈfaSHˌizəm | (also Fascism)
an authoritarian and nationalistic right-wing system of government and social organization.

• (in general use) extreme right-wing, authoritarian, or intolerant views or practice.

The term Fascism was first used of the totalitarian right-wing nationalist regime of Mussolini in Italy (1922–43); the regimes of the Nazis in Germany and Franco in Spain were also Fascist. Fascism tends to include a belief in the supremacy of one national or ethnic group, a contempt for democracy, an insistence on obedience to a powerful leader, and a strong demagogic approach.

1920s: from Italian *fascismo*, from *fascio* "bundle, political group", from Latin *fascis* (see fasces).

—definition of "fascism" in the Oxford online dictionary

FOREWORD
FACING THE CHALLENGES:
THE URGENCY OF NOW

AMERICAN NIGHTMARE: FACING THE CHALLENGE OF FASCISM IS A SCREAM IN THE NIGHT. It is, in the words of Rabbi Abraham Joshua Heschel, a prophetic scream, one designed to pierce America's political nihilism and ethical lethargy. Henry A. Giroux's critically engaging, persuasively brilliant, ethically astute and politically forthright text speaks courageously during this moment in U.S. history as our fragile democratic experiment stands to be dismantled by the emergence of an insidious form of neo-fascism embodied in the character, ideology, decision-making, rhetoric, tweets, populism, demagoguery, and person of Donald Trump.

As Giroux's book title unequivocally states, Trump's grip on power is, indeed, a collective nightmare. The monstrous reality that we now face, however, is not like the hauntings experienced during our nightly dreams. After all, even if sweating and flailing result from an experienced nightmare, we awaken from it, happily so, realizing that we were only dreaming. Trumpism is not a dream; it's a painful reality. And lest we think otherwise, toward the very end of Giroux's powerful text, he reminds us, "The time to wake up is now."

As one of our most vocal and prolific contemporary public intellectual gadflies, Giroux refuses to allow us to sleep or become seduced by a totalitarian figure whose somnolent discourse has forced many, primarily white people, to abdicate their responsibility to contest evil when they see it. Then again, perhaps the seduction is so great, perhaps the feeling of hopelessness is so overwhelming, perhaps the activated racist and xenophobic hatred is so deep, that many have sold their souls to a Faustian figure who promises a utopia predicated upon a dystopian America in which white nation-building finally expunges those people deemed "disposable," those dangerous ethical values deemed "un-American," and those politically resistant practices deemed "unfit" for the maintenance of a totalitarian order.

Trumpists' racially coded slogan "Make America Great Again" has very little meaning to those who have always known the United States as a place that has systematically failed to be true to its ideals or those creeds written on parchment. What Trump really seems to be signaling is to *make America white again*. Taking cues from his favorite president, Andrew Jackson, Trump's discourse evokes ethnic cleansing, a racially "pure" nation where white people enjoy privileges and the rest are consigned to a trail of tears, as it were. Trump's nationalism is predicated upon the logic of Nordicism, an ideology of white purity, and the goal of keeping the country clean of undesirables from "shithole countries." For Trump, making America great again seems to involve keeping the border door open exclusively for white people from countries like Norway. "Dystopia," as Giroux makes clear, "is no longer the stuff of fiction; it has become the new reality."

Like Martin Luther King Jr., Giroux writes with a sense that social injustice is both a chronic intergenerational condition, and urgent to address in the here and now. Like James Baldwin, he recognizes that action requires commitment and that commitment is dangerous within the context of hegemonic orders that subject critical consciousness to erasure. And like Rabbi Abraham Joshua Heschel, he knows that America is in a state of moral emergency, standing on the precipice of self-destruction. Not only is this warning, this impeding doom, articulated by Giroux's critically observant discourse and astute historical, social, and political analysis, but the book's cover photograph conveys a semiosis of ghostly doom through the powerful artistic genius of Roger Ballen. Giroux's choice of imagery critically frames, for many of us, our contemporary mood. He writes, "The nightmare we had thought might one day arrive is here." Looking at the cover photography, which is thematically connected to the analyses throughout text, one is confronted by disturbed gazes. The faces are spectral figures, apparitions that are haunting to look at. And yet, one is forced to ask if those figures are in fact ourselves looking into the chasm of authoritarianism, neo-fascism, and unadulterated white nativism. The faces appear frozen, monstrous even. Like Trump's vision for America, the cover image functions to communicate a foreboding force waiting to seize and destroy all that is possible should we succumb to fascist silence and paralysis instead of building networks of solidarity with those who don't look like us, and uplift and fight on behalf of those who have been politically, socially, and economically marginalized and oppressed.

As the Spanish artist Francisco Goya might say, Trump's America is producing conditions where ethical inaction and conformity call forth monsters. Giroux makes it painfully clear that under Trumpism, a pervasive contempt for reason has become a poisonous feature of our contemporary political moment. Giroux's argument is not that this unreason—or even anti-reason—has never existed before in U.S. history. Rather, he argues that what we are witnessing is an open manifestation of racism, xenophobia, and militarism, accompanied by a divisive, hateful, violent, and exclusionary discourse perhaps not seen since President Andrew Jackson's vicious crusade to erase Native American civilization and subjugate people of color by keeping them permanently enslaved.

For Giroux, we are also witnessing a global expression of cynicism regarding the value of democracy itself. Not only in America, but also in Western Europe, as Giroux makes clear, people have "become more cynical about the value of democracy as a possible system, less hopeful that anything they do might influence public policy, and more willing to express support for authoritarian alternatives."

For Giroux, there is also a pervasive tendency toward skepticism regarding the radical possibilities inherent within our collective social imagination. He links this to a growing authoritarianism that wages a war on critical thought itself, social diversity, education, dissent, solidarity, and community.

We are witnessing a failure to risk, a refusal to be in danger, a fear to speak courageously against a burgeoning authoritarian regime that desires to evacuate reason and to masquerade as the "new normal," where ignorance and doublespeak are valorized. There is nothing historically new about the normalization of official irrationality, conformity, or fascism. It is the toxic absurdity of dictatorship. None of this is lost on Giroux, whose critical analysis exposes our contemporary moment as one that is indicative of the theater of the absurd where Trump lives out his middle-school fantasies of size, popularity, and supremacy.

And Giroux recognizes just how Trumpism is orchestrated to give social legitimacy to a herd mentality and sycophantic worship. Within this context, parrhesia, or courageous speech, is in fact dangerous. Michel Foucault understood that parrhesia was a mandate that one speak the truth regardless of the danger. Giroux's engaging text neither minces words nor underestimates the deep existential and political gravity of our situation. In short, like the parrhesiastes, he refuses to remain silent, but risks speaking the truth. He writes, "Resistance is no longer an option: it is now a matter of life or death." There is profound urgency in Giroux's voice, in his writing, in his clarion call for resistance. To say that there is no option means that what is required is the insistence of critically informed action.

Of course, many of us, Black people, for example, have always known the painful truth of that disjunction. But now the entire planet is imperiled by an impulsive and unstable commander-in-chief who casually threatens to use nuclear weapons in Twitter taunts to foreign leaders.

Giroux suggests that the United States needs to be brought "to a halt" through multiple forms of resistance. After all, capitalism is able to sustain itself precisely through exploitation, commodification, and consumption. Indeed, it is also able to consume oppositional spaces, often allowing resistance to take place just enough to sustain political hope and a sense of optimism that things will improve. Giroux is aware of capitalism's consumptive allure and Trump's desire for absolute power. Giroux, in fact, reminds us that capitalism and democracy are not the same. Hence, Giroux demands more. He writes, "Those who believe in a radical democracy must find a way to make this nation ungovernable by the powers that currently claim governing authority." By this, Giroux does not mean chaos, but a fundamental undoing of various social, political, economic, epistemic, and pedagogical logics that continue to atomize who and what we are and that continue to separate us. The idea is that civil society, through solidarity and resistance, possesses the power to foreclose Trumpian attempts to impose supremacy and what Giroux insightfully calls "dead zones of the imagination." He writes that these zones are "wedded to a society addicted to consumerism, war, militarism, economic exploitation, and self-promotion." He links the production of such zones to Trump's masterful deployment of "pedagogies of repression."

Giroux is fundamentally rethinking the very concept of how we suffer, of how the ways in which we are oppressed are mutually entangled and require collective action. In this context, Giroux suggests oppositional ways of rethinking and re-imagining the concept of sociality. This cuts at the very social ontological core of what we mean by "the human." This is partly why he writes, "Single-issue movements will have to join with others in supporting both a comprehensive politics and a mass collective movement." Central to Giroux's political outlook and revolutionary élan vital is the importance of oppositional politics; an oppositional politics undergirded, driven, and shaped by critical *collective* praxis. This collectivity is linked to Giroux's brilliant concept of democracy in exile, which is "the space in which people, families, networks, and communities fight back."

Dr. Martin Luther King Jr. spoke of creating spaces of unified power and collective agency. It is this critical and collective consciousness that pre-fascist societies and hegemonic totalitarian regimes fear. Giroux is deeply cognizant of both the potential embedded within oppositional collective praxis and the danger that they represent for a Trumpian white supremacy and unbridled ignorance and divisiveness. He is aware of and passionately speaks for a form of "critical consciousness in which individuals and groups allow themselves to embrace the condition of exile—with its underlying message of being flawed—in solidarity with their brothers and sisters who are targeted because of their politics, gender, religion, residency status, race, sexual preference, and country of origin." This condition of exile speaks powerfully to the very process of decentralization and the construction of new and oppositional modes of re-mapping the ways in which we have been divided and rendered forlorn—made to suffer alone.

Giroux's *American Nightmare* is a text of critically informed hope, one that sustains our humanity and compassion. It is also a call for greater solidarity, for the building of bridges, and for forms of intellectual and ethical self-defense that will help us rise up and face the challenges of fascism. Giroux concludes his complex, insightful, and provocative text with the words of one of the most prominent and prophetic writers in American history. I, too, end with the words of James Baldwin: "People who shut their eyes to reality simply invite their own destruction, and anyone who insists on remaining in a state of innocence long after that innocence is dead turns himself into a monster."

—George Yancy, Professor
of Philosophy, Emory University
May 1, 2018

STARING INTO THE AUTHORITARIAN ABYSS

With the rise of Donald Trump to the pinnacle of U.S. political and military power, America has descended, as never before, into a drama styled after theater of the absurd. Unbridled anti-intellectualism, deception, and "vindictive chaos" have created the conditions for repeating elements of a morally reprehensible past in the guise of "Making America Great Again." Advancing an alarmist agenda bolstered by "alternative facts," the Trump presidency has unleashed a type of anti-politics that unburdens people of any responsibility to challenge—let alone change—the fundamental precepts of a society torn asunder by open bigotry, blatant misogyny, massive inequality, and violence against immigrants, Muslims, the economically disadvantaged, and communities of color.[1] Immersed in crisis, America now mimics a failing state as the credibility of its democratic institutions and the trustworthiness of its leadership openly depreciate on the global stage.[2]

Despite all his fabrications and posturing, Trump's contempt for democratic processes has been exceeded only by his commitment to nepotistically favoring his family and fellow members of the country-club elite. Trump's ascendancy has revealed the degree to which acute political illiteracy, corruption, and contempt for reason have become defining features of present-day U.S. culture. His rise has involved using threats of violence and intimidation to shock and incite everyday people, and is preceded by a serious decline of American public life. Taken with relentless lying and targeted attacks on dissent, the result is a political climate that recalls those of past pre-fascist societies. Trump is not simply unfit to be president, he is a "political weapon of mass self-destruction for American democracy," says Henry Aaron, a senior fellow at Brookings.[3] Seen in this light, Trumpism is symptomatic of the decline of the United States into a new, commercially integrated, American-style fascism. While sectors of Trumpist fascism may re-use imagery from European symbols of the 1930s, its actual roots extend directly from the absolute white supremacy of the settler-colonial origins of the United States and its subsequent racialized economic history of destroying and erasing Native American civilizations and enslaving, breeding, and subordinating Africans and people of color for generations. It will take great struggle for the American public to come to terms with the voices and narratives of this history, and even greater struggle to overcome the ways Trumpism is giving new social legitimacy and political form to these racist legacies today.

The danger signs are not just in the United States.

Movements in North America and across Europe are exhibiting growing support for right-wing extremist politicians and political movements, though there was one respite with the 2017 presidential election in France with centrist Emmanuel Macron's victory over far-right leader Marine Le Pen. Unemployment, wage stagnation, vision-less futures, a growing sense of precarity and insecurity for working and lower middle classes, and an increasing sense of atomization and alienation—all of it fueled by austerity measures, a growing worldwide culture of fear, and a permanent war culture—are undermining not only the foundations of democracy, but a belief in the value of democracy itself.[4] Many people now find themselves living in societies in which they experience a kind of social homelessness, detached from and invisible to the policies and language of those in power.

As Hannah Arendt, Simone Weil, and Erich Fromm, among others, have reminded us, rootlessness creates the conditions for an escape from freedom and social responsibility, and finds meaning in the foundations of totalitarianism. After reviewing a number of Harvard University reports analyzing historical and current attitudes on the part of millennials in North America and Europe, Gwynn Guilford concludes that young people have grown weary of democracy. Not only have many millennials lost their faith in democracy, but many are less willing to oppose military coups and no longer view civil rights as absolutely essential; more than a quarter dismiss the importance of free elections to democracy.[5] Roberto Stefan Foa and

Yascha Mounk argue that support for authoritarianism is increasingly apparent. They write:

> Citizens in a number of supposedly consolidated democracies in North America and Western Europe have not only grown more critical of their political leaders. Rather, they have also become more cynical about the value of democracy as a political system, less hopeful that anything they do might influence public policy, and more willing to express support for authoritarian alternatives. The crisis of democratic legitimacy extends across a much wider set of indicators than previously appreciated.[6]

The growing protest movements against fascism in general, and against the Trump regime in particular, offer hope against this dismal prediction. But the fight against the politics of hate operates in a difficult historical moment, one in which many people feel abandoned by both the ruling elite and the political left. The language of intolerance now seriously threatens the survival of the institutions that make a critical formative culture possible. Marsha Gessen describes how "Donald Trump has an instinct for doing . . . violence to language:"

> He is particularly adept at taking words and phrases that deal with power relationships and turning them into their opposite. This was, for

example, how he used the phrase "safe space" when talking about vice-president-elect Mike Pence's visit to the musical Hamilton. Pence, if you recall, was booed and then passionately—and respectfully—addressed by the cast of the show. Trump was tweeting that this should not have happened. Now, the phrase "safe space" was coined to describe a place where people who usually feel unsafe and powerless would feel exceptionally safe. Claiming that the second most powerful man in the world should be granted a "safe space" in public turns the concept precisely on its head. Trump performed the exact same trick on the phrase "witch hunt," which he claimed was being carried out by Democrats to avenge their electoral loss. Witch hunts cannot actually be carried out by losers, big or small: the agent of a witch hunt must have power. And, of course, he has seized and flipped the term "fake news" in much the same way.[7]

The world is now witnessing how the conditions that have been undermining U.S. democracy over the last forty years have brought us to a place where resurgent forms of nativism, racism, and misogyny, have consolidated and aligned as a social base for an authoritarian, corporate, political-economic order. Trump's emergence signals the successful merger of white ultra-nationalism with the forces of unfettered corporate power. And it is this lethal combination that poses, as the *Washington Post* observed, a "unique threat to democracy."[8]

While U.S. courts initially blocked Trump's various versions of an immigration ban, he has unleashed and emboldened a rising culture of hate and violence that has led to attacks on immigrants, Blacks, Jews, transgender people, and institutions and individuals deemed anti-American. Synagogues have been bombed, white supremacist slogans have been painted on schools, students have shamelessly shouted racial slurs at classmates, and militant right-wing groups have attacked those attending anti-Trump rallies. A particularly violent display of racism took place on May 26, 2017, in Portland, on a light-rail train. Three men were stabbed by Jeremy Joseph Christian, a white supremacist, as they attempted to intervene after Christian hurled religious slurs at two females, one of whom was wearing a hijab. Two of the men were killed. While appearing at his first court date, flanked by two deputies in the courtroom, Christian unapologetically yelled, "Get out if you don't like free speech. . . . You call it terrorism, I call it patriotism. You hear me? Die." He followed up with "Death to the enemies of America. Leave this country if you hate our freedom."[9]

For those who defend equality, justice, and democracy as fundamental principles and essential elements of American society, the time for equivocation and half measures is over. Trump is more than an opportunistic clown who leveraged his reality-show celebrity for political gain; he has been a vehicle for right-wing populism by rousing

uneducated white fear and committing it to a pro-corporate economic agenda.[10] As Gessen has demonstrated, this
is a populism that relies on the blunt hammer of ignorance,
a "rejection of the complexity of modern politics," and a
disdain for expertise.[11]

Trump is wedded to both the spectacle and use of
power—a position made all the more dangerous given that,
unlike his Russian counterpart, Vladimir V. Putin, Trump
is a "poorly educated, under-informed, incurious man
whose ambition is vastly out of proportion to his understanding of the world."[12] He is also a racist, a demagogue,
and a neoliberal fundamentalist who is contemptuous of
dissent, truth, and the basic norms of political life. As is
evident in the rise of numerous modes of fascism since the
1920s, authoritarianism takes many forms, and aligns itself with the worse dimensions of the historical contexts
in which it gains political and ideological currency. Trump
is the endpoint of a social order that values self-interest
over compassion, profit over basic human needs, and corruption over justice. Trump is not simply a liar. He has
no regard for the truth, empathy, or reality itself. Trump's
world is the underside of a fascistic movement that feeds
on fantasies, paranoia, alternative realities, conspiracy theories, and self-aggrandizement. Trump's authoritarianism
is on display on many levels: in the menacing tone of his
populist rallies, in his public humiliation of his own staff,
in his open threat of Republican rivals, in his relentless
falsehoods and fabrications, in his alignment with bigots
and nationalists, and in his embrace of violence, coercion,

and militarism. Paraphrasing former White House advisor Steve Bannon, Trump unabashedly presents himself to his base as the blunt instrument of a populist authoritarian movement. As David Goldberg has pointed out, what is most disturbing today—and Trump personifies this position—"is the license to say and act in blatantly racist ways with little restraint, magnified by a deafening lack of condemnation and constraint by those in a position to delimit the expression."[13]

What Trump makes clear is the dystopian side of an ideology that enshrines existing relations of power as a matter of common sense while endorsing ignorance as a virtue. Coupled with a systemic culture of fear, ignorance sustains itself by looking everywhere for enemies while occupying the high ground of political purity and an empty moralism. I think the artist Sable Elyse Smith is right in arguing that ignorance is more than the absence of knowledge or the refusal to know, it is also a form of violence that is woven into the fabric of everyday life by powerful disimagination machines, and its ultimate goal is to enable us to not only consume pain and to propagate it, but also to relish in it as a form of entertainment and emotional uplift. This is a culture of social abandonment and terminal exclusion. Justice in this discourse is disposable, along with the institutions that make it possible. What is distinctive about Trump is that he defines himself through the ideology of ignorance while employing it to fill government positions and produce death-dealing policies. Trump is a master at putting into play pedagogies of repression that reproduce what I have called dead zones of the imagination, zones endemic to a society addicted to consumerism, war, militarism, economic exploitation, and self-promotion.[14] Trump is not the stranger in the night banging menacingly on our front door. Far from an abnormality, he is the overt and unapologetic symbol of a feral capitalism that has been decades in the making. He is the theatrical postmodern self-absorbed Frankenstein monster that embodies and makes clear a history of savagery, greed, and predatory cruelty that has reached its endpoint—a poisonous form of American authoritarianism. As John Steppling writes, "he is the sun-lamped face of capital."[15]

Dystopia is no longer the stuff of fiction; it has become the new reality. But underlying Trumpism's dark and poisonous assaults on the imagination is a truth worth remembering. At the center of resistance, politics, and hope is the power of educating people to a more promising reality, one that unmasks the falsehood and fear upon which fascism depends. Authoritarians live in fear of criticism, dissent, community, solidarity, and the social imagination. Brad Evans captures it well in his comment on the importance of language and books:

> If you don't provide people with the intellectual tools to empower critically minded subjects, you end up with incarcerated minds. A world without books is a world foreclosed. Every great tyranny begins by declaring a war upon the imagination and the appropriation or imprisonment of those

deemed to be its most creative. The question is why? Imagining other worlds runs counter to the fascistic impulse to impose a forced unity upon a people. Tyrants always try to suffocate and replace the richness of the human condition with dogmatic images of thought.[16]

And it is precisely in the recognition and struggle against the imagination, the war on truth, and the attack on democratic public spheres that the power and horror of authoritarian rule becomes visible and therefore vulnerable. Albert Camus understood this threat well. He warned us about how the plague of authoritarianism can reappear in updated forms. For Camus, the disease of fascism could best be initially fought with the antibody of consciousness, one that embraced the past as a way of protecting the future. The words that form the concluding paragraph of *The Plague* are as relevant today as they were when they were written more than half a century ago. Camus writes:

[As] he listened to the cries of joy rising from the town, Rieux remembered that such joy is always imperiled. He knew what those jubilant crowds did not know but could have learned from books: that the plague bacillus never dies or disappears for good; that it can lie dormant for years and years in furniture and linen chests; that it bides its time in bedrooms, cellars, trunks, and bookshelves; and that perhaps the day would come

when, for the bane and the enlightening of men,
it would rouse up its rats again and send them
forth to die in a happy city.[17]

One place to begin is with reason and truth, and how fundamental they are to creating critically engaged citizens and communities. As both reason and truth come under attack, it is essential to advance democracies in exile—or what has been called the project of a parallel polis—oppositional political and pedagogical social formations that spread within authoritarian societies to preserve and advance social justice, egalitarianism, political tolerance, cultural diversity, and vibrant democracy-centered community.

A Politics of the Indefensible

In the age of Trump, there is a great deal of evidence to suggest that any appeal to reason, critical thought, and informed judgment would be at odds with the Republican-dominated political culture, if not the 91 percent of his political base who support his performance regardless of what he says or does.[18] Many Americans seem to display a growing fondness for misinformation, an attitude that reinforces the disintegration of the civic culture and even the communicative function of language, which Trumpists strongly reinforce. As Lucy Marcus has observed, "Nowadays, facts and truth are becoming [more] difficult to uphold in politics (and in business and even sports)."[19] Indeed, falsehood and deception no longer appear marginal to political debate; they now seem to shape much of what is spoken in the public sphere, even by U.S. presidential candidates. This includes the former Democratic presidential candidate Hillary Clinton, whose email scandal is surely symptomatic of a deeper level of dishonesty than her apparent penchant for serial lying.[20] Matters of corporate power, economic injustice, state violence, widespread poverty, institutional racism, a broken criminal justice system, the school-to-prison pipeline, and the existence of the mass incarceration state, among other important matters, rarely entered her discourse during the 2016 presidential campaign, and yet these are major issues negatively affecting the lives of millions of children and adults in the United States.

The politics of deceit has reached alarming new heights with Trump, whose campaign and presidency have been the source of endless falsehoods. When Trump is caught in a falsehood, he simply ignores the facts and just keeps on lying or switches the topic. Matthew Yglesias in *Vox* has argued that Trump's misrepresentations are not lies in the sense of trying to mislead his audience. On the contrary, Yglesias argues, "Trump provides the public with a steady diet of bullshit [with the intent] of both endlessly reinscribing polarization in American politics . . . corroding America's governing institutions, [and] poisoning civic life."[21] Yglesias claims that Trump has no interest in accuracy or persuasion, and that his endless stream of fictions are part of his attempt to create a separate language meant to distinguish his fan base from his enemies, to enforce what he calls "trust and loyalty in his followers."[22] Yglesias is only partly right.

Trump persistently tests his subordinates by seeing who "around him will debase themselves to repeat" his lies.[23] But Trump's violence to language is used to do more than test the fealty of officials and underlings. He also uses language and lies to both persuade and distract people from reality, to "create enough confusion about basic facts" in order to normalize his preferred policies as sensible so that he can legitimate his right-wing policies and corrupt politics.[24] Trump's lies are part of the spectacle of distraction fueled by a long history in which large sectors of corporate media have been all too willing to surrender their pursuit of the truth for pursuit of commercial enrichment.[25]

Trumpists seem to care little about whether their public servants, particularly the president, deceive them or not. Nationwide support for militant right-wing politicians resonates strongly with Trump's attacks on trade policies that produced massive unemployment, deindustrialization, despair, and little hope for them or their families for the future. Trump's critique of companies moving their facilities abroad, his call for competitive bidding in the drug industry and military-industrial complex, fuel their disdain for the ruling elite, outlandish CEO salaries, and a two-party system that bailed out the banks but left American towns to rot in despair and misery. Principles of equality, egalitarianism, and meritocracy, however frail, are no longer espoused by the major political parties. Many of Trump's supporters respond to his criticism of crumbling infrastructures that affect their towns, neighborhoods, and cities, and recognize that such neglect was more often than not the result of government indifference to the needs of low-income areas and the common good. The despair that has ravaged the towns and cities of many Trump supporters is real. As Anne Case and Angus Deaton have shown in their studies, the mortality rates from drugs, alcohol, and suicide, which they call "deaths of despair," have reached alarming heights among working-class whites with no more than a high school diploma. They also observe that this pattern has spread across the country, and there is no end in sight. In addition, they observe that deteriorating economic conditions are a powerful force, but that they are only part of the story.

> Many commentators have suggested that poor mortality outcomes can be attributed to contemporaneous levels of resources, particularly to slowly growing, stagnant, and even declining incomes; we evaluate this possibility, but find that it cannot provide a comprehensive explanation. . . . We propose a preliminary but plausible story in which cumulative disadvantage from one birth cohort to the next, in the labor market, in marriage and child outcomes, and in health, is triggered by progressively worsening labor market opportunities at the time of entry for whites with low levels of education. This account, which fits much of the data, has the profoundly negative implication that policies, even ones that successfully improve earnings and jobs, or redistribute

income, will take many years to reverse the mortality and morbidity increase, and that those in midlife now are likely to do much worse in old age than those currently older than 65.[26]

Decades of big business rigging the political economy have taken a terrible toll on the lives of American workers. Trumpism deviously taps the resulting insecurity of white workers and weaponizes it into a sense of contempt for liberals, immigrants, Muslims, Mexicans, climate change, affordable health care, and the left in general. White Americans support Trumpist narratives because they validate anger and blame, and openly reconnect with the officially sanctioned Jacksonian national security vision—white supremacy. This is an important issue that many analysts often overlook.

Trump and Bannon, prior to their split following the publication of *Fire and Fury*, Michael Wolff's explosive exposé of Trump's mindset, more often than not used fighting words in place of ideas as pathways toward political solutions. Trumpism, as a form of nascent fascism, is being built around aggression, hatred, and violence, while coding white supremacy as an acceptable form of historical national heritage. At the same time, through his tweets and mass rallies, Trump has offered his mostly white audiences a consistent narrative that gives them a sense of visibility and symbolic community. Unfortunately, Trump's style often appeals to his supporters' juvenile fantasies. Many commentators have argued that Trump's followers are

ignorant to continue to support him in light of his perpetual lies and fabrications. Roger Berkowitz argues that
most Trump supporters don't care about his lies or that his
economic moves are designed to make the rich even richer.
What they prefer is a consistent narrative of a reality in
which they are a part. He writes:

> The reason fact-checking is ineffective today—
> at least in convincing those who are members of
> movements—is that the mobilized members of a
> movement are confounded by a world resistant to
> their wishes and prefer the promise of a consistent
> alternate world to reality. When Donald Trump
> says he's going to build a wall to protect our bor-
> ders, he is not making a factual statement that an
> actual wall will actually protect our borders; he
> is signaling a politically incorrect willingness to
> put America first. When he says that there was
> massive voter fraud or boasts about the size of
> his inauguration crowd, he is not speaking about
> actual facts, but is insisting that his election was
> legitimate. "What convinces masses are not facts,
> and not even invented facts, but only the consis-
> tency of the system of which they are presumably
> part." Leaders of these mass totalitarian move-
> ments do not need to believe in the truth of their
> lies and ideological clichés. The point of their
> fabrications is not to establish facts, but to create
> a coherent fictional reality. What a movement

demands of its leaders is the articulation of a consistent narrative combined with the ability to abolish the capacity for distinguishing between truth and falsehood, between reality and fiction.[27]

Every day that Donald Trump remains employed as a public servant is a day he takes us closer to fascism. While Clinton hardly critiqued the imperialist role played by the United States around the globe, Trump's bellicose posturing, particularly toward countries such as nuclear-armed North Korea, puts the entire world at risk.

In the aftermath of the 2016 election, it became clear that Trump and Bannon wanted to intensify a domestic war, though not just against the political establishment, but against people of color, the economically disadvantaged, transgender people, and undocumented immigrants. Trump's attorney general, Jeff Sessions, has reversed the prison reforms of the last decade and is instructing prosecutors to reinstate maximum sentencing laws, three-strikes-you're-out legislation, and other regressive and racist legislations that re-establish the worst dimensions of the police state. Eric Holder, Barack Obama's attorney general from 2009 to 2015, has stated that Sessions' policies are draconian and condemned them as an "absurd" hold-over of "failed 20th-century ideology . . . unwise and ill-informed," quipping that his "tough on crime" stance, in reality "is dumb on crime."[28] In actuality, it is much more, and serves as a disturbing reminder of the ongoing war on economically disadvantaged youth and communities of color.

The whole world is watching the Donald operate the nation's affairs like a TV game show, hyping himself and belittling rivals with the relish of a fifth grader. How have we arrived here? For one, the U.S. political establishment's foreign policy approach, which has for decades involved calls for regime change and war, has now become the dominant framework governing American society—and has been fortified by its recent alliance with state-sanctioned torture, armed ignorance, and a deep hatred of democracy. With Trump's presidency, the crisis of politics has been accelerated by a crisis of historical conscience, memory, ethics, and agency. In the process, legitimacy has been extended to a populist notion of "common sense" in which facts are dismissed and "alternative facts" dominate. In a culture of immediacy, spectacle, and sensationalism, Trump behaves as if he is still starring in his own TV show. But more dangers lie ahead than our collective immersion in the shallow appeal of politics as theater.

Under the economic, religious, and political extremists Trump has been installing in positions of power, intolerance and militarization will intensify. Financial capital will be deregulated in order to be free to engage in behavior that puts most of the American public and the planet in danger. Institutions that embody the common good, such as public schools, will be defunded or privatized, and as a culture of greed and selfishness reaches new heights, there will be a further retreat from civic literacy and a growing abandonment by the state of any allegiance to the public interest. The free-market mentality that gained prominence under the presidency of Ronald Reagan will advance under Trump and will continue to drive politics, destroy many social protections, further privilege the wealthy, and de-regulate economic activity. How else to explain Trump's tax reform bill, which offers a $1.5 trillion tax cut that largely favors the ultra-rich and major corporations and would eventually leave 83 million middle-class and poor families paying more in taxes? Moreover, the increase in the deficit caused by these tax cuts enables the Republicans to wage and justify a major assault on the welfare state and its chief social provisions, such as social security, Medi-care, and Medicaid. And what other rationale is there for Trump's war on the environment, evident not only in his withdrawing from the Paris climate agreement but also in his opening up billions of acres of land on both the Pacific and Atlantic coasts for oil drilling? This is beyond shame-ful. It constitutes an act of war on the planet and the health of millions of adults and children.

Trump's reign will continue to usher in an extreme version of pro-corporate capitalism in which all human ac-tivities, practices, and institutions will be subject to market principles and commercialization. Under the Trump re-gime, the powers of the state will be unleashed against new targets as well as old: political rivals, Blacks, Muslims, un-documented immigrants, transgendered people, women's reproductive rights, "porous" borders, the environment, protest, the press, the U.S. Justice system. Americans are witnessing the emergence of new forms of authoritarian-ism and fascism that are challenging the very ability for society to function as a civilian democracy. This is precisely why Trumpism cannot be further normalized.

It is crucial to acknowledge that the path we are currently on will lead to more misery and conflict. It will bring more violence to our doorsteps, unleashing and trapping many people in reactionary spirals of escalation and retaliation. Such violence is seen in increasingly frequent mass shootings, the killing of unarmed civilians by the police, and the senselessness of daily violence in all its forms. If you are Black, this means living each day with the possibility of being either harassed, incarcerated, or shot by the police.[29] Violence, or the threat of violence, seems to be increasingly the default response of the state to every domestic and foreign problem. Trump has even publicly ridiculed his secretary of state for attempting to de-escalate nuclear confrontation with North Korea. "I told Rex Tillerson, our wonderful Secretary of State," said Trump in a tweet, "that he is wasting his time trying to negotiate with Little Rocket Man." Another says, "Save your energy Rex, we'll do what has to be done!"[30]

Unsurprisingly, it has been reported that Secretary of State Rex Tillerson (since fired) once called Trump a "fucking moron." Ignorance and power form a foundation for fascism. Commenting on his book *Fire and Fury*, Michael Wolff stated that he "interviewed more than 200 people in Trump's inner and outer orbit and they reached a joint conclusion. They all say, 'He is like a child,' and what they mean by that is he has a need for immediate gratification," the author told NBC.[31] In short, most of the people interviewed considered Trump to be stupid and incompetent. What they left out is that he is also dangerous, particularly at a time when violence runs through U.S. politics and culture like an electric current. Violence is at the heart of every fascist society. To paraphrase the historian Richard J. Evans, what we are witnessing under Trump is the emergence of a society that is plunging into "a new, militarized, and brutalized world where violence in the service of politics [becomes] the norm."[32]

Wolff's gossipy tale may be revealing, if not entertaining, in exposing Trump's character and mode of (non) governance, but it also is a distraction that feeds the mainstream media's obsession with his mental health rather than a much-needed focus on the slew of dangerous policies he promotes that inflict violence and misery upon immigrants, the poor and vulnerable, and those marginalized by class, race, sexual orientation, and gender. Of course, the more serious issue ignored by the mainstream media should be a focus on what kind of political and economic system produces demagogues like Trump, the people who support him, and a gangster capitalism with its organized culture of violence. Reference here to Nazi Germany may be overblown, but under Trump there are echoes and warnings resembling a fascist past that "shut down the country's democratic institutions, destroyed the freedom of its press and media, and created a one-party state in which opposition was punishable by imprisonment, banishment, or even death."[33] As Richard Evans, the renowned historian of modern Germany, observes, democracies die in different ways, but what they often have in common as they fall is the shift of violence to the center of civic and political life. Trump may not be Hitler, but the Nazis and the legacy of fascism offer a "warning from history" that cannot be dismissed.[34] While the United States under Trump may not be an exact replica of Hitler's Germany, the mobilizing ideas, policies, and ruthless social practices of fascism, wrapped in the flag and discourses of racial purity, ultra-nationalism, and militarism, are at the center of power in Trump's United States.

Violence increasingly finds its way onto the screens of Americans' phones and devices. War culture, alive and well on U.S. soil, becomes commercialized via constant news programming of extreme violence captured in videos of a lone gunman indiscriminately shooting scores people at an outdoor concert in Las Vegas or at a church in a small community in Texas. Such mass shootings now occur daily in the United States, and have for years. A pervasive culture of violence means that "seventy-eight children under 5 died by guns in 2015—thirty more than the forty-eight law enforcement officers killed by guns in the line of duty."[35] It also means that in the United States, mass shootings occur, on average, more than once per day.[36] In Chicago alone, in the first eight months of 2016, twelve people were shot daily. According to a Carnegie-Knight News21 investigation, the effects on youth are devastating:

> For every U.S. soldier killed in Afghanistan during 11 years of war, at least 13 children were

shot and killed in America. More than 450 kids didn't make it to kindergarten. Another 2,700 or more were killed by a firearm before they could sit behind the wheel of a car. Every day, on average, seven children were shot dead. A News21 investigation of child and youth deaths in America between 2002 and 2012 found that at least 28,000 children and teens 19 years old and younger were killed with guns. Teenagers between the ages of 15 and 19 made up over two-thirds of all youth gun deaths in America.[37]

Gary Younge observes that every day in the United States "seven kids and teens are shot dead," which adds up to 2,500 dead children a year. It's clear that neither mainstream political party has what is needed: "a thoroughgoing plan for dealing with America's gun culture that goes well beyond background checks."[38] While such a plan would be an improvement, it would not be enough. The level of gun deaths and violence exhibited in the United States has deep roots in systemic structures of racism, inequality, and poverty that bear down particularly hard on young people. Not only is the United States "the only country in the world that continues to sentence children to life in prison without parole," but the criminal justice system functions to make it more difficult for young people to escape the reach of a punishing and racist legal system.[39] According to a 2016 report published by the Juvenile Law Center, there are close to a million children who appear in juvenile court each year and are subjected to a legal system rife with racial disparities and injustices, which are further entrenched by the extraction of fees for court-related services. This report, titled "Debtor's Prison for Kids? The High Cost of Fines and Fees in the Juvenile Justice System," states:

> Approximately one million youth appear in juvenile court each year. In every state, youth and families face juvenile justice costs, fees, fines, or restitution. Youth who can't afford to pay for their freedom often face serious consequences, including incarceration, extended probation, or denial of treatment—they are unfairly penalized for being poor and pulled deeper into the justice system. Many families either go into debt trying to pay these costs or must choose between paying for basic necessities, like groceries, and paying court costs and fees. Research shows that costs and fees actually increase recidivism and exacerbate economic and racial disparities in the juvenile justice system.[40]

An updated form of the debtors' prison, one of the hallmark horrors of the nineteenth century, has materialized in the United States with young people as its target. This is a justice system operating as a legalized extortion racket, and an appalling illustration of how our society has come to accept the neoliberal priority of profit over people.

It is clear we now live at a time in which institutions

that were meant to limit human suffering, and to protect young people and other vulnerable groups from the excesses of the police state and the market, have been either weakened, defunded, or abolished. The consequences can also be seen in the ongoing and ruthless assault on public education in the United States, with the transformation of schools into "microcosms of the American police state."[41] Schools have become, in many cases, surveillance zones that increasingly subject students to pedagogies of control, discipline, and detention. Designed to provide profits for the security industries, they impose violence and repression on young people, with the direst effects impacting students from low-income neighborhoods and communities of color. At the same time, what students learn—and the pedagogies through which they are taught—have been emptied of critical content, and now impose on students mind-numbing curricula and the primacy of the test. The dismantling of schools as sites for creativity, critical thinking, and learning constitutes both a war on the imagination and the establishment of a set of disciplinary practices meant to criminalize the behavior of children who do not submit to overbearing control. No longer considered democratic public spheres intended to create critically informed and engaged citizens, many schools now function as intermediary sites that move between the roles of warehousing students in low-income communities and creating pathways that will lead them into the machinery of the criminal justice system and eventually prison. Under such circumstances, public schooling is unmoored from the culture of education and bound instead with a culture of punishment and militarization.

Children matter in any discussion of politics because they remind us of the need not only to create a more democratic future, but also to take seriously the collective struggle and modes of resistance that can make it happen. Likewise, the degree to which a nation turns its back on its young people, selling out their futures and allowing the social fabric to be torn to shreds, is a bellwether of that country's deepening descent into an abyss of political self-annihilation. Rather than being viewed as a social investment, economically disadvantaged youth, particularly youth of color, are now seen as excess in the United States—threatening, suspect, and undeserving of either a society in which they are protected or a future in which they are treated with respect. Instead of educating them, the United States spends large sums of money to imprison them; instead of building schools, we invest more and more in prisons; instead of providing quality health care, jobs, and housing for them, we consign them to dilapidated schools, push them into the underground economy, and criminalize their behaviors. There are few safe spaces left for economically disadvantaged youth, especially youth of color, only the likelihood of increased encounters with police and jail. This suggests not only a politics that has turned into a pathology, but a dystopian logic that is as cruel as it is morally indifferent.

If children matter, as many politicians are quick to insist, then it is crucial to recognize that such concerns are highly disingenuous when they are not backed up by efforts to halt the sacrificing of youth to the most brutal elements of an unbridled capitalism. This means regulating big business in the public interest, not the other way around. It means fighting for a sovereign social order that is able to hold a system of governance accountable to serve the interests of the common good, not those of a small financial elite. It means investing resources in a diverse and open society that addresses the needs of young people of all colors and economic levels. Accomplishing this not a matter of reform, it is a matter of justice—economic, political, environmental, racial, and social justice—at all levels.

The current state of electoral politics in the United States makes it abundantly clear that an allegedly more progressive Democratic Party seems incapable of addressing the underlying conditions that have brought us to this calamitous moment in American history. The Republican Party took a different approach than the Democrats did, successfully deploying the slogan "Make America Great Again" while unleashing big business in full force, undermining whatever social and environmental protections are left, relentlessly attacking affordable health care, and waging nothing less than an informational, financial, and political war against the average American family. As the Trumpists embark on their mission to eradicate the welfare state, it also builds on Obama's efforts to expand the surveillance state, but with a new and deadly twist. This is evident, for example, in the Congressional Republicans' successful efforts to pass a bill that overturned privacy protections for internet users, thereby allowing corporations to monitor, sell, and use everything that people put on the internet, including their browsing history, app usage, and financial and medical information. Early on, we already see emerging the Orwellian side of Trump's administration as it not only strives to make it easier for the surveillance state to access information, but also sells out the American public to corporate strategists who view everything in terms of money, no matter what the consequences for other people, the nation, or the environment.

Meanwhile, state-backed and corporate-sponsored ignorance produced primarily through the disimagination machines of both social and legacy media now function chiefly to accommodate the public to its own atomization and commodification, suppress selected elements of history, express disdain for critical thought, reduce dissent to a species of fake news, and undermine the social imagination. Manufactured ignorance erases histories of repression, exploitation, and revolt. What is left is a space of fabricated absences that makes it easy, if not convenient, to forget that Donald Trump is not just some impulsive rich guy who marketed his way into politics through empty Kardashian-type celebrity and consumer culture. Trump, Bannon, and their so-called alt-right sphere of influence represent a genuine threat to democracy, the public interest, and ethical culture. The isolated analyses of Trump's tweets and comments simply work to distract people's attention away from seeing the whole pattern now emerging, an orchestrated proto-fascist campaign to consolidate power and dismantle democracy by tearing it to pieces one joint and one limb at a time.

What this context makes clear, and what I argue throughout this book, is that resisting the whitewashing of history is a core issue. History unexpurgated provides us with a vital resource that helps inform the ethical ground for resistance, an antidote to Trump's politics of disinformation, division, diversion, and fragmentation. Moreover, history reminds us that in the face of emerging forms of authoritarianism, solidarity is essential. People need to network and organize in public spheres and institutional structures that allow their actions to be organized collectively and magnified outward. As historian Timothy Snyder observes:

> And the reason why institutions are so important is that they're what prevent us from being those atomized individuals who are alone against the overpowering state. That's a very romantic image, but the isolated individual is always going to lose. We need the constitutional institutions as much as we can get them going. It's a real problem now, especially with the legislature. We also need the professions, whether it's law or medicine or civil servants, to act according to rules that are not the same thing as just following orders. And we need to be able to form ourselves up into nongovernmental organizations, because it's not just that we have freedom of association. It's

that freedom itself requires association. We need association to have our own ideas confirmed, to have our confidence raised, to be in a position to actually act as individuals.[42]

Currently, historical knowledge is under attack. How else to explain the recent Arkansas legislator who is pushing legislation to ban the works of Howard Zinn? How else to explain the aggressive attempts by extremists in both political parties to undermine public and higher education? Authoritarian policies and practices once again feed a war culture, while moral paralysis paves the way for further gains by the forces of intolerance. These are moves that will not be stopped through half measures. If there is one thing that the important lessons of history and the radical imagination of writers such as George Orwell have taught us, it is that we must refuse to be complicit in the mockery of truth now put on display by Trumpists and commercial far-right operations such as Infowars and Breitbart News that profit from propagating it. The nightmare we had thought might one day arrive is here. The challenge is to develop nationwide solidarity and resistance networks required to overcome it with non-violence, imagination, and community.

Rethinking Resistance as the Rise of Democracies in Exile

Within weeks of assuming the powers of civilian president and military commander-in-chief, Trump issued an executive order banning all Syrians and people from seven predominantly Muslim nations from entering the United States. At the end of his first year in office, Trump reversed an immigration policy that allowed 200,000 people from El Salvador to "live and work legally in the United States since a pair of devastating earthquakes struck their country in 2001."[43] Coupled with Trump's rescinding protections for 800,000 Dreamers—children who have grown up in the United States but were born in other countries—it is difficult not to view such acts as both racist and as acts one associates with fascist regimes. Such policies put Trump's embrace of white supremacy on full display, making visible his authoritarian intentions, while also setting in place an additional series of repressive practices for the creation of a police state. This is a grim reality, indicating that the United States has conclusively entered a period of what Alex Honneth terms "failed sociality"[44]—a failure in the power of civic imagination, political will, and a functioning democracy.

Given its design and rhetoric of exclusion, not only does Trump's immigration order further threaten the security of the United States, it also legitimates a form of state-sponsored racial and religious cleansing. Chicago Cardinal Blase Cupich, hardly a radical, was accurate in stating that the design and implementation of the initial order banning Muslims and Syrians from the United States was "rushed, chaotic, cruel, and oblivious" to the demands and actualities of national security, and that it had "ushered in a dark moment in U.S. history."[45] Dark indeed, because the order surely signals not only a governing authority that has stopped questioning itself, but one that openly assaults religious and racial communities.

Trumpism offers fascist purification rituals motivated by social intolerance and the attempt to re-create a system of white privilege that extends from and perpetuates founding narratives of Anglo settler-colonialism. Trumpist glorification of President Andrew Jackson and a "Jacksonian national security"[46] vision signals the advance of the same historical white supremacy that codified the Second Amendment to decentralize and individualize white people's armed enforcement of Black enslavement and the extermination of Native Americans. Understanding this, many Americans accurately interpret the Trumpist slogan "Make America Great Again" as "Make America White Again." The celebrated writer Ta-Nehisi Coates further exposes Trump's fascist intolerance. He writes:

> It is often said that Trump has no real ideology, which is not true—his ideology is white supremacy, in all its truculent and sanctimonious power. His political career began in advocacy of birtherism, that modern recasting of the old American precept that black people are not fit to be citizens of the country they built. But long before birtherism, Trump had made his worldview clear. He fought to keep blacks out of his buildings, according to the U.S. government; called for the death penalty for the eventually

exonerated Central Park Five; and railed against "lazy" black employees. "Black guys counting my money! I hate it," Trump was once quoted as saying. "The only kind of people I want counting my money are short guys that wear yarmulkes every day." . . . The triumph of Trump's campaign of bigotry presented the problematic spectacle of an American president succeeding at best in spite of his racism and possibly because of it. Trump moved racism from the euphemistic and plausibly deniable to the overt and freely claimed.[47]

Trumpism openly legitimizes armed white supremacy and social intolerance. Those considered flawed and disposable due to race, residency status, political affiliation, gender, sexual preference, and religious practice are subjected to increased suspicion, surveillance, exclusion, and increased vulnerability to hate crimes. Intolerance to diversity of all kinds feeds violence as a method for maintaining dominance and militancy on all levels. While Ta-Nehisi Coates makes clear that "not every Trump voter is a white supremacist," he qualifies that statement with the insightful comment that "every Trump voter felt it acceptable to hand the fate of the country over to one."[48] That is both the defining ideology of the Republican Party under Trump and the residual fungus of authoritarianism mushrooming in the United States today. Unfortunately, Coates does not mark the history of collective struggles waged by people of color against the legacy of white supremacy. His condemnation runs the risk of cynicism and omits, as Cornel West points out, "the centrality of Wall Street power, U.S. military policies, and the complex dynamics of class, gender, and sexuality in Black America."[49] Coates's analysis of white supremacy needs further development in regard to how white privilege operates with other forms of domination.[50]

American citizens are not exempt, either, from the cruelty and misery of massive exploitation dispensed by a society in the thrall of wealth and neoliberal capitalism, which now merges the spectacle of exclusion with a politics of disposability reminiscent of the fascist regimes of the 1930s.[51] This is nowhere more evident than in Trump's modes of racial and religious cleansing based on generalized notions of identity that strongly echo the principles of historical policies of extermination seen in the past. This is not to suggest that Trump's immigration policies have risen to that standard of violence as much as to identify that they contain within them the impetus and elements of a past authoritarianism that herald it as a possible model for the future.[52] This form of radical exclusion suggests previous elements of fascism are crystallizing into new forms.

In response to Trump's executive order targeting Muslims and Syrian refugees escaping the devastation of war, carnage, and state violence, thousands of people across the country initially mobilized with great speed and energy to reject not just an unconstitutional ban, but also what this and other regressive policies portend for the days ahead. Many writers have focused on the massive disruption this shoot-from-the hip piece of legislation will produce for students, visa holders, and those entering the United States after finishing a long vetting process. As an editorial in the *Washington Post* pointed out, Trump's immigration order is "breathtaking in scope and inflammatory in tone."[53] Moreover, it lacks logic and speaks to "the president's callousness and indifference to history, to America's deepest lessons about its own values."[54] The fact that it was issued on Holocaust Remembrance Day further points to Trump's moral incapacity; it may also point to the machinations of former chief White House strategist Steve Bannon, who played a key role in drafting it. Trump's ongoing reversal of a number of immigration policies put in place by the Obama administration has been opposed by the United States Chamber of Commerce, members of Congress, and numerous immigrant advocacy groups. Such opposition falls on deaf ears in an administration filled with racist animus and an allegiance to the legacy and principles of white supremacy.

Now is the moment to challenge one of the most destructive governments ever to emerge in the United States. Now is the time to talk back, occupy the streets, organize, and resist. Today it might be immigrants and Muslims who are under attack—maybe a neighbor, a librarian, a journalist, a teacher—but tomorrow it could be any of us. The need to engage in massive forms of resistance and civil disobedience is urgent. If we expect the planet to survive, and hope to offer the next generation something better than life in a state of permanent war, we must act.

The metaphor of an American nightmare provides us with a rhetorical space where a kind of double consciousness, based in both resistance and hope, can emerge. This is a consciousness that identifies and rejects structures of domination and repression. It is an expression of what Vaclav Havel once called "the power of the powerless," but it also gestures beyond this, to what the poet Claudia Rankine calls a new understanding of community, politics, and engaged collective resistance in which a radical notion of the social contract is revived. This is a critical consciousness in which individuals and groups allow themselves to embrace the condition of exile—with its underlying message of being flawed—in solidarity with their brothers and sisters who are targeted because of their politics, gender, religion, residency status, race, sexual preference, and country of origin. She writes of exile as an opportunity to address the resentment and retribution that have historically underlain denials of our common humanity. For Rankine, being "flawed differently" offers a metaphor for embracing our differences. It offers diversity as a strength in our collective resistance against the pre-fascist "America First" script in which whiteness is sustained as the dominating feature of a violent society that has descended directly from genocidal settler-colonialism.

Democracies in exile embrace being flawed differently as a way to insist that "You want to belong, you want to be here. In interactions with others you're constantly waiting to see that they recognize that you're a human being. That they can feel your heartbeat and you can feel theirs. . . .

There's a letting go that comes with it. I don't know about forgiving, but it's an 'I'm still here.' And it's not just because I have nowhere else to go. It's because I believe in the possibility. I believe in the possibility of another way of being. Let's make other kinds of mistakes; let's be flawed differently."[55]

To be "flawed differently" provides a rhetorical signifier to understand and work against the poisonous legacies and totalitarian strictures of racial purity that are still with us, and rejects the toxic reach of a government dominated by morally repulsive authoritarians with their hired legions of lawyers, think tanks, pundits, and intellectual thugs.

Being "flawed differently" means we bleed into each other, flawed in our rejection of certainty and our condemnation of the false ideals of racial and religious purity. Flawed differently, we revel in our diversity, united by a never-ending search for a just society. Our "flaws" increase rather than diminish our humanity, as we celebrate our differences mediated by a respect for the common good. But we also share in our resistance to a demagogue and his coterie of reactionaries who harbor a rapacious desire for obliterating differences, for concentrating power in the hands of a financial elite, and the economic, political, and religious fundamentalists who slavishly beg for recognition and crumbs of power.

Being "flawed differently" means mobilizing against the suffocating circles of certainty that define the ideologies, worldviews, and policies that are driving the new authoritarianism, expressed so clearly by a Trump administration official who, with an echo of fascist Brownshirt bravado, told the press to shut up and be quiet.[56]

Being "flawed differently" provides a rhetorical signpost for being in collective exile, working to create new democratic public spheres, noisy conversations, and alternative spaces informed by compassion and a respect for the other. It is not a retreat. On the contrary, it echoes Naomi Klein's insistence that in moments of crisis and peril, we broaden the spaces of resistance that provide a collective voice to the struggle against authoritarianism.[57]

Trump's constant use of lies, fear, belittlement, and humiliation wages war on the ideals, values, and practices of a viable democracy. Under such circumstances, a fierce, courageous, and broad-based nonviolent resistance is the only option—a necessity forged within and by an unshakable commitment to economic, political, and social justice. As I argue throughout this book, this must be a form of collective resistance that is not episodic but systemic, ongoing, loud, noisy, educative, and disruptive. Under the reign of Trump, the words of Frederick Douglass ring especially true: "If there is no struggle, there is no progress. This struggle may be a moral one; or it may be a physical one; or it may be both moral and physical; but it must be a struggle. Power concedes nothing without a demand. It never did and it never will."[58]

There is no choice but to stop the authoritarian machinery of political death from consolidating further. It has to be brought to an end in every space, landscape, and institution in which it tries to shunt and obstruct the pathways to justice and democracy. Reason and thoughtfulness have to awake from the narcoticizing effects induced by a culture of spectacles, consumerism, militarism, populist ignorance, and the narrow preoccupations of unchecked self-interest. The body of democracy is fragile, and the wounds now being inflicted upon it are alarming.

Under the current circumstances, it is crucial to confront the nightmare with insurgency. Such confrontation can be waged and won through our capacity for solidarity, cooperation, kindness, and community. Such capacity inspires us to organize and take action in our local communities, and to imagine a more just and democratic future, one that can only emerge through a powerful and uncompromising collective struggle. As Hannah Arendt once predicted, totalitarianism's curse is upon us once again, and it has emerged in forms unique to the tyranny of the times in which we live. Trump has brought the terrors of the past into full view, feeding off the fears, uncertainties, and narratives that make diversity seem threatening. In response, we must create a new language for politics, resistance, and hope. This must be a language that exposes and counters the drift toward fascism that Trumpism clearly accelerates.

In the conclusion I return to the issue of creating spaces of resistance defined through the metaphor of democracy in exile. Developing such spaces serves to energize efforts in which increasingly totalitarian practices are revealed, analyzed, challenged, and undone. It is worth noting that my previous book, *America at War with Itself*, tracked the rise of authoritarianism in the United States.

American Nightmare continues the analysis while providing a detailed exploration of the numerous instances of the ideals and practices of multicultural democracy being denounced, subverted, or directly attacked by a unique form of U.S. authoritarianism.

The United States now occupies a historical moment in which there will likely be an intensification of violence, oppression, impunity, and corruption. These are serious forces that must be confronted if a radical democratic future is not to be foreclosed. Roger Ballen's image, "The Stare," on the cover of this book is eerie and prophetic, signifying the deep sense of alienation, loneliness, and anxiety that haunts the United States at the present moment. At the same time, the eyes look out from a space of danger, watching and witnessing the emergence of a menacing political environment that must be confronted, resisted, and destroyed. "The Stare" brings to light a democracy in the shadows, a haunting phenomenon, unwilling to look away and determined to prevent a further darkening of social justice and ethical culture. Hopefully, the image will also bring home for the reader the need not only to acknowledge current conditions, but also to confront and counter their potential to further the allure of fascism.

CHAPTER ONE

AMERICA'S NIGHTMARE: REMEMBERING ORWELL'S *1984* AND HUXLEY'S *BRAVE NEW WORLD*

"The ideal subject of totalitarian rule is not the convinced Nazi . . . but people for whom the distinction between fact and fiction, true and false, no longer exists."

—Hannah Arendt

Under the Trump regime, Americans have entered into a dark period that cannot be understood without acknowledging the ways fascism has manifested in the past. Under Trump, justice has become the enemy of democratic leadership. As digital time replaces the time needed for informed judgments, everything takes place in the immediate present.[1] Most evident in an age of celebrity and presidential tweets, thinking is reduced to information that is consumed instantly while consciousness becomes the enemy of contemplation. Our collective capacity to remember and to name injustice, and to imagine a reality different from the one that now confronts us, recedes with each new imposition of falsehood, obstruction, and diversion. Historical memory should always serve as a mode of moral witnessing and protection against tyranny. When it no longer does so, it signals a crisis of politics, agency, and civic literacy. This is particularly true today.

What follows is an attempt to assert the significance of historical memory as fundamental to the preservation of democracy in the face of an unprecedented shift toward authoritarianism and fascism. Reviving the memory of real and imagined horrors of a previous generation, strikingly represented in Orwell's and Huxley's fiction, is a way to understand the present descent of the United States into an authoritarian nightmare. Doing so offers a form of intellectual self-defense against Trumpism's violence against truthfulness, accountability, reason, science, and liberal modernity. I begin with Orwell.

Orwell's Nightmare

Before we credit Donald Trump with using George Orwell's great novel as his codebook, we must note that Orwell's terrifying vision of a totalitarian society has actually been a waking dream in the United States for many years—a country that maintains the largest prison system in the world, "with 2.2 million people in jail and more than 4.8 million on parole."[2] Originally published in 1949, *1984* provided a stunningly prophetic image of the totalitarian machinery of the surveillance state that was brought to life in 2013 through Edward Snowden's exposure of the mass spying conducted by the U.S. National Security Agency.

Orwell's genius was not limited to this prediction alone. In addition, his work explores how modern democratic populations are won over by authoritarian ideologies and rituals, revealing how language specifically functions in the service of, deception, abuse and violence. He warned in exquisite and alarming detail how "totalitarian practice becomes internalized in totalitarian thinking."[3] Hannah Arendt added theoretical weight to Orwell's fictional nightmare by arguing that totalitarianism begins with contempt for critical thought and that the foundation for authoritarianism lies in a kind of mass thoughtlessness in which a citizenry is "deprived not only of its capacity to act but also its capacity to think and to judge."[4]

For Orwell, the mind-manipulating totalitarian state took as its first priority a war against what it called "thought crimes," nullifying opposition to its authority not simply by controlling access to information but by undermining the very basis on which critical challenges could be waged and communicated. Orwell illustrated his point by providing examples of how language could be used to weaken the critical formative culture necessary for producing thinking citizens central to any healthy democracy. According to Orwell, totalitarian power drained meaning of any substance by turning language against itself, exemplified infamously through the slogans of the Ministry of Truth, such as: "War Is Peace," "Freedom Is Slavery," and "Ignorance Is Strength." In recognizing how language fundamentally structures as much as it expresses thought, Orwell made clear how language could be distorted and circulated to function in the service of violence, deception, and corruption, and serve to utterly collapse any ethical distinction between good and evil, truth and lies.

The intersection, if not merger, of American politics with Orwell's disquieting vision was evident in the frenzied media circus focused on Trump's language that took place after Trump assumed the presidency. In a strange but revealing way, Orwell's novel *1984* surged to Amazon.com's number-one best seller in the United States and Canada. This followed two significant political events. First, Kellyanne Conway, Trump's advisor, in a move echoing the linguistic inventions of Orwell's Ministry of Truth, coined the term "alternative facts" to justify why then press secretary Sean Spicer lied in advancing disproved claims about the size of Trump's inauguration crowd.[5] With apologies to his late father who was a pastor, Bill Moyers has called Conway the "Queen of Bullshit."[6] "Alternative facts," or what should be called more precisely outright lies, is an updated term for what Orwell called "Doublethink," when people blindly accept contradictory ideas or allow truth to be subverted in the name of an unquestioned common sense. In the second instance, within hours of assuming the presidency, Trump penned a series of executive orders that caused Adam Gopnik, a writer for *The New Yorker*, to rethink the relevance of *1984*. Gopnik was compelled to go back to Orwell's book, he writes, "Because the single most striking thing about [Trump's] matchlessly strange first week is how primitive, atavistic, and uncomplicatedly brutal Trump's brand of authoritarianism is turning out to be."[7]

Unfortunately, the machinery of manipulation, intimidation, and distortion now commands the pinnacle of U.S. political and military power. In this Orwellian universe, facts are purged of their legitimacy, and the distinction between right and wrong disappears, promoting what Viktor Frankl once called "the mask of nihilism."[8] In this worldview, there are only winners and losers. Under such circumstances, "greed, vengeance, and gratuitous cruelty aren't wrong, but are legitimate motivations for political behavior."[9] This is a discourse that dictates a future in which authoritarianism thrives and democracies die. It is the discourse of a dystopian society marked by a deep-seated anti-intellectualism intensified by the incessant undermining and collapse of civic literacy and civic culture. Offering no room for deciphering fact from fiction, the flow of disinformation works to dismantle self-reflection while it serves to infantilize and depoliticize large segments of the polity. This is a hallucinatory discourse that reduces politics to marketing, self-promotion, and a theater of retribution and cruelty. Such systematic efforts on the part of the Trump administration to mislead, fabricate, and falsify undermine the very capacity to think, judge, and exercise informed judgment. This is what David Theo Goldberg has called the landscape of "make-believe," which functions as a vast disimagination machine.[10]

As Orwell often remarked, historical memory is dangerous to authoritarian regimes because it has the power to both question the past and reveal it as a site of injustice. Currently, Orwell's machinery of organized forgetting is reinforced in American popular culture by a burgeoning landscape of mega-malls and theme parks, media-driven spectacles of violence, and a deluge of consumerism, self-interest, and sensationalism for those who can afford participation. In this sink-or-swim society, the ongoing financial starvation and evisceration of public schools and public universities ensures that the lessons of history are neutered or displaced altogether by an instrumentalist curriculum whose hallmark objective is to confer "job-ready skills." For the citizens in *1984*, the Ministry of Truth made it a crime to read any history outside the official narrative. But history was also falsified so as to render it useless as a crucial pedagogical practice both for understanding the conditions that shaped the present and for remembering what should never be forgotten. As Orwell shows, this is precisely why tyrants consider historical memory dangerous: history can readily be put to use in identifying present-day abuses of power and corruption.

The Trump administration offered a pointed example of this Orwellian principle of historical falsification when it recently issued a statement regarding the observance of International Holocaust Remembrance day. In the statement, the White House refused to mention its Jewish victims, thus erasing them from a monstrous act directed against an entire people. *Politico* reported that the official White House statement "drew widespread criticism for overlooking the Jews' suffering, and was cheered by neo-Nazi website the *Daily Stormer*."[11] Accounts of these events read like passages out of Orwell's *1984* and speak to what historian Timothy Snyder calls the Trump administration's efforts to look to authoritarian regimes of the 1930s as potential models.[12]

This act of erasure is but another example of the willingness of Trumpism to empty language of any meaning, a practice that constitutes a flight from historical memory, ethics, justice, and social responsibility. Under such circumstances, government takes on the workings of a disimagination machine, one characterized by an utter disregard for the truth and often accompanied, as in Trump's case, by "primitive schoolyard taunts and threats."[13] In this instance, Orwell's "Ignorance Is Strength" materializes in the Trump administration's weaponized attempt not only to rewrite history but also to obliterate it, all of which contributes to what might be called a "drugged complacency."[14] Trump's claim that he loves the poorly educated and his willingness to act on that assertion by flooding the media and the wider public with an endless proliferation of peddled falsehoods reveal his contempt for intellect, reason, and truth. Trump derides intelligence and revels in ignorance; he does not read books, appears addicted to watching television, and is aligned ideologically with dictators who turned books to cinders, destroyed libraries, shut down the free press, and disparaged and punished artists, intellectuals, writers, and socially responsible scientists.[15]

As the master of phony stories, Trump is not only at war with historical remembrance, science, civic literacy, and rationality, he also wages a demolition campaign against democratic ideals by unapologetically embracing humiliation, racism, and exclusion for those he labels as illegals, criminals, terrorists, and losers, categories implicitly equated with Muslims, Mexicans, women, the disabled, and the list only grows. As John Wight observes, Trump's language of hate is "redolent of the demonization suffered by Jewish people in Germany in the 1930s, which echoes a warning from history."[16]

Orwell's point about duplicitous language was that, to some extent, all governments lie. The rhetorical manipulation one associates with Orwellian language is by no means unique to the Trump administration—though Trump and his acolytes have taken on an unapologetic register in redefining it and deploying it with reckless abandon. The draconian use of lies, propaganda, misinformation, and falsification has a long legacy in the United States, with other recent examples evident under the presidencies of Richard Nixon and George W. Bush. Nixon's claim that he was not a crook in the face of his lies over Watergate took place at a time in American history when a politician could still pay a price for lying. Since his impeachment that has become increasingly less true.

Under the Bush-Cheney administration, for example, "doublethink" and "doublespeak" became normalized, as state-sponsored torture was strategically renamed "enhanced interrogation." Barbaric state practices such as sending prisoners to countries where there are no limits on torture were framed in the innocuous language of "rendition."[17] Such language made a mockery of political discourse and eroded public engagement. It also contributed to the transformation of institutions that were meant to limit human suffering and misfortune, and to protect citizens from the excesses of the market and state violence, into something like their opposite.[18]

Yet the attack on reason, dissent, and truth itself finds its Orwellian apogee in Trump's endless proliferation of lies, including claims that China is responsible for climate change; former President Obama was not born in the United States; the murder rate in the United States is at its highest in forty-seven years; former President Obama wiretapped Trump Tower; and voter fraud prevented Trump from winning the popular vote for the presidency. Such lies, big and small, don't function simply as mystification: they offer justification for aggressive immigration crackdowns, for effectively silencing the Environmental Protection Agency, and for upending Obamacare. Too often the relentless fabrications serve to distract the press, which then focuses its energies on exposing the untrustworthiness of the person and not on the symbolic, legal, and material violence that such pronouncements and harsh policies invariably unleash.

Allow me to underscore one more striking example. In moments that speak to an alarming flight from moral and social responsibility, Trump has adopted terms strongly affiliated with the legacy of anti-Semitism and Nazi ideology. Historian Susan Dunn refers to his use of the phrase "America First" as a "sulfurous expression" connected historically to "the name of the isolationist, defeatist, anti-Semitic national organization that urged the United

States to appease Adolf Hitler."[19] It is also associated with its most powerful advocate, Charles Lindbergh, a notorious anti-Semite who once declared that America's greatest internal threat came from Jews who posed a danger to the United States because of their "large ownership and influence in our motion pictures, our press, our radio, and our government."[20] Though Trump denies he has given a platform to neo-Nazi groups, the shocking uptick in bomb threats to dozens of Jewish community centers across the United States speaks for itself.[21]

Moreover, once he was elected, Trump took ownership of the notion of "fake news," inverting its original usage as a criticism of his perpetual lying and redeploying it as a pejorative label aimed at journalists who criticized his policies. Even Trump's inaugural address was filled with lies about rising crime rates and the claim of unchecked carnage in America, though crime rates are at historical lows. His blatant disregard for the truth reached another high point soon afterwards with his nonsensical and false claim that the mainstream media lied about the size of his inaugural crowd, or the subsequent assertion that the leaks involving his national security advisor were "real" but the news about them was "fake." The *Washington Post* fact-checked Trump's address to the joint session of Congress and listed thirteen of his most notable "inaccuracies," or what can rightfully be called lies.[22] Trump's penchant for lies and his irrepressible urge to tell them are beyond what Gopnik calls "Big Brother crude" and the expression of a "pure raging authoritarian id," they also speak to a more systematic effort to undermine freedom of speech and truthfulness as core democratic values.[23] Trump's lies signal more than a Twitter fetish aimed at invalidating the work of reason and evidence-based assertions. Trump's endless threats, fabrications, outrages, and "orchestrated chaos" produced with a "dizzying velocity" also point to a strategy for asserting power, while encouraging if not emboldening his followers to think the unthinkable ethically and politically.[24] As Charles Sykes, a former conservative radio host, observes, while it may be true that all political administrations lie, what is unique to the Trump administration is "an attack on credibility itself."[25] Trump's endless lies do more than undermine standards of credibility, they also embolden pro-Trump media, particularly Fox News, Breitbart, and right-wing talk radio, to abandon all standards of proof, verification, and evidence in order to advance Trump's agenda and pounce upon those who criticize him.

In fact, there is something delusional if not pathological about Trump's propensity to lie, even when he is constantly outed for doing so. For instance, in a thirty-minute interview with the *New York Times* on December 28, 2017, the *Washington Post* reported that Trump made "false, misleading or dubious claims . . . at a rate of one every 75 seconds."[26] Trump's abuse of truth corresponds directly to his abuse of power. Trump's aim is to dominate social and political reality with narratives of his own making, irrespective of how ridiculous doing so often appears. As a result, Trump has undermined the relationship between engaged citizenship and the truth, and has relegated matters of debate and critical assessment to a spectacle of bombast, threats, and intimidation. There is more in play here than Trump's desire to blur the lines between fact and fiction, the truth and falsehoods. Trump's more serious aim is to derail the architectural foundations of reason in order to construct a false reality and alternative political universe in which there are only competing fictions and the emotional appeal of shock theater. This is the conduct of dictators, one that makes it difficult to name injustices or conduct democratic politics.[27]

But the language of fascism does more that institutionalize falsehood and ignorance, it normalizes political short-term memory, paralysis, and spectatorship. At the same time, it makes fear and anxiety the everyday currency of exchange and communication. Destabilized perceptions in Trump's world are coupled with the shallow allure of celebrity culture. In this environment, vulgarity and crassness attempt to steamroll civic courage and measured arguments. Masha Gessen is right in arguing that Trump's lies are different than ordinary lies and are more like "power lies." In this case, these are lies designed less "to convince the audience of something than to demonstrate the power of the speaker."[28] Peter Baker and Michael Tackett sum up a number of bizarre and reckless tweets that Trump produced to inaugurate the New Year. They write:

> President Trump again raised the prospect of nuclear war with North Korea, boasting in strikingly playground terms on Tuesday night that he

commands a "much bigger" and "more powerful" arsenal of devastating weapons than the out-
lier government in Asia. "Will someone from his
depleted and food starved regime please inform
[North Korean leader Kim Jong Un] that I too
have a Nuclear Button, but it is a much bigger
& more powerful one than his, and my Button
works!" It came on a day when Mr. Trump, back
in Washington from his Florida holiday break,
effectively opened his new year with a barrage of
provocative tweets on a host of issues. He called
for an aide to Hillary Clinton to be thrown in jail,
threatened to cut off aid to Pakistan and the Pal-
estinians, assailed Democrats over immigration,
claimed credit for the fact that no one died in a
jet plane crash last year and announced that he
would announce his own award next Monday for
the most dishonest and corrupt news media.[29]

Echoes of earlier fascist societies are not only audi-
ble in Trump's falsehoods, petulance, and crudeness, but
are also evident in his embrace of elements of white supremacy. As I previously mentioned, his racism was on full
display in the issuance of his executive order banning citizens from seven Muslim-majority countries—Iran, Iraq,
Syria, Yemen, Somalia, Sudan, and Libya. Trump's plan
for America is constructed around an imagined assault (alleged terrorists from the countries named in the ban were
accountable for zero American deaths) that legitimates a

form of state-sponsored racial and religious purging.[30] Fear is now managed and buttressed by asserting the claims of white supremacists and militant right-wing extremists that racial domination should be accepted as a general condition of society and its securitization.

Under Trump, the cruelty, misery, and massive exploitation associated with neoliberal capitalism merges with a politics of exclusion and disposability. Social cleansing based on generalized notions of identity echoes principles seen in past regimes and which gave birth to unimaginable atrocities and intolerable acts of mass violence and genocide.[31] This is not to suggest that Trump's immigration policies have risen, as yet, to that level of genocidal vitriol, but to propose that they contain elements of a past totalitarianism that "heralds a possible model for the future."[32] What I am arguing is that this form of radical exclusion based on the denigration of Islam as a closed and timeless culture marks a terrifying entry into a political experience that suggests that older elements of fascism are crystallizing into new forms.

The malleability of truth has made it easier for those in power, particularly Trump, to wage an ongoing and ruthless assault on immigrants, the social state, workers, unions, higher education, students, poor minorities, and any vestige of the social contract. Under Trump, the interests of corporate power, a permanent war culture, the militarization of everyday life, the privatization of public wealth, the elimination of social protections, and the elimination of ecological protections will be accelerated. As democratic institutions decay, Trump does not even pretend to defend the fiction of democracy. He only blurts and tweets his own fiction-rich narratives to better attack the enemy of the moment, be it Hillary Clinton, CNN, or the supreme leader of North Korea.

There can be little doubt about the ideological direction of the Trump administration given his appointment of billionaires, generals, white supremacists, representatives of the corporate elite, and general incompetents to the highest levels of government. Public spheres that once offered at least the glimmer of progressive ideas, enlightened social policies, non-commodified values, and critical dialogue and exchange have and will be increasingly commercialized—or replaced by private spaces and corporate settings whose ultimate commitment is to increasing profit margins. What we are witnessing under the Trump administration is more than an aesthetics of vulgarity, as the mainstream media sometimes suggest. Instead, we are observing a politics fueled by a market-driven view of society that has turned its back on the very idea that social values, public trust, and communal relations are fundamental to a democratic society. It is to Orwell's credit that in his dystopian view of society, he opened a door for all to see a "nightmarish future" in which everyday life becomes harsh, an object of state surveillance and control—a society in which the slogan "Ignorance Is Strength" morphs into a guiding principle of the highest levels of government, mainstream media, education, and popular culture.

Huxley's World of Manufactured Ignorance

Aldous Huxley's *Brave New World* offers a very different and no less critical lens with which to survey the landscape of state oppression, one that is especially relevant with the rise of Trumpism. Huxley believed that social control and the propagation of ignorance would be introduced by those in power through a vast machinery of manufactured needs, desires, and identifications. For him, oppression took the form of voluntary slavery produced through a range of technologies, refined forms of propaganda, and mass manipulation and seduction. Accordingly, the real drugs of a control society in late modernity were to be found in a culture that offers up immediate pleasure, sensation, and gratification. This new mode of persuasion seduced people into chasing commodities, and infantilized them through the mass production of easily digestible entertainment, orchestrated rallies, and a politics of distraction that dampened, if not obliterated, the very possibility of thinking itself. For Huxley, the political subject had lost his or her sense of agency and had become the product of a scientifically and systemically manufactured form of idiocy and conformity.

If Orwell's dark image is the stuff of government oppression—"a boot stamping on a human face—forever," Huxley's dystopia is the stuff of entertaining diversions, staged spectacles, and a cauterizing of the social imagination. We can see how such a future becomes possible when core cultural and educational institutions such as public schools are defunded to the point where they serve mostly a warehousing function, no longer providing a bulwark against civic illiteracy. In addition, the educational function of wider cultural apparatuses now offers a new mechanism for social planning and engagement, to be found in the hallucinatory power of a mind-deadening entertainment industry, the culture of extreme sports, and other forms of public pedagogy that extend from Hollywood movies and video games to mainstream television, news, and social media. These cultural platforms commercialize attention and impose spectacles of dehumanizing violence. They also degrade women through representations of hyper-aggressive masculinity, driving both the infantilization produced by consumer culture and the power of a fatuous commercial culture that encourages the adoration of celebrity lifestyles, all of which temporarily confers enormous temporary media power on people like Lady Gaga, Donald Trump, and the Kardashians.

Behind Trump's inflated strongman persona lies his blatant disregard for the truth, his willingness to taunt and threaten individuals at home and abroad, and his rush to enact a series of regressive executive orders—an authoritarian machinery through which the ghost of fascism reasserts itself with a familiar blend of fear, humiliation, and revenge. Unleashing policies that make good on the promises he made to his angry, die-hard, ultra-nationalist, and white supremacist supporters, the billionaire populist plays on the desires and desperation of his base by targeting a range of groups he believes have no place in American society. Muslims, Syrian refugees, and Salvadoran immigrants are among those he has quickly singled out with a number of harsh discriminatory policies. The underlying ignorance and cruelty behind such policies were amplified when Trump suggested that he intended to pass legislation amounting to a severe reduction of environmental protections, a promise he shamefully acted on by withdrawing the United States from the Paris Climate Accord. Moreover, he signed an executive order to massively expand offshore drilling areas "in the Arctic and Atlantic Oceans, as well as assess whether energy exploration can take place in marine sanctuaries in the Pacific and Atlantic."[33]

And little did his cheering crowds suspect that they'd be paying for the wall through massive taxation on imports from Mexico. He also asserted his willingness to resume the practice of state-sponsored torture, despite warnings from military experts of serious blowback for Americans, and to deny federal funding to those cities willing to provide sanctuary to undocumented immigrants.

And this was just the beginning. Trump has since reaffirmed his promise to lift the U.S. ban on torture by appointing Gina Haspel as the CIA's new deputy director. Haspel not only played a direct role in overseeing the torture of detainees at a black site in Thailand, she also participated in the destruction of videotapes documenting their brutal interrogations.[34] Trump's enthusiasm for committing war crimes has only been matched by his eagerness to roll back many of the regulatory restrictions put in place by the Obama administration in order to prevent the financial industries from repeating the economic crisis of

2008. The wealthiest Americans, banks, and other major financial institutions quietly appreciate Trump as they wait for millions more in tax handouts, and are poised to happily embrace minimal government regulations. Should we be surprised? Shock might be a more appropriate response given that the 2017 Republican tax bill benefits the rich and major corporations and hurts everyone else. As Robert L. Borosage points out in *The Nation*, "At a time when inequality has reached Gilded Age extremes, the Republicans will give fully one-half of the tax cuts to the top 1 percent. That's not an economic strategy. That's a plutocrats' raid on the Treasury."[35]

As Huxley predicted, historical memories of fascist methods used to seduce and exploit the masses—the ready supply of simplistic answers, vulgar spectacles, fear-mongering, and veneration of strong leaders—have faded. Under such circumstances, it is difficult to underestimate the depth and tragedy of the collapse of civic culture and democratic public spheres, especially given the profound influence of a corporate commercialism that offers nothing to counter the top-down culture of authoritarianism advanced under Trump.

A clear indication of how the apparently trivial media games played by Trumpists can quickly mutate into the censoring gag of authoritarianism took place when Steve Bannon stated in an interview that "the media should be embarrassed and humiliated and keep its mouth shut and just listen for a while. . . . You're the opposition party. Not the Democratic Party. . . . The media is the opposition party. They don't understand the country."[36] Unsurprisingly, Bannon also openly admired the power of Dick Cheney, Darth Vader, and Satan.[37] Such comments suggest not only a war on the press, but the intention to suppress dissent. It is a blatant refusal to see the essential role of robust and critical media in a democracy. In the Trumpist view, real journalism, which at its best functions as "the enemy of injustice, corruption, oppression and deceit,"[38] is another opponent to be ridiculed and silenced.

How else to explain a U.S. president calling journalists "among the most dishonest human beings on earth,"[39] going so far as to claim that critical media are "the enemy of the American people"?[40] These are ominous and alarming comments that not only imply journalists can be charged with treason, but echo previous totalitarian regimes that waged war on both the press and democracy itself. As Roger Cohen, a columnist for the *New York Times*, observes:

> "Enemy of the people," is a phrase with a near-perfect totalitarian pedigree deployed with refinements by the Nazis. . . . For Goebbels, writing in 1941, every Jew was "a sworn enemy of the German people." Here "the people" are an aroused mob imbued with some mythical essence of nationhood or goodness by a charismatic leader. The enemy is everyone else. Citizenship, with its shared rights and responsibilities, has ceased to be.[41]

A public shaped by manufactured ignorance and indifferent to the task of discerning the truth from lies has largely applauded Trump's expressions of fascist bravado, especially when he incites hatred and violence. Trump's call to build a wall between the United States and Mexico and his consideration of using the National Guard to round up undocumented immigrants arouse applause among his followers.[42] As does Trump's penchant for disparaging all his critics as losers, which perpetuates the way failed contestants were treated on his commercial TV show, *The Apprentice*.[43] Dissenting journalists and others are refused access to government officials, derided as purveyors of "fake news," become objects of retribution while being told to "shut up," and, in the course of being symbolically fired, are relegated to zones of terminal exclusion.[44]

What is clear is that elements of twentieth-century fascism that haunt the current age no longer appear as mere residue, but instead as an emerging threat. Trumpists epitomize the danger posed by authoritarians who long to rule a society without resistance, dominate its major political parties so as to dismantle any opposition, and secure uncontested control of its most important political, cultural, and economic institutions. In the United States, the consolidation of power and wealth in the hands of the financial elite, along with the savagery and misery that characterize the merger of neoliberalism and authoritarian politics, is no longer the stuff of movies and books. Those members of Congress who railed against both Obama's alleged imperial use of executive orders and later, during the

Republican primaries, denounced Trump as unfit for office, now exhibit a level of passivity and lack of moral courage that testify to their complicity with the dark shadow of authoritarianism signified by Trump's political ascent and actions taken during his first year in power.

The Trump Echo Chamber

During the early Trump presidency, we saw increasing numbers of supine media pundits, political opponents, and mainstream journalists tying themselves in "apologetic knots" while they "desperately look for signs that Donald Trump will be a pragmatic, recognizable American president once he takes the mantle of power."[45] Even the high-profile celebrity Oprah Winfrey stated, and without irony, in an interview with *Entertainment Tonight*, "I just saw President-elect Trump with President Obama in the White House, and it gave me hope."[46] This is quite a stretch given Trump's history of racist practices, his racist remarks about Blacks, Muslims, and Mexican immigrants during the primaries and the presidential campaign, and his appointment of a number of cabinet members who embrace a white nationalist ideology. *New York Times* opinion writer Nicholas Kristof sabotaged his self-proclaimed liberal belief system by asserting, in what appears to be acute lapse of judgment, that Americans should "Grit [their] teeth and give Trump a chance."[47] Bill Gates made clear his own often hidden reactionary worldview when speaking on CNBC's *Squawk Box*. The Microsoft co-founder slipped into a fog of self-delusion by stating that Trump had the potential to emulate JFK by establishing an upbeat and desirable mode of "leadership through innovation."[48] As comedian John Oliver pointed out on his show *Last Week Tonight*, Trump is not ordinary. Oliver brought his point home by shouting repeatedly, "THIS IS NOT NORMAL," and, of course, he is right. What does it mean to call it "ordinary" when the leader of a contemporary Western nation and global superpower proclaims a politics rooted in racist exclusion, white supremacy, and reactionary populism?

The initial complacency of much of the mainstream media further signaled that the storm clouds of authoritarianism were gathering unchecked and pointed to a retreat from responsible reporting and discourse if not a flight from any vestige of social responsibility.[49] But as the Trump administration assumed power, producing a litany of reactionary policies, embarrassing lies, insults aimed at America's allies, and attacks on the mainstream media, outlets such as MSNBC, CNN, the *Washington Post*, and the *New York Times* engaged in a series of relentless critiques of Trump, his systemic derangement of any viable notion of governance, and his authoritarian policies. As a result, watchdog journalists came under heavy criticism from Trump and his allies, who labeled their work "fake news" and "enemies of the American People." In fact, the Trump administration has repeated this view of the media so often that "almost a third of Americans believe it and "favor government restrictions on the press."[50]

Yet, in spite of the growing criticism of the Trump administration, especially around the publication of Michael

Wolff's scathing book, *Fire and Fury: Inside the Trump White House*, the ongoing legitimation and normalization of the Trump regime continued mostly through the efforts of conservative media apparatuses such as Fox News, Breitbart News Network, and Rupert Murdoch's media empire coupled with the almost unmitigated and sycophantic support of many prominent Republican politicians in the Senate and House of Representatives. Michelle Goldberg writing in the *New York Times* argues that Wolff's book makes clear "that Trump is entirely unfit for the presidency [and] everyone around him knows it. [Yet,] most members of Trump's campaign and administration are simply traitors. They are willing, out of some complex mix of ambition, resentment, cynicism and rationalization, to endanger all of our lives—all of our children's lives—by refusing to tell the country what they know about the senescent fool who boasts of the size of his 'nuclear button' on Twitter."[51]

Normalizing Trump's influence does more than sabotage democracy, political integrity, moral responsibility, and justice; it also diminishes the public-interest institutions necessary for a future of collective well-being and economic and political justice. *New York Times* columnist Charles Blow observes insightfully that under Trump,

> [The fact that] the nation is soon to be under the aegis of an unstable, unqualified, undignified demagogue [who surrounds] himself with a rogue's gallery of white supremacy sympathizers, anti-Muslim extremists, devout conspiracy

theorists, anti-science doctrinaires and climate change deniers is not normal, [and] I happen to believe that history will judge kindly those who continued to shout, from the rooftops, through their own weariness and against the corrosive drift of conformity.[52]

Blow is right. Any talk of working with a president who has surrounded himself with militarists, racists, anti-intellectuals, political sycophants, and neoliberal fundamentalists should be resisted at all costs. Trump and his companion ideologues fantasize about destroying all vestiges of the welfare state and the institutions that produce the public values that support the social contract. It is well worth remembering that neo-Nazis applauded when Trump welcomed into his inner-circle White House staff Steve Bannon, a notorious and combative bigot.[53] They were also the most vocal group bemoaning his dismissal in August 2017.

Normalization is both a code for a retreat from any sense of moral and political responsibility, and an act of political complicity with authoritarianism, and should be condemned outright. Holding on to any sense of what might be considered just and ethical suggests a responsibility to recognize when a government is put in the hands of a demagogue. When the inconceivable becomes conceivable, the call for normalization of what attempts to pass for the ordinary amounts to surrender to the forces of authoritarianism. What is being propagated by Trump's apologists is not only a reactionary and demagogic populism that will underpin the fundamental tenets of an emerging American-style authoritarianism, but also a shameless whitewashing of the racism and repression of dissent at the center of Trump's politics. In addition, little has been said about how Trump and his coterie of semi-delusional, if not heartless, advisors embrace a version of Ayn Rand's view that selfishness, a war against all competition, and unchecked self-interest are the highest human ideals. Arguments holding up Trump as a moderate, if not openly defending his normality, appear to overlook with facile indifference how fascist rhetoric has reared its ugly head again in many parts of the world, to grave effect, and that the Trump administration has clearly demonstrated an affinity with that sort of hateful vocabulary. How else to explain the support that Trump has received from a number of ruthless dictators who lead reactionary governments in countries such as the Philippines, Turkey, and Egypt, among others? The danger this complacency suggests is all the more ominous given the current breakdown of civic literacy and the general public's increasing inability to deal with complex issues, on the one hand, and the attempt by those who hold power to ruthlessly promote a depoliticizing discourse of lies, simplicity, and manufactured distortions on the other.

Hannah Arendt, Sheldon Wolin, Timothy Snyder, and Robert O. Paxton, the great theorists of totalitarianism, believed that the fluctuating elements of fascism are still with us and that as long as they are, they will crystallize in different forms. Far from being fixed in a frozen moment of historical terror, these theorists believed not only in the persistence of totalitarianism's "protean origins," but that its endurance "heralds [totalitarianism] as a possible model for the future."[54] Arendt, in particular, was keenly aware that a culture of fear, the dismantling of civil and political rights, the ongoing militarization of society, the attack on labor, an obsession with national security, human rights abuses, the emergence of a police state, a deeply rooted racism, and the attempts by demagogues to undermine education as a foundation for producing a critical citizenry were all at work in American society.

Historical conjunctures might produce different forms of authoritarianism, but they all share a hatred for democracy, dissent, and human rights. More recently, Robert O. Paxton, in his seminal work *The Anatomy of Fascism*, provides a working definition of fascism that points to both its anti-democratic moments and those elements that link it to both the past and the present. Paxton's purpose is not to provide a precise definition of fascism, but to understand the conditions that enabled fascism to work and make possible its development in the future.[55] Accordingly, he argues that fascism may be defined as follows:

A form of political behavior marked by obsessive preoccupation with community decline, humiliation or victimhood and by compensatory cults of unity, energy and purity, in which a mass-based party of committed nationalist militants, working in uneasy but effective collaboration with traditional elites, abandons democratic liberties and pursues with redemptive violence and without ethical or legal restraints goals of internal cleansing and external expansion.[56]

Under Trump, there are ominous echoes of the fascism that developed in Europe in the 1920s and 1930s. Paxton is particularly useful in describing what he calls nine "mobilizing passions" of fascism that provide a common ground for most fascist movements. These include, in abbreviated form, (1) a sense of overwhelming crisis; (2) the primacy of the group and subordination of individuals to it; (3) the belief that one group is a victim, justifying action beyond moral and legal limits; (4) dread of the group's decline; (5) call for purer community by consent of violence if necessary; (6) need for the authority of a natural leader (7) supremacy of leader's instincts over reason; (8) beauty of violence and efficacy of the will devoted to group's success; (9) right of chosen people to dominate others without restraint.[57]

All of these "mobilizing passions" bear a resemblance to the fascist script that Trump has made in his repeated claims that the United States is in a period of decline; his nationalist slogan to "make America great again"; his official displays of coded bigotry and intolerance, as in his symbolic association with Andrew Jackson; his portrayal of himself as a strongman who alone can save the country; his appeal to aggression and violence aimed at those who disagree with him; his contempt for dissent; his deep-rooted anti-intellectualism, or what Arendt called "thoughtlessness" (e.g., denial that climate change is produced by humans), coupled with his Twitter-driven elevation of impulsiveness over reason; his appeal to xenophobia and national greatness; his courting of anti-Semites and white supremacists; his flirtation with the discourse of racial purity; his support for a white Christian public sphere; his denigration of Muslims, Blacks, undocumented immigrants, Native Americans, women, and transgender people; his contempt for weakness; and his adolescent, size-matters enthusiasm for locker-room masculinity.

But fascism did not come to the United States with the emergence of Donald Trump. In fact much of what pass for American history has a close relationship to what might be called the neo-fascist age of Trump. As David Neiwert observes:

> Fascism is not just a historical relic. It remains a living and breathing phenomenon that, for generations since World War II, had only maintained a kind of half-life on the fringes of the American right. Its constant enterprise, during all those years, was to return white supremacism to the mainstream, restore its previous legitimacy, and restore its own power within the nation's political system. . . . [The] long-term creep of radicalization of the right [has] come home to roost. . . . With Trump as its champion, it has finally succeeded. [58]

In his book *On Tyranny*, the renowned historian Timothy Snyder also acknowledges that fascism is not static and expresses its most fundamental attacks on democracy in different forms, which is all the more reason for people to develop what he calls an active relationship to history to prevent a normalizing relationship to authoritarian regimes such as the United States under Trump's rule.[59] Surely, a critical understanding of history would have gone a long way in recognizing the elements of a fascist discourse in Trump's inaugural speech.

Trump's authoritarian mindset was on full display during his inaugural speech and in the actions he undertook during his first few days in office. In the first instance, he presented a dystopian view of American society laced with racist stereotyping, xenophobia, and the discourse of ultra-nationalism. Frank Rich called the language of the speech "violent and angry—'This American carnage stops right here'—reeking of animosity, if not outright hatred . . . the tone was one of retribution and revenge."[60] As soon as the speech ended, however, the normalizing process within the mainstream media began with the expected tortured clichés from various Fox News commentators calling it "muscular," "unifying," "very forceful," and "just masterful," and Charles Krauthammer stating that it was "completely nonpartisan."[61] The fog of self-delusion and denial was in full swing at CNN when historian Douglas Brinkley called Trump's inaugural address not only "presidential" but "solid and well-written" and the "best speech" Trump has made "in his life."

Just before Trump's election, the CEO of the CBS television network, Les Moonves, stated that his network's inordinate and disastrous coverage of Trump "may not be good for America but it's damn good for CBS." Moonves openly gloated because the network was not only pumping up its ratings but was also getting rich by covering Trump. As he put it, "the money's rolling in. . . . this is going to be a very good year for us. . . . It's a terrible thing to say, but bring it on, Donald. Go ahead. Keep going."[62] Moonves made it clear that the objectives of mainstream media in general have little to do with the public interest, pursuing the truth, or holding power accountable. On the contrary, their real goal is to leverage corruption, lies, and misrepresentation to garner attention, even to the point of transforming the press into an adjunct of authoritarian ideologies, policies, interests, and commodified values—if that is what it takes to increase their profit margins. But more dangers lie ahead for the country than the transformation of critical and independent media into an echo chamber for an entertainment industry that serves up Trump as its main spectacle, or for that matter the media's growing refusal to recognize the fascist ideology driving the Trump administration. A growing criticism of Trump by the critical mainstream media is to be welcomed, but it does not go far enough and runs the risk of normalizing a president that has turned governance into leverage for his family to rake in profitable business deals. For instance, the press has said too little about Jared Kushner's real estate company receiving a $30 million investment from Menora Mivtachim, which according to the *New York Times* is "an insurer and "one of Israel's largest financial institutions."[63] In blatant disregard for conflict of interest, the investment came at a time when Kushner was acting as the point person in mediating peace talks between the Palestinians and the Israeli government. Such shameless and irresponsible acts of misconduct began as soon as Trump took office.

Once in command of the U.S. military and the White House, Trump not only enacted measures to facilitate building a wall on the Mexican border and to prevent people from seven Muslim-majority countries from entering the United States, putting his xenophobia in action, but he also cleared the way for resurrecting the construction of the Keystone XL and Dakota Access pipelines. Trump's broad assault on U.S. environmental protections is indicative of his equal disregard for domestic issues and certain populations, when the accumulation of capital is at stake. Pushing through the pipelines suggests a barefaced disdain for the rights of Native Americans who protested the building of a pipeline that both crossed their sacred burial lands and posed a risk to contaminating the Missouri River, the primary water source for the Standing Rock Sioux. In response to Trump's inaugural address and early policy measures, Roger Cohen wrote a forceful commentary suggesting that Trump's fascist tendencies reverberate with the familiar tactics of former dictators and that his presence in American politics augurs ill for democracy. He stated:

But the first days of the Trump presidency . . . pushed me over the top. The president is playing with fire. To say, as he did, that the elected representatives of American democracy are worthless and that the people are everything is to lay the foundations of totalitarianism. It is to say that democratic institutions are irrelevant and all that counts is the great leader and the masses he arouses. To speak of "American carnage" is to deploy the dangerous lexicon of blood, soil and nation. To boast of "a historic movement, the likes of which the world has never seen before" is to demonstrate consuming megalomania. To declaim "America first" and again, "America first," is to recall the darkest clarion calls of nationalist dictators. To exalt protectionism is to risk a return to a world of barriers and confrontation. To utter falsehood after falsehood, directly or through a spokesman, is to foster the disorientation that makes crowds susceptible to the delusions of strongmen.[64]

As language is hacked by propaganda, the American public is inundated with empty slogans such as "post-truth," "fake news," and "alternative facts." This culture is part of what Todd Gitlin calls "an interlocking ecology of falsification that has driven the country around the bend."[65] Under such circumstances, Trump uses language for humiliation and ridicule, not truth-telling or governing.

Given these conditions, the celebration of the principle of an alleged free press hides more than it promises.

Noam Chomsky, Bill Moyers, and Robert McChesney, among others, have previously observed that corporate media work in conjunction with the financial elite and the military-industrial-academic complex. The normalization of Trump is about more than dominant media outlets being complicit with corrupt power or willfully retreating from any sense of social responsibility; it is also about aiding and abetting power in order to increase the bottom line and attract other cowardly forms of influence and recognition. This is evident in the fact that some dominant elements of the mainstream press not only refused to take Trump seriously, they also concocted embarrassing rationales for why they would not hold him accountable for what he says. For instance, Gerard Baker, the editor-in-chief of the *Wall Street Journal,* publicly announced that in the future he would not allow his reporters to use the word "lie" in their coverage. National Public Radio (NPR) also issued a statement arguing that it would not use the word "lie," on the grounds that "the minute you start branding things with a word like 'lie,' you push people away from you."[66] In this truly Orwellian comment, NPR is suggesting that reporting lies on the part of governments and politicians should be avoided by the media on the grounds that people might be annoyed by having to face the contradiction between the truth and misinformation. This is more than a refusal of journalism's democratic purpose to uphold people, institutions, and power to some measure of justice; it also legitimizes the kind of political and moral cowardice that undermines informed resistance, the First Amendment, and the truth. While such actions may not rise to the level of book burning that was characteristic of various totalitarian regimes in the past, they do mark a form of self-censorship and misinformation seen in pre-fascist societies.

Although in much of the mainstream media, especially its more reactionary elements, Trump appears to have more friends than foes, this has not prevented him from demonstrating several times over that he is capable of using bullying repression and censorship to undermine the press. Hence, it was no surprise when Trump, at his first president-elect press conference, not only refused to take questions from a CNN reporter because his network had published material critical of Trump, but also justified his refusal by labeling CNN "fake news"—a slogan he appropriated not to challenge the veracity of the media, but to disparage his critics. Yet the general response of the mainstream media was to adopt Trump's stance, and likewise to rage against the rise of "fake news," suggesting that, by doing so, their own integrity could not be questioned. Of course, the term "fake news" is slippery and can be deployed to political ends—a maneuver which is on full display particularly when used by Trumpists to dismiss anyone or any organization that might hold them accountable for their fabrications. A particularly egregious and telling example of Trump's refusal to deal with anyone who questions his authority was his firing of James Comey, the director of the FBI, followed by Comey's appearance soon afterwards before a congressional committee.

Testifying before a Senate Intelligence Committee, Comey claimed that in meetings with the president, Trump had not only asked him if he wanted to keep his job, but also demanded what amounted to a loyalty pledge from him. Comey saw these interventions as an attempt to develop a patronage relationship with him and viewed them as part of a larger attempt to neutralize an FBI investigation into former national security advisor Michael Flynn's links to Russia. What Comey implies, but does not state directly, is that Trump attempted to turn the FBI into a complicit and subservient agent of corrupt political power. Comey also stated that he did not want to be alone with the president, going so far as to ask Attorney General Jeff Sessions to make sure that such meetings would not take place in the future, because he did not trust Trump. Comey also accused Trump of lying about the FBI being in disarray, slandering him, and misrepresenting the reasons for his firing. And most important, Trump had possibly engaged in an obstruction of justice. In fact, Comey was so distrustful of Trump that he took notes of his exchanges with him and leaked some of the memos to a friend at Columbia University, who passed on the contents to a reporter at the *New York Times*. Comey stated outright he leaked the information because he thought Trump would lie about their conversations, and he wanted to prompt the appointment of a special counsel.

Suffering from what appears to be malignant narcissism and a pathological contempt for the truth, Trump has tweeted that Comey's testimony had vindicated him and that Comey was a liar and a leaker. Of course, Trump made no mention of the fact that Comey leaked non-classified information because he did not trust anyone at the Department of Justice, especially since it was led by Trump crony Jeff Sessions. Since it goes without saying that Trump is a serial liar, there is a certain irony in Trump accusing Comey, a lifelong Republican and highly respected director of the FBI, of lying. As Mehdi Hasan, appearing on *Democracy Now!*, observes:

> From a political point of view, we know that one of the biggest flaws in Donald Trump's presidency, his candidacy, his ability to be president, is that he's a serial fabricator. Now you have the former top law enforcement officer of this country going in front of the Senate, under oath, saying he—that, you know, "Those are lies, plain and simple," he said, referring to Trump's description of his firing. He said, "I was worried he would lie." He says, "I was worried about the nature of the man." . . . And there was a quite funny tweet that went viral last night, which said, you know, "Trump is saying he's a liar. Comey is saying Trump's a liar. Well, who do you believe? Do you believe an FBI director who served under two— who served under three presidents from two parties? Or do you believe the guy who said Obama was born in Kenya?" And, you know, that's what faces us today.[67]

Trump's presidency normalizes official intolerance, bigotry, and falsehood. Under Trump, lying and fake news are used for dominating rivals, journalists, and the American public. A scammer and a bully, Trump assumes the inflated swagger of an insufferably pompous game show host. Like a boy in middle school, he is obsessed with size, popularity, and winning. In addition to democracy itself, his biggest fears seem to be openness, honesty, and criticism of his performance. We will likely see more of this, as traditional democratic public spheres such as higher education also feel the brunt of Trump's politics of retribution. Writing about the "creeping rot" of the Trump administration and how it emulates and accentuates a society lost in a neoliberal abyss of self-interest, unchecked individualism, and mass contempt, James Traub rightly argues that "Perhaps in a democracy the distinctive feature of decadence is not debauchery but terminal self-absorption."[68] We live at a time when notions of shared responsibility, share citizenry, and an embrace of the public good become objects of disdain, especially in the conservative media and other right-wing cultural pathways.

Any analysis of the forces behind the election and normalization of Trump's fraudulence must, once again, include the powerful role of the reactionary media in the United States. A remarkable article by former conservative radio talk show host Charles Sykes argues that over the last few decades, right-wing media have played a major role in discrediting and delegitimizing the fact-based media. In doing so, the conservative media have destroyed "much of the right's immunity to false information." According to Sykes, conservatives, including himself, created a "new post-factual political culture" that has become so powerful that even when the Trumps are caught lying, they believe they can do so with impunity because "the alternative-reality media will provide air cover" for their lies, allowing these fabrications effectively to pollute "political discourse" and discredit other "independent sources of information."[69]

Evidence of this major assault on truth can be measured in part by the Orwellian magnitude of the lies the Trump family and their employees produce.[70] For instance, Kellyanne Conway attempted recently to justify Trump's executive order banning people from seven Muslim-majority countries by referring to what she called the "Bowling Green massacre," an alleged terrorist attack by Iraqi refugees that was to have taken place in 2011. According to Conway, Obama instituted a six-month ban on Iraqi resettlements. The attack never happened, no Iraqis engaged in any such activity, and the Obama administration never instituted such a ban. It got even more absurd, as when former White House press secretary Sean Spicer claimed that Iran had committed an act of war by attacking a U.S. naval vessel. In reality, Houthi rebels had attacked a Saudi vessel off the coast of Yemen. Trump's lying appears to have no limits and exceeds the boundaries of sanity, as was evident in his statement to a senator and an advisor, according to the *New York Times*, that the notorious 2005 *Access Hollywood* ("grab 'em by the pussy") tape was not authentic, though he acknowledged in October 2016 that it was his voice on the tape, and later apologized for his egregious sexist comments.[71]

Normalization has many registers, and how media broadcast Trump's statements serves, in many ways, to further normalize his constant fraudulence. For instance, the *Wall Street Journal*'s refusal to address critically Trump's endless lies and insults is matched by the highbrow *New Yorker*'s publication of a piece on Trump that largely celebrates how he is viewed by conservative intellectuals such as Hillsdale College president Larry Arnn.[72] Arnn supports Trump because they share the view that "the government has become dangerous." If Arnn were referring to the rise of the surveillance and permanent war state, it would be hard to disagree with him. Instead, he was referring to the government's enforcement of "runaway regulations." What Arnn and Kelefa Sanneh, the author of the *New Yorker* article, ignore or conveniently forget is the fact that the real danger the government poses is the direct result of its being in the hands of demagogues such as Trump who are truly dangerous and threaten other countries, American society, and the rest of the world. When Sanneh mentions Trump's connection to the "alt-right," he underplays the group's fascist ideology and refuses to use the term "white supremacist" in talking about such groups, reverting instead to the innocuous-sounding term "white identity politics."[73] Trump's misogyny, racism, anti-intellectualism, Islamophobia, and hatred of democracy are barely mentioned. Sanneh even goes so far as to suggest that since Trump has disavowed the "alt-right," his connection to neo-fascist groups is tenuous. This is more than an apology dressed up in the bland discourse of ambiguity. Such reporting is a shameful retreat from journalistic integrity—an assault on the truth that constitutes an egregious act of normalization.[74]

Under Trump's regime, compassion and respect for the other will almost certainly be viewed with contempt, while society will increasingly become more militarized and corporations further deregulated in order to engage in behaviors that put the American public and the entire planet in danger. A form of social and historical amnesia appears set to descend over American society. A culture of civic illiteracy will likely become more widespread and legitimated, along with a culture of fear that will enable an increasingly harsh law-and-order regime. Indeed, Neal Gabler argues that the normalization of Trump's "alt-right" political network presents a greater threat than Trump himself.[75] Frank Rich goes further by insisting that things might get worse *after* Trump because of the "permanent mass movement" he and Bannon fomented. According to Rich,

Trump's unexpected triumph in 2016, claiming the Oval Office for unabashedly nationalist right-wing populism, changed history's trajectory. His capture of the presidency and a major political party makes it highly unlikely that his adherents will now follow the pattern of their dejected forebears, who retreated to lick their wounds and regroup in the shadows after their electoral defeats. These radicals are not some aberrational fringe. The swath of America that has now been reinvigorated and empowered by landing a tribune in the White House for the first time is a permanent mass movement that has remained stable in size and fixed in its beliefs for more than half a century. How large a mass? At the high end, Trumpists amount to the third or so of the country that has never wavered in support of the Trump presidency.[76]

A society driven along by reactionary zeal will mean support for policies to be enacted in which public goods—such as schools—will be privatized. There will likely be a further retreat from political engagement, civic courage, and social responsibility, one matched by a growing abandonment by the state of any allegiance to the common good. The free-market mentality that gained prominence under the presidency of Ronald Reagan will likely accelerate under Trump and continue to drive politics, destroy many social protections, celebrate a hyper-competitiveness, and deregulate economic activity. Under Donald Trump's reign, almost all human activities, practices, and institutions are at risk of becoming subject to market principles and militarized. The only relations that will matter will likely be those defined in commercial, not civic, terms.

Under Trump, it is likely that the full power of the surveillance state will be deployed to target protesters, people of color, Muslims, and undocumented immigrants. Surely, all the signs are in place, given the coterie of warmongers, Islamophobes, white supremacists, and anti-public demagogues Trump has placed in high-ranking government positions. Americans may be on the verge of witnessing how democracy unravels, and this is precisely why Trump's authoritarian presidency must not be normalized. Trump's repressive policies will not change as his presidency unfolds. His impulsive narcissism, indifference to the truth, and intensive use of the spectacle will further increase his view of himself and his policies as unaccountable, especially as he institutes a mode of governance that bullies his opponents and deals with his audience directly through social media.

With the new authoritarian state, perhaps the gravest threat we might encounter is widespread indifference to Trump's undemocratic use of power. It is precisely the pervasive spread of political indifference that puts at risk the fundamental principles of justice and freedom that lie at the heart of a robust democracy. The Trump family's rise to power signals the unimaginable. Dynastic politics, official lying, and militant nationalism all occur openly under Donald Trump's rule. Democracy is under attack. Americans are expected not to behave as empowered citizens, but as obedient subjects and grateful consumers who should repeat slogans and cheer for the supreme leader no matter what. This is the brave new surveillance/punishing state that merges Orwell's Big Brother with Huxley's mind-altering modes of entertainment, education, and propaganda.

Fortunately, a number of diverse groups, including unions, immigrant rights groups, constitutional law organizations, anti-fascist networks, Black liberation groups, congregations and faith-based organizations, legal coalitions and reproductive rights groups, along with teachers, actors, and artists openly oppose Trump's authoritarian ideas and policies. As George Yancy has pointed out, such opposition is unique in that it makes the political more pedagogical by elevating protests, modes of resistance, and criticism to the level of the cultural rather than allowing such critiques to reside in the voice and presence of isolated outspoken people of conscience.[77] Moreover, numerous publications, activists, and public intellectuals such as Cornel West, Angela Davis, Anthony DiMaggio, and Robin D.G. Kelley, and groups such as Action Together, Swing Left, Dream Defenders, Black Youth Project 100, and the Black Lives Matter movement are producing instructive articles on both the nature of resistance and what forms it might take.[78]

The nightmare is upon us. Donald Trump is driving the United States toward neo-fascist rule. The new authoritarianism is glaringly visible and deeply brutal, and points to a bleak future in the most immediate sense. Certainly, we are in the midst of what Hannah Arendt called "dark times." Individual and collective resistance is the only hope we have to move beyond this ominous moment in our history. The question that we once confronted us was, what will U.S. society look like under Trump? Now we must ask, what will U.S. society look like in the aftermath of a Trump regime that goes unchallenged? For most Americans, it may well mimic Huxley's lurid world in which corruption is rampant, ignorance is a political weapon, and pleasure is utilized as a form of control, offering nothing more than the swindle of commercialized fulfillment, if not something more self-deluding and defeating.

Both Huxley and Orwell presented their visions of closed dystopian societies as warnings. They did so in the hope of motivating us to preserve and advance openness in government and society. Orwell believed in the power of people to resist the seduction of authoritarian propaganda with spirited forms of broad-based resistance willing to grasp the reins of political emancipation. For Huxley, there was only hope to be found in a pessimism that had exhausted itself, leaving people to reflect on the implications of a totalitarian power that controls pleasure as well as pain, and the utterly disintegrated social fabric that would be its consequence. Orwell's optimism, tempered by a sense of educated hope, was one that granted people the capacity to reclaim their agency, expand a narrow conception of self-interest, place themselves in the bigger picture, connect their individual well-being to the well-being of others, and make a commitment to struggle for an alternative future. History is open, and only time will tell who was more accurate.

CHAPTER TWO

AUTHORITARIANISM AND THE LEGACY OF FASCIST COLLABORATION

"The twentieth century was excellent proof evil was alive and well, and this has reinforced the positions of modern Manichaeans. They saw a world that could be temporarily abandoned by God, but not by Satan."

—Zygmunt Bauman and Leonidas Donskis

Donald Trump's presidency has sparked a heated debate about the past, particularly over whether the Trump administration should be judged on a continuum with fascist regimes whose "protean origins" reach back to the beginnings of the modern nation-state, but which a number of contemporary thinkers believe are "still with us."[1] This is a compelling argument, one that combines the resources of historical memory with analyses of the distinctive temper of the current historical moment in the United States. For instance, an increasing number of critics across the ideological spectrum have identified Trump as a fascist or neo-fascist whose administration echoes some of the key messages of an earlier period of fascist politics. On the left/liberal side of politics, this includes writers such as Chris Hedges, Robert Reich, Cornel West, Drucilla Cornel, Peter Dreier, and John Bellamy Foster.[2] Similar arguments have been made on the conservative side by writers such as Robert Kagan, Jet Heer, Meg Whitman, and Charles Sykes.[3]

Historians of fascism such as Timothy Snyder and Robert O. Paxton have argued that Trumpism is not comparable to Nazism, but that there are sufficient similarities between them to warrant some concerns about surviving elements of a totalitarian past crystalizing into new forms in the United States.[4] Paxton, in particular, argues that the Trump regime is closer to a plutocracy than to fascism. I think Paxton's analysis overplays the differences between fascism and the kind of far-right political formations currently taking shape under the influence of Donald Trump.[5] If Trump has his way, traditional state power will succumb to the influence of wealthy individuals and corporations. We have already seen that the social cleansing and state violence inherent in totalitarianism have been amplified under Trump.

Both Hannah Arendt and Sheldon Wolin, the great historians of totalitarianism, argued that the dangerous conditions that produce totalitarianism are still with us. Wolin, in particular, insisted that the United States was evolving into an authoritarian society.[6] In contrast, other historians and pundits have downplayed or simply denied the association of totalitarianism with the United States.

With respect to Trump, they argue he is either a sham, a right-wing populist, or simply a reactionary. Three notable examples of the latter position include cultural critic Neal Gabler, Corey Robin, and Victoria de Grazia. Gabler argues that Trump is mostly a self-promoting con artist and pretender president whose greatest crime is to elevate pretentiousness, self-promotion, and appearance over substance, all of which proves that he lacks the capacity and will to govern.[7] Corey Robin argues that Trump bears no relationship to Hitler or the policies of the Third Reich, and in doing so not only dismisses the threat that Trump poses to the values and institutions of democracy, but plays down the growing threat of authoritarianism in the United States. For Robin, Trump has failed to institute many of his policies and hence is just a weak politician with little actual power. Not only does Robin focus too much on the person of Trump, but he is relatively silent about the forces that produced him and the danger these proto-fascist social formations now pose to those who are the objects of the administration's racist, sexist, and xenophobic taunts and policies. Trump and his Vichyesque collaborators have put in place a culture of fear and cruelty that evokes a distinctly authoritarian regime and cannot be dismissed by simply focusing on Trump as some sort of reckless clown.[8]

As Robin D.G. Kelley pointed out to me in a personal correspondence, Corey Robin "falls into the trap of confusing the president's behavior with what his administration is doing and what political and cultural changes are taking place all around us." By focusing exclusively on

Trump the failed politician, Robin both normalizes the conditions that produced Trump and the varied forces at work in producing an emerging if not actually existing authoritarianism. Under the Trump administration, life is stripped of all transcendent values and is reduced to those vile discourses, policies, and values that reproduce nativistic, white supremacist politics and a society inhabited by a ruling elite whose life, borrowing a phrase from Byung-Chul Han, "equals that of the undead. They are too alive to die and too dead to live."[9]

Those arguments suggesting we have to choose between whether Trump is just a twittering clown or a Hitler in the making miss the point of how dangerous the current historical moment is and the degree to which Trump is a symptom of the rise of illiberal democracy in many other countries and a political party at home that embraces distinctly American authoritarian impulses and elements of fascism.[10]

An extended version of this argument can be found in the work of historian Victoria de Grazia, who has argued that Trump bears little direct resemblance to either Hitler or Mussolini and is just a reactionary conservative.[11] Trump is not Hitler in that he has not created concentration camps, shut down the critical media, or rounded up dissidents; moreover, the United States at the current historical moment is not the Weimar Republic. But it would be irresponsible to consider him a clown or aberration, given his hold on power and the ideologues who support him.

At best, Trump and his deeply bigoted advisors speak to the social, cultural, and economic anxieties of many working-class Americans, particularly white Americans. Their efforts to consolidate power, repress dissent, thwart investigation, and engage in a politics of fabrication increasingly pose a national security crisis that resembles aspects of the fascism that emerged in the 1930s. On the other hand, Trumpism is a unique product of our times, our commercial culture, and the media. Before his death in 1975, Italian film director Pier Paolo Pasolini suggested that commercialism could lead to new, non-traditional forms of fascism. "I consider consumerism to be a Fascism worse than the classical one," Pasolini said, "because clerical Fascism didn't really transform Italians, didn't enter into them. It was a totalitarian state but not a totalizing one."[12] Corporate commercialism today *is* totalizing. The result is an advertising-saturated culture that permits a rich con artist like Donald Trump to abandon any pretense of civility, accountability, or integrity and simply play by the rules of celebrity and advertising to hype, scam, and market his way to power.

Decontextualizing Trump's rise to power and personalizing his presidency are more than ahistorical fantasies, they also underestimate the ways in which neoliberalism has devalued and waged a full-scale assault on the ideologies, values, institutions, and modes of solidarity necessary for a functioning democracy. As Wendy Brown observes:

> On the one hand, I would argue that only when democracies have already been devalued, weakened, and diminished in meaning—as they have

been under neoliberalism—could a full-scale assault on democracy from the right take place as
we see today. So this authoritarian—I'm wary of
using the term "populist"—contempt for liberal
democratic institutions and values we see sweeping across the Euro-Atlantic world has a lot to
do with three decades of devaluing and diminish-
ing democracy. . . . So this is not a radical break
from neoliberalism. . . . Trump was certainly not
able to mobilize conservatives and Evangelicals
to vote for him because we've suddenly become
"overrun" with immigrants from the South. The
ground for Trump's rise was tilled not just by
neoliberalism's destruction of viable lives and futures for working and middle-class populations
through the global outsourcing of jobs, the race
to the bottom in wages and taxes, and the destruction of public goods, including education.
This ground was also tilled by neoliberalism's
valorization of markets and morals and its deval-
uation of democracy and politics, Constitutional-
ism and social justice.[13]

Trump's ability to attract followers was based in part
on his call to "drain the swamp," suggesting he would address the corrupt merger of politics, money, and corporate
power in Washington. Rather than drain the swamp, he
has expanded it and elevated corporate power and privilege to new and almost unprecedented levels. Not only

has he initiated tax reforms that egregiously benefit corporations and the ultra-rich, he has also given new life to Pasolini's insights about the deadening force of consumerism. For example, Trump has pushed legislation that would overturn "a Consumer Financial Protection Bureau rule that permits class-action lawsuits against banks and credit unions."[14] Senator Elizabeth Warren called the bill "a giant wet kiss to Wall Street."[15] It is hard to make this stuff up. It gets worse. What appears indisputable is that the Trump family's occupation of the White House not only furthers the interests of the Trump family business, it furthers decades of effort from the larger financial elite to undermine the democratic institutions that seek to hold them accountable to the same laws of the land that average Americans must live by. The threat of authoritarianism has become the crisis of our times.[16] Democracy, openness, and accountability are under attack.

History, once again, offers us a context in which a global constellation of forces is coming together in ways that speak to tensions and contradictions animating everyday lives. Little coherent and critical language is in use to address these forces. Fear, angst, paranoia, and incendiary passion escalate as a result. It would be wise to revisit one of the key questions that emerges from the work of Hannah Arendt: *Are the events of our time are leading us to become a totalitarian society?*

Whether or not Trump is a fascist in the manner of earlier totalitarian leaders somewhat misses the point. Though the legacies of past authoritarian regimes persist in contemporary politics, there is no exact blueprint for fascism. As Adam Gopnik observes:

> To call [Trump] a fascist of some variety is simply to use a historical label that fits. The arguments about whether he meets every point in some static fascism matrix show a misunderstanding of what that ideology involves. It is the essence of fascism to have no single fixed form—an attenuated form of nationalism in its basic nature, it naturally takes on the colors and practices of each nation it infects. In Italy, it is bombastic and neoclassical in form; in Spain, Catholic and religious; in Germany, violent and romantic. It took forms still crazier and more feverishly sinister, if one can imagine, in Romania, whereas under Oswald Mosley, in England, its manner was predictably paternalistic and aristocratic. It is no surprise that the American face of fascism would take on the forms of celebrity television and the casino greeter's come-on, since that is as much our symbolic scene as nostalgic re-creations of Roman splendors once were Italy's.[17]

The fact is that Trumpism fetishizes the Andrew Jackson presidency, a gateway to normalizing historical social intolerance and violent white supremacy as forms of official national heritage. Taken with nationalist appeals, these forces coalesce into contemporary manifestations of a pro-fascist system, an increasingly militarized, top-down order in which what the supreme leader says goes, irrespective with how closely it comports with fact, consensus, law, or the common good. Historian Timothy Snyder also suggests that the real issue is not whether Trump is a literal model of other fascist leaders but whether his approach to governing and the new political order he is producing are fascistic. He writes:

> I don't want to dodge your question about whether Trump is a fascist or not. As I see it, there are certainly elements of his approach which are fascistic. The straight-on confrontation with the truth is at the center of the fascist worldview. The attempt to undo the Enlightenment as a way to undo institutions, that is fascism. Whether he realizes it or not is a different question, but that's what fascists did. They said, "Don't worry about the facts, don't worry about logic, think instead in terms of mystical unities and direct connections between the mystical leader and the people." That's fascism. Whether we see it or not, whether we like it or not, whether we forget, that is fascism. Another thing that's clearly fascist about Trump were the rallies. The way that he used the language, the blunt repetitions, the naming of the enemies, the physical removal of opponents from rallies, that was really, without exaggeration, just like the 1920s and the 1930s.[18]

To date, the ascendency of Trumpism has been compared to the discrete emergence of deeply reactionary nationalisms in Italy, Germany, France, and elsewhere. Broadening the lens with which we view events happening in the United States allows for a deeper historical understanding of the international scope and interplay of forces that characterize globalization. We are currently seeing socially grounded responses and authoritarian responses (of which ultra-nationalism is one) to the intensifying impact of neoliberal capitalism. Such impact includes catastrophic climate change, technological disruption, acute inequities in wealth and power, mass migrations, permanent warfare, and the increasing possibility of a nuclear war. In the United States, indications of authoritarianism are present in Trump's eroding of civil liberties, the undermining of the separation of church and state, health care policies that reveal an egregious indifference to life and death, and attempts to shape the political realm through a process of chronic fabrication and intolerance, if not, as Snyder insists, tyranny itself.[19]

History not only grounds us in the past by showing how democratic institutions rise and fall, it is also replete with memories and narratives of resistance that pose a dangerous threat for any fascist system. This is particularly true today given the ideological features and legacies of fascism that are deeply woven into Trumpism's rhetoric of retribution, intolerance, and demonization; its mix of shlock pageantry, coercion, violence, and impunity; and the constant stoking of ultra-nationalism and racial agitation.

Keeping historical memory alive is a form of resistance because it questions everything and complicates one's relationship to power, oneself, others, and the larger community. It also functions "to give witness to the truth of the past so that the politics of today is vibrantly democratic."[20] Historical memory matters because it offers a form of moral witnessing, and serves as a crucial asset in preventing new forms of fascism from becoming normalized. The conditions leading to fascism do not exist outside of history in some ethereal space in which everything is measured against the degree of distraction it promises. Historical memory is a prerequisite to the political and moral awakening necessary to successfully counter authoritarianism in the United States today.

The echoes of fascism in Trump's actions have been well documented, but what has been overlooked is a sustained analysis of his abuse and disparagement of historical memory, particularly in light of his relationships with a range of extreme right-wing networks at home, and dictators and political demagogues across the globe. Trump's ignorance of history was on full display in his misinformed comments about former U.S. president Andrew Jackson and nineteenth-century abolitionist Frederick Douglass. Trump's comments about Jackson having strong views on the Civil War were widely ridiculed given that Jackson died sixteen years before the war took place. Trump was also criticized for comments he made during Black History Month when he spoke about Frederick Douglass as if he were still alive, though he died 120 years ago. For the mainstream press, these historical missteps largely reflect Trump's ignorance of American history.

But there is more at stake than simply ignorance. Trump's comments provide a window into his ongoing practice of stepping outside of history so as to deny its relevance for understanding both the economic and political forces that brought him to power, and the historical lessons to be drawn in light of his embrace of authoritarian elements. His alleged ignorance is also a cover for enabling a "post-truth" culture in which dissent is reduced to fake news, the press is dismissed as the enemy of the people, and a mode of totalitarian education is enabled whose purpose, as Hannah Arendt has written, is "not to instill convictions but to destroy the capacity to form any."[21]

Trump's disrespect for journalists appears to have found a home in the wider culture of control and violence. For instance, Peter Maass notes that "journalists physically [are] prevented from asking questions of officials, arrested when trying to do so, and in a now-infamous example from Montana, body-slammed to the ground by a Republican candidate who didn't want to discuss his party's position on health care. [This] is most likely a prelude" to more ominous forms of repression.[22] Maass argues that Trump's targets in the future will be "government officials who provide us with the news for our stories."[23]

Robert Reich sees a broader potential reach of such repression, arguing that Trump has supplemented his attack on the press and government officials with huge budget cuts that roll back civil rights enforcement. For instance, he states that the Trump administration has initiated massive cuts in the investigative arm of the Civil Right Division, the Department of Labor's Office of Federal Contract Compliance, "which investigates discrimination by companies with federal contracts, [and] the Department of Education's Office of Civil Rights—charged with investigating discrimination in America's schools."[24] He has also called for eliminating "the Environmental Protection Agency's environmental justice program—which combats higher rates of pollution in communities of color."[25] Instead of fighting the out-of-control opioid crisis in the United States, Trump and Sessions have decided to enforce pot prohibition and force states to recriminalize marijuana possession and distribution.[26] In spite of how difficult it may be for Sessions to wage this war, it does signal his willingness to criminalize harmless behaviors as part of a broader attempt to expand the reach of the carceral state.

Donald Trump's supportive relationships with dictators and demagogues around the world also speaks volumes. As the *New York Times* editorial board stated on November 13, 2017:

Authoritarian leaders exercise a strange and powerful attraction for President Trump. As his trip to Asia reminds us, a man who loves to bully people turns to mush—fawning smiles, effusive rhetoric—in the company of strongmen like Xi Jinping of China, Vladimir Putin of Russia and Rodrigo Duterte of the Philippines. Perhaps he sees in them a reflection of the person he would like to be. Whatever the reason, there's been nothing quite like Mr. Trump's love affair with one-man rule since Spiro Agnew returned from a world tour in 1971 singing the praises of thuggish dictators like Lee Kuan Yew, Haile Selassie, Jomo Kenyatta, Mobutu Sese Seko and Gen. Francisco Franco.[27]

Mutual endorsements of and by a range of international dictators include Abdel-Fattah el-Sisi, the Egyptian president; Turkish president Recep Tayyip Erdogan, Vladimir Putin, president of Russia; Rodrigo Duterte, president of the Philippines, and the unsuccessful French presidential candidate Marine Le Pen. All of these politicians have been condemned by a number of human rights groups including Human Rights Watch, Amnesty International, and Freedom House.[28] Less has been said about the support Trump has received from controversial right-wing bigots and politicians from around the world such as Nigel Farage, the former leader of the right-wing UK Independence Party; Matteo Salvini, the right-wing Italian politician who heads the North League; Geert Wilders, the founder of the Dutch Party for Freedom; and Viktor Orban, the reactionary prime minister of Hungary. All of these politicians share a mix of ultra-nationalism, xenophobia, Islamophobia, anti-Semitism, homophobia, and hatred of Muslim immigrants. While the mainstream press and others have expressed moral outrage over these associations, they have refused to examine these relationships within a broader historical context. Trump's affinity for indulging right-wing demagogues is part of the formative culture for enforcing hierarchy intolerance, exclusion, and cruelty.

Historical memory suggests that a better template for understanding Trump's embrace of rogue states, dictators, and neo-fascist politicians can be found in the history of collaboration between individuals and governments, and between the fascist regimes of Italy and Germany before and during the Second World War. For instance, one of the darkest periods in French history took place under Marshall Philippe Pétain, the head of the Vichy regime, who collaborated with the Nazi regime between 1940 and 1944. The Vichy regime was responsible for "about 76,000 Jews [being] deported from France, only 3,000 of whom returned from the concentration camps. . . . Twenty-six percent of France's pre-war Jewish population died in the Holocaust."[29] For years, France refused to examine and condemn this shameful period in its history by claiming that the Vichy regime was an aberration, a position that was taken up in the 2016 French presidential election by Marine Le Pen, the neo-fascist National Front Party leader. Not only did Le Pen deny the French government's responsibility for the roundup of Jews sent to concentration camps between 1940 and 1944, but she also used a totalitarian script from the past by appealing to economic nationalism in order "to cover up her fascist principles."[30]

The deeply horrifying acts of collaboration with

twentieth-century fascism were not limited to France, but included collaborators in Belgium, Croatia, the Irish Republican Army, Greece, Holland, and other countries. At the same time that millions of people were being killed by the Nazis, many businesses collaborated with them in order to profit from the fascist machinery of death. Businesses that collaborated with the Nazis included Kodak, which used enslaved laborers in Germany. Hugo Boss manufactured clothes for the Nazis. IBM created the punch cards and sorting system used for identifying Jews and others in order to send them to the gas chambers. BMW and chemical manufacturer IG Farben utilized forced labor in Germany, along with another car company, Audi, which "used thousands of forced laborers from the concentration camps . . . to work in their plant."[31]

The political and moral stain of collaboration with the Nazis was also evident in the United States in both FDR's and the American business community's initial supportive views of Mussolini. Moreover, as Noam Chomsky has pointed out,

> In 1937 the State Department described Hitler as a kind of moderate who was holding off the dangerous forces of the left, meaning of the Bolsheviks, the labor movement . . . and that of the right, namely the extremist Nazis. [They believed] Hitler was kind of in the middle and therefore we should kind of support him.[32]

One telling manifestation of America's deeply rooted affinity with fascistic principles was the America First movement of the 1930s. America First was the motto used by Americans friendly to Nazi ideology and Hitler's Germany. Its most famous spokespersons were Charles Lindbergh and William Randolph Hearst. The movement had a long history of anti-Semitism, made apparent in Lindbergh's claim that American Jews were pushing America into war. Historian Susan Dunn has argued that the phrase "America First," which was appropriated and used by Donald Trump before and after his election, is a "toxic phrase with a putrid history."[33]

The awareness of these historical correspondences functions to deepen our understanding of Trump's current associations with right-wing demagogues, and should serve as a warning that offers up a glimpse of both the contemporary recurrence of fascist overtones from the past and our current immersion in what Richard Falk has called "a pre-fascist moment."[34] Trump's endorsements of right-wing demagogues such as Duterte, Le Pen, and Erdogan are more than an aberration for a U.S. president: they suggest an ominous disregard for human rights and human suffering, and the imminent suppression of dissent including the very principles of democracy itself. As Michael Brenner observes, "authoritarian movements and ideology with fascist overtones are back—in America and in Europe. Not just as a political expletive thrown at opponents, but as a doctrine, as a movement, and—above all—as a set of feelings."[35]

It is against this historical backdrop of collaboration that Trump's association with various dictators should be analyzed. Trump's infatuation with Rodrigo Duterte is particularly telling. Duterte is a ruthless dictator who has savagely imposed a campaign of terror on the people of his country. He has been condemned by U.N. officials and human rights organizations across the globe for conducting a brutal anti-drug campaign. According to Felipe Villamor of the *New York Times*, "Mr. Duterte has led a campaign against drug abuse in which he has encouraged the police and others to kill people they suspect of using or selling drugs."[36]

Duterte's brutality does not seem to concern Trump, and warning signs of his own authoritarian proclivities abound in his invitation to Rodrigo Duterte to visit the White House. A leaked transcript of Trump's call inviting him to the White House revealed that Trump offered Duterte full support for his savagely bloody war on drugs—a war in which the police and vigilantes have killed thousands of people, most of whom are from the economic underclass.[37] According to the leaked transcript published by the *Intercept*, Trump said, quote, "I just wanted to congratulate you because I am hearing of the unbelievable job on the drug problem. Many countries have the problem, we have a problem, but what a great job you are doing and I just wanted to call and tell you that."[38] Villamor quotes Duterte stating that "Donald J. Trump had endorsed his brutal antidrug campaign, telling Mr. Duterte that the Philippines was conducting it 'the right way.' Mr. Duterte, who spoke with Mr. Trump by telephone . . . said Mr. Trump was 'quite sensitive' to 'our worry about drugs. He wishes me well, too, in my campaign, and he said that, well, we are doing it as a sovereign nation, the right way.'"[39]

What Trump failed to address was that Duterte has supported and employed the use of death squads both as mayor of Davao and as the president of the Philippines. He has established what is essentially a nationwide killing machine that includes giving "free license to the police and vigilantes" to kill drug users and pushers while allowing children, innocent bystanders, and others to be caught in the indiscriminate violence.[40] The *New York Times* has reported that under Duterte's rule "more than 7,000 suspected drug users and dealers, witnesses and bystand-ers—including children—have been killed by the police or vigilantes in the Philippines."[41] It is terrifying to believe that a U.S. president would endorse such policies. Trump's alleged support of Duterte also raises questions about how much violence he might use in the United States against dissident journalists. Duterte has told journalists, "You are not exempted from assassination, if you're a son of a bitch."[42] David Kaye, a U.N. special rapporteur on freedom of opinion and expression, stated in response to Duterte's threat that "justifying the killing of journalists on the basis of how they conduct their professional activities can be un-derstood as a permissive signal to potential killers that the murder of journalists is acceptable in certain circumstanc-es and would not be punished."[43] During his 2017 tour of Asia, Trump met with Duterte and reaffirmed his "great relationship" with the Philippine dictator while making no mention of human rights, "although the pair did discuss their mutual distaste for Barack Obama."[44] Trump's fondness for dictators appears to have no limits, especially in the case of Duterte, a monster whom the *New York Times* has described as relishing "the image of killer-savior. He boasts of killing criminals with his own hands. On occasion, he calls for mass murder."[45] On the subject of drug addicts, he has stated, "I would be happy to slaughter them."[46]

Duterte has called former U.S. President Obama "the son of a whore,"[47] has drawn comparisons between himself and Hitler,[48] and has stated—now proven by the leaked transcript—that Trump approves of his drug war,[49] in addition to threatening to assassinate journalists.[50] Duterte's likening himself to Hitler offers a horrifying view of his embrace of lawlessness as a governing principle and his use of the machinery of death to enforce his rule. Comparing himself to Hitler, Duterte's own words speak for themselves:

> Hitler massacred 3 million Jews. Now, there is 3 million—what is it? Three million drug addicts, there are. I'd be happy to slaughter them. At least if Germany had Hitler, the Philippines would have [me]. You know, my victims, I would like to be all criminals.[51]

Duterte's legalized brutality is captured by photographer Daniel Berehulak, who while in the Philippines states that he had "worked in 60 countries, covered wars in Iraq and Afghanistan, and spent much of 2014 living inside West Africa's Ebola zone, a place gripped by fear and death, [but] what I experienced in the Philippines felt like a new level of ruthlessness: police officers summarily shooting anyone suspected of dealing or even using drugs, vigilantes taking seriously Mr. Duterte's call to 'slaughter them all.'"[52]

Trump's open support for Duterte may arise out of his admiration for Duterte's militant approach to crime, hatred of the press, and enforcement of one-man rule. It may also have to do with the Trump family's various business ventures in the Philippines, including ownership of a new $150 million tower in Manila's financial district.[53] All of these issues represent elements of Trump's extreme allegiance to his own insatiable self-interest and to a number of anti-democratic policies he has crafted, possibly both. Either way, Trump is degrading democracy in the United States, while his ties with Duterte should serve as a caution regarding how much further he might want to go.

Trump's tacit support for Le Pen's failed bid for the presidency of France rests on his sympathies with her anti-immigration policies, ultra-nationalism, and her claim to speak for the people. Like Le Pen, Trump has turned deflection into an art, as he directs attention away from real problems such as rising inequality, a carceral state, human rights violations, climate change, and a persistent racism that demonizes and scapegoats others. Trump wants to join hands with those other right-wing leaders who declare a similar intent to build walls and beef up the security state. His affinity for collaboration with Le Pen is matched only by his affinity for his white nationalist and white supremacist devotees, both of which feed his own narcissistic impulses, bigotry, hatred of Muslims, and what Juan Cole calls "neo-fascism" cloaked in the guise of "economic patriotism."[54]

At the same time, Trump's disdain for human rights, a critical press, and dissent has endeared him to Vladimir Putin in Russia, President Recep Tayyip Erdogan of Turkey, and Egypt's bloodthirsty dictator, President Abdel Fattah el-Sisi. Erdogan, Putin, el-Sisi, and Trump are ideological bedfellows who harbor a great deal of contempt for the rule of law, the courts, or any other check on their power. Erdogan, in particular, has not only imposed a state of emergency on his country and installed himself as a virtual dictator, but has also purged and arrested dissidents in the critical media and in academia. After Erdogan assumed dictatorial powers through what many believe was a rigged election, Trump congratulated him in a phone call. Erdogan and Trump are ideological intimates, only Erdogan has carried his authoritarian policies to a greater extreme. He is on record as describing his political system as an "illiberal state," where there can "be no room for cosmopolitan, free thought."[55] He has made good on his embrace of authoritarian rule by jailing his opposition, including journalists, academics, and civil servants. He has been particularly ruthless in attacking the autonomy of Turkey's universities and has pledged to close the internationally renowned Central European University in Budapest.[56]

El-Sisi is a brutal military dictator "who overthrew his

country's democratically elected president in a 2013 coup, killed more than 800 protesters in a single day, and has imprisoned tens of thousands of dissidents since he took power."[57] Soon after el-Sisi came to power on July 3, 2013, he put into place many of the policies that were essential to his establishing an authoritarian government. As Joshua Hammond points out:

> That fall, Sisi launched a sweeping crackdown on civil society. Citing the need to restore security and stability, the regime banned protests, passed antiterrorism laws that mandated long prison terms for acts of civil disobedience, gave prosecutors broad powers to extend pretrial detention periods, purged liberal and pro-Islamist judges, and froze the bank accounts of NGOs and law firms that defend democracy activists. Human rights groups in Egypt estimate that between 40,000 and 60,000 political prisoners, including both Muslim Brotherhood members and secular pro-democracy activists, now languish in the country's jails. Twenty prisons have been built since Sisi took power.[58]

Trump's response to his human rights violations and the turning of Egypt into a police state was to publicly announce that he was "very much behind President el-Sisi. He's done a fantastic job in a difficult situation."[59] Trump has also offered to meet with Thailand's prime minister,

Prayuth Chan-ocha, a junta head who is responsible for jailing dissidents after he took power through a coup. But the masterpiece of Trump's terms of endearment for his fellow leaders is undoubtedly his description of one of the most brutal and disturbed dictators in the world, North Korean leader Kim Jong Un, as "a smart cookie." While it is difficult to know what he admires about Kim Jong Un, he does mimic much of his authoritarian behavior, particularly his addiction to the threat of violence. For instance, when Kim Jong Un stated that he has a "Nuclear Button is on his desk at all times," Trump responded with a mix of breath-taking immaturity and the threat of unimaginable violence stating, "Will someone from his depleted and food starved regime please inform him that I too have a Nuclear Button, but it is a much bigger & more powerful one than his, and my Button works!"[60]

Trump has repeatedly praised Vladimir Putin, which is not surprising given Trump's business ties with Russia. As Trump made clear in 2013 on the *Late Show with David Letterman*, "I have done a lot of business with the Russians."[61] Many people believe that Trump's business connections far exceed what he is willing to admit. His refusal to publicly disclose his tax returns has been criticized as a way for Trump to hide shady business dealings, including financial ties with Russia.[62] While Trump's business connections with Russia are not clear, there is a deeper concern about the degree to which Trump might be indebted to economic and political interests in Russia. Jeremy Venook rightly observes:

Trump's track record in doing business in Russia doesn't definitively demonstrate that he currently has connections to the country. . . . It also doesn't in any way mean that he colluded with Russia during the campaign, which is the reason for the FBI's investigation. But the problem underlying the inquiry into Trump's financial ties isn't simply whether he currently has projects there; it's whether his dealings leave him indebted to the Russian government or the nation's oligarchs, which could compromise his decision-making.[63]

The processes by which Donald Trump rose from being a petty celebrity and self-promoting wheeler-dealer to president of the United States and commander in chief of its global military apparatus will be studied for years to come. The key issue is not whether black swans like the Trump family will continue to appear—they will. Rather, the issue is understanding the underlying social, political, and commercial forces that enable them to achieve power and impose their interests over those of the common good. When individualized resentment, brute force, and scapegoat-centered violence are normalized, we move closer to becoming a militarized police state and a fascist society. As we do, it becomes too easy to forget the totalitarian tendencies that drove the United States to invade Iraq, commit torture, perpetrate war crimes, degrade the ecosystem, and conduct extensive surveillance of its own population. The Trump family is only a symptom, not the cause, of our troubles.

Amid the anxiety regarding Trump's power over the country, we must recognize that indignation can be channeled into various forms of productive resistance, or it can be appropriated and manipulated as a breeding ground for resentment, hate, bigotry, and racism. What is clear is that Trump knew how to turn such an odious appeal into both a performance and a spectacle—one that mimicked the darkest anti-democratic impulses of the modern era. Many on the left called any critique of Trump prior to his election victory "hysterical," since they assumed he could never win, and instead portrayed Hillary Clinton as the new Satan who had to be demonized at all costs. This kind of binary thinking is not only bad politics but may have inadvertently fed the zeal for authoritarian rule that has advantaged the spread of Trumpism. As Bob Herbert mentioned to me:

> Trump threatens everything we're supposed to stand for. He's the biggest crisis we've faced in this society in my lifetime. The Supreme Court is lost for decades to come. His insane tax cuts will only expand (and lock in) the extreme inequality we're already facing. I don't need to provide a laundry list for you. The irony of ironies, of course, is that the very idiots, racists, misogynists, and outright fools who put him in the presidency will be among those hammered worst by his madness in office.[64]

Under Trump's power and influence, the state of democracy in the United States will be set back for years, especially given Trump's propensity for vengeance, crushing dissent, and sheer animosity toward anyone who disagrees with him. We have already seen this with a wave of policies that include his withdrawing the United States from the Paris Climate Accord; his attacks on Black youth coupled with his call for an increase in racial profiling as a centerpiece of his law-and-order plank; his call to lower taxes for the rich, deregulate business restrictions, and eliminate social welfare programs; making good on his pledge to appoint a die-hard conservative to the U.S. Supreme Court, and his expanding of the police state as he further militarizes the borders and accelerates mass deportations. We need a broad-based movement for a radical democracy, one that brings together various isolated movements to struggle for a democracy appropriate for the twenty-first century, based on participatory democracy and a massive redistribution of wealth and power.

While the light of our present democracy, however flawed, dims, we cannot let anger and resentment distort our organizing and political work. It is time to wake up and repudiate the notion that the interests of corporations and those of citizens are one and the same. They are not. We must use our indignation to fight collectively for a democracy that refuses to forget the atrocities of the past so that it might secure a better future. Such a struggle is a process, a call to continue organizing to safeguard the promise of democracy for the generations ahead. Such a struggle must also address the ways new configurations of power are imposing a harsh culture of cruelty that will further heighten the contradiction between the possibility of democracy that the United States has stood for and the present-day confluence of political authoritarianism, white supremacy, corporate power, and creeping fascism.

CHAPTER THREE

BEYOND THE POLITICS OF INCIVILITY

"All human beings have this burden in life to constantly figure out what's true, what's authentic, what's meaningful, what's dross, what's a hallucination, what's a figment, what's madness."

—Maxine Hong Kingston

As I have pointed out thus far in this book, we live at a time of unending crises. Historically, such crises have mobilized a sense of vigilance, a challenge that infused politics with a consciousness of collective struggle and ethical responsibility. The crisis faced by the New Deal and the Great Society of FDR and Lyndon Johnson, respectively, now appear, in a culture of immediacy and forgetting, as an ephemeral moment in history. Time has become a burden rather than a luxury as more and more individuals lose their ability to think, judge, and embrace time as a space of contemplation. As Jonathan Crary points out, "Time for human rest and regeneration is now simply too expensive to be structurally possible within contemporary capitalism."[1] More is at risk here than the death of agency and the collapse of civic culture. Crises no longer seem manageable in a world in which propaganda, violence, and isolation have become normalized as aspects of the everyday environment. A culture of anxiety and intolerance has reinforced a culture of privatization as people retreat into the commercialized comforts of entertainment, shopping, and social media. Engineered privatization appears to push people into a state of cynicism if not a distrust and withdrawal from the public realm and politics itself.

Times have changed as power has increasingly become managed by financial forces that float beyond territorial boundaries. As nation-based politics are separated from global forces, nation states are increasingly reduced to containing crises rather than solving them. Decisions that affect millions are now made by a global elite, while the burden and responsibility for the effects of such decisions fall upon individuals forced to act alone. As the late Zygmunt Bauman notes, "It is left now to individuals to seek, find and practice individual solutions to socially produced troubles—and to do all that by individual, singly undertaken and solitary tools and resources that are blatantly inadequate to the task."[2]

As neoliberalism normalizes its market ethos and retreats into a savage fundamentalism, there is neither a state to provide safety nets nor a theoretical road map that can be used to reject the notion that there are no systemic problems, only individual troubles. As agency loses its collective possibilities, people become susceptible to representations of celebrity and strength that can "take on the daunting task of putting things right."[3] One consequence is that hope is privatized and removed from its social moorings and collective potential.[4] Hobbes' toolbox of fear, insecurity, and state repression is reinforced by a neoliberal order that celebrates selfishness, competition, commodification, unchecked individualism, and social divisions. Expectations become personalized, detached from the larger world, and the connection between the personal and the social withers.[5] Under such circumstances, language is depreciated, dissent is diminished, and agency is reduced to the dictates of self-interest in which everyone looks out for themselves. Individual initiative, self-help, and the discourse of the isolated self are now reinforced by a neoliberal culture of anti-politics, one that offers no language for connecting private troubles with broader systemic issues.[6] Michael Lerner is right in arguing that it would be wrong to assume that Trump's supporters only care about economic issues such as poverty, stagnant wages, and the loss of jobs. Certainly, these are important concerns, but the inability of many people to understand the underlying political and economic conditions that produce these problems is thwarted by the power of neoliberal ideology. As Lerner points out, neoliberalism is internalized and serves to convince many Americans of its destructive tenets:

> Human nature cannot be changed, and . . . the only rational way to live is to give priority to

looking out for number one and seeing others as valuable primarily for what they can do to advance our own self-interest. Sadly, the more people accept this way of being, the more they act in ways that actually undermine the possibility of sustaining long-term friendships, loving relationships, and families. . . . These painful feelings that we have failed ourselves are intensified by the pop-psychology and pop-spirituality of capitalist society that teach that you create your own reality so you have no one to blame for your own lack of fulfillment but yourself. All this obscures the economic, political, and cultural institutions of the society over which most people have little control and which increasingly reward materialism and selfishness in almost every way.[7]

Under the Trump regime, totalitarianism takes new form, but its paralyzing impact on society is recognizable.[8] Problems such as widespread poverty, crumbling infrastructures, deteriorating public schools, persistent racism, militarization, climate pollution, and the immediate fear of terrorism, among others, affect us all, but rather than move toward collective struggles and a militant sense of hope, Americans appear isolated, angry, and incapable of acting collectively to address major social problems. As social bonds appear untrustworthy, there is a growing and appalling, if not heartless, indifference to the social contract and common good.

Under varied regimes of neoliberalism, loneliness and anxiety are expanding all over the world and have amounted to what some have called a plague of social isolation. People do not know their neighbors, and loneliness preys on the young and old. The deterioration of physical and mental health is intensified by austerity measures that serve to erode social provisions aimed at providing support services and communal spaces for people to interact and build community together.[9] Young girls now get plastic surgery to improve their selfies,[10] and an increasing number of older people claim their only company is the television.[11] Competitive self-interest, extreme individualism, endless competition, and the reduction of citizens to consumers exacerbates the crisis of atomization and further renders politics inoperable. Digital culture floods society with a relentless stream of data, images, and representations. Thus, time and distance appear stuck in what Byung-Chul Han calls a "digital medium [whose] temporality is the immediate present."[12] We now live in an age of the digital panopticon marked not only by the rise of the surveillance state but also by a "pornographic display of intimacy [in which] social networks wind up being exhibition rooms for highly personal matters. . . . The digital medium *privatizes* communication by shifting the site where information is produced . . . creating a medium of the immediate present. [One consequence is that] the *future*, as the time of the political, is disappearing."[13]

Any attempt to address the politics of atomization in the United States must begin by reclaiming the language of the social and affirming the project of an inclusive, diverse, and open democracy. This suggests addressing the ways neoliberalism works to hide the effects of power, politics, and racial injustice. For instance, one viable intervention would be to expose gratuitous forms of mystification in which those who produce violence against people of color are portrayed as the real victims. This would warrant a critical analysis of the appropriation and attempts to derail the message of the Black Lives Matter movement by mainstream and conservative media that seem partial to the police. What is both troubling and must be made problematic by progressives is that neoliberalism wraps itself in what appears to be an unassailable appeal to common sense. Defined as the paragon of all social relations, neoliberalism attempts to eliminate an engaged critique about its most basic principles and social consequences by embracing the "market as the arbiter of social destiny."[14] More is lost here than neoliberalism's willingness to make its own assumptions problematic. Also lost is the ability to see how the war against the social, against hope, and against public values gives way to the nightmare of authoritarianism.

In the Trump administration, we see what Goya called "the sleep of reason" give way to the collective failure of conscience, "the catastrophe of indifference," and a facile willingness to tolerate fascism. The ghost of such memories should never vanish if Americans do not want to see their own democracy, however fragile, yield even more to a new and terrifying form of authoritarianism. The language of privatization erases history, memory, and politics itself and offers no resources to learn from the rise of totalitarianism, but does do a great deal in enabling us to forget about it. As the historian of totalitarianism Timothy Snyder observes:

> Today, our political order faces new threats, not unlike the totalitarianism of the twentieth century. We are no wiser than the Europeans who saw democracy yield to fascism, Nazism, or communism. Our one advantage is that we might learn from their experience. . . . My sense is that we've seen institutions like our own fail. Twentieth-century authoritarians have learned that the way to dismantle systems like ours is to go after one institution and then the next, which means that we have to have an active relationship both to history, so that we can see how failure arises and learn from people who tried to protect institutions, but also an active relationship to our own institutions, that our institutions are only as good as the people who try to serve them.[15]

Many commentators have been quick to argue that Americans have fallen prey to a culture of incivility and bad manners. In this case, the discourse of "bad manners" parades as insight and functions, regardless of intention, to hide the effects of a range of forms of oppression. The rhetoric of "incivility," when used as a pejorative ideological label, serves to discredit political rhetoric as ill-tempered, rude, and uncivilized. Politics, in this sense, shifts its focus from substance to style—reworking the notion of critical thinking and action through a rule book of alleged collegiality—which becomes code for the elevated character and manners of the privileged classes. As John Doris points out, "the discourse of character often plays against a background of social stratification and elitism."[16] In other words, the privileged and rich are deemed to possess admirable character and to engage in civil behavior. At the same time, those who are poor, unemployed, homeless, or subject to police violence are not seen as the victims of larger political, social, and economic forces that bear down upon them; on the contrary, their problems are reduced to the depoliticizing discourse of bad character, defined as individual pathology, and whatever resistance they present is dismissed as rude, ignorant, and uncivil. Ruling elites have used the discourse of incivility to criticize dissent as it has emerged across ideological and racial lines, encompassing unruly conservative working-class whites as well as progressive Black youth groups. This type of elitism has a long history in the United States, but its appeal to character, moral uplift, and good manners was flipped on its head by Trump, who embodied and showcased the worse dimensions of incivility as a way to critique a political establishment despised by many of his followers.

Trump has marshalled the assumptions underlying the discourse of incivility to support his presidential campaign and political agenda, which warrant far more alarm than suggested by terms such as "ill mannered." More than other candidates, Trump not only showcased and appropriated "incivility" in his public appearances as a mark of solidarity with many of his white male adherents, he tapped into their resentment and transformed their misery into a racist, bigoted, misogynist, and ultra-nationalist appeal to the darkest forces of authoritarianism. Still, millions of U.S. Americans voted to live under Trump, and as David Remnick observes, this represents more than a tragedy in the making:

> The election of Donald Trump to the Presidency is nothing less than a tragedy for the American republic, a tragedy for the Constitution, and a triumph for the forces, at home and abroad, of nativism, authoritarianism, misogyny, and racism. Trump's shocking victory, his ascension to the Presidency, is a sickening event in the history of the United States and liberal democracy. On January 20, 2017, we will . . . witness the inauguration of a con who did little to spurn endorsement by forces of xenophobia and white supremacy. It is impossible to react to this moment with anything less than revulsion and profound anxiety.[17]

Clearly, Trump's "incivility" was a winning strategy that not only signaled the degree to which the politics of extremism has become more acceptable to Americans, but has also turned politics into a commercial spectacle that can deliver larger audiences to advertisers. Trump's use of incivility as a tool of resistance against establishment politicians played a major role in his winning the White House. But it would be wrong to subordinate Trump's politics to his persona, or to categorize either as mere rudeness. Trump has turned politics into what Guy Debord once called a "perpetual motion machine" built on fear, anxiety, militancy, and a full-fledged attack on women, the welfare state, and low-income communities.

Tom Engelhardt has persuasively argued that Trump's presidency will alter the political and economic trajectory of the country toward an increasingly anti-democratic or authoritarian mode of governance. Such alterations clearly anticipate the "dark times" that Hannah Arendt associated with totalitarianism. In early 2017, Engelhardt wrote:

> Donald Trump's administration, now filling up with racists, Islamophobes, Iranophobes, and assorted fellow billionaires, already has the feel of an increasingly militarized, autocratic government-in-the-making, favoring short-tempered, militaristic white guys who don't take criticism lightly or react to speed bumps well. In addition, on January 20th, they will find themselves with immense repressive powers of every sort at their fingertips, powers ranging from torture to surveillance that were institutionalized in remarkable ways in the post-9/11 years with the rise of the national security state as a fourth branch

of government, powers which some of them are clearly eager to test out.[18]

What happens to a democracy when justice loses its mooring and no longer serves as a common moral guidepost and central organizing principle for society? What happens to rational debate, civic culture, public interest and the common good? The discourse of incivility now takes on a dual function. Not only is it used to smear legitimate dissent, it is also used as a rhetorical tool to advance an incendiary populism by insulting and humiliating others. Thus Trump's combative language serves to further enforce dominant ideologies and relations of power by using uncivil discourse as a tool of inflammatory theatrics. For instance, when Trump's opponents engage him using argument, evidence, and informed judgment, or display a strong response to injustice, their positions are reliably dismissed or belittled as inferior, disloyal, and small. It has been precisely in this manner that Trump has attacked right-wing senators such as McCain, Corker, and Flake who challenge Trump's lack of fitness to serve and protect the national interest. In this discourse, matters of power, class conflict, white supremacy, and state-sponsored violence against immigrants, Muslims, and communities of color simply disappear.

When removed from a context of social justice, the discourse of incivility reduces politics to the realm of the personal and affective, while cancelling out broader political issues such as the *underlying conditions* that might produce anger, or the dire effects of misguided resentment, or a passion grounded in the capacity to reason. Donald Trump plays the part of president like a crooked slumlord used to rigging the terms in his favor.

Under Trump, the United States has become motivated less by indignation than by a snide culture of retribution, which personalizes problems and tends to seek vengeance on those viewed as a threat to American history and heritage—often alt-right code for *white* history and heritage. One can argue further that the condemnation of incivility in public life no longer registers favorably among those who are less interested in mimicking the discourse and manners of the ruling elite than in expressing their resentment as the struggle for power, however rude such expressions might appear. Rather than an expression of a historic, if not dangerous, politics of unchecked personal resentment (as seen among many Trump supporters), a legitimate politics of indignation rooted in solidarity is desperately needed.

In this instance, we must not confuse anger that is connected to chronic injustice with resentment emanating from personalized pettiness. We see elements of legitimate anger among the many supporters of Bernie Sanders, as well as the Black Lives Matter movement and the Indigenous-led movement to stop the Dakota Access Pipeline. Anger can be a disruption that offers the possibility for critical analysis, calling out the social forces of oppression and violence in which so many current injustices are rooted. Meanwhile, resentment operates out of a friend/enemy distinction that produces convenient scapegoats. It is the festering stuff of fear, loathing, and deep-seated racism that often erupts into spectacles of spontaneous violence, hate-mongering, and implied threats of state repression. In this instance, ideas lose their grip on reality and critical thought falls by the wayside. Echoes of such scapegoat-driven animosity can be heard in Trump's "rhetorical cluster bombs," in which he states publicly that he would like to punch protesters in the face, punish women who have abortions, have the police beat up suspects, and execute terrorists before their guilt has even been established by a fair trial.[19] Genuine civic attachments are now cancelled out in the bombast of vileness and shame, which has been made into a national pastime and the central feature of a spectacularized politics.[20]

Critical reflection no longer challenges a poisonous appeal to "common sense" or casts light on the shadows of racism, hatred, and bigotry. Manufactured ignorance opens the door to an unapologetic culture of bullying and violence aimed at an ever-growing group of people who do not fit into the racially coded propaganda to "Make America Great Again."[21] This is not about the breakdown of civility in American politics or the bemoaned growth of incivility. From its settler-colonial inception in Native American land, U.S. society has been economically enriched by enslavement of Black people and the genocide of Indigenous nations. Today's racist ideologies extend from the settler-colonial days and find official normalization in the presidency of Andrew Jackson, an American who bred and enslaved Black people for profit and led the massacre of Native American communities. Today's alt-right openly codes its bigotry in its advocacy for a "Jacksonian national security vision." To drive the point home, Trump has hung a portrait of the enslaver president in the Oval Office and made a public display of visiting Jackson's grave during his first weeks in office. "I have to tell you," said Trump of Jackson, "I'm a big fan."[22] When, in November 2017, Trump met Navajo American veterans in the White House, the spot chosen for the photo op was directly in front of the portrait of Andrew Jackson, the president who signed into law the infamous Indian Removal Act.[23] Trump continuously signals his unapologetic support for what historian Cedric Robinson, in a different context, called the "rewhitening of America"—tacit support for a political and social order that extends the legacy of white domination that dates back to the settler-colonial inception of the nation.[24]

The alt-right movement has served to successfully align the anger of the white underclass with the greed and self-interest of the Mar-a-Lago country club set. Operating together, these divergent far-right forces are mounting a sustained attack on public values and the common good. Trump did not invent these forces. Trump's following goes back as far as the 2008 GOP campaign that launched Sarah Palin and the incendiary Tea Party insurrection. Trump simply brought them to the surface and made them the centerpiece of his campaign and presidency. As anti-democratic pressures mount, the commanding institutions of capital are divorced from matters of politics, ethics, and responsibility. The goal of making the world a better place has been replaced by dystopian narratives about how to survive alone in a world whose destruction is just a matter of time. Under the influence of neoliberalism the lure of a better and more just future has given way to questions of mere survival. Entire populations once protected by the social contract are now considered disposable, dispatched to the garbage dump of a society that equates one's humanity exclusively with one's ability to consume.[25]

The not-so-subtle signs of the culture of seething resentment are everywhere, and not just on Breitbart News and in neo-Nazi street protests. Young children, especially those whose parents are being targeted by Trump's rhetoric, report being bullied more. State-sanctioned violence is accelerating against Native Americans, Black youth, Latinos, and others now deemed inferior in Trumpist America.[26] Hate crimes are on the rise, seeping into public spaces and institutions once largely protected from such assaults For instance, as W.J.T. Mitchell observes, "Populist ignorance and cynical demagoguery are now at the gates of higher education, demanding to get in under the banner of 'free speech' and 'civility.'"[27]

There can be little doubt that higher education is now under siege, especially by an army of alt-right trolls such as the followers of David Horowitz, who plaster campuses with posters of left-wing and progressive academics he labels "the enemies of America," create networks in the world of social media such as Frontpage Mag and

CanaryMission.org, which provide profiles of all the persons named on his posters. Moreover, in corporate media and online, the endless peddling of lies becomes fodder for higher ratings, enabled by a suffocating pastiche of talking heads, too many of whom surrender to "the incontestable demands of quiet acceptance."[28] Politics has been reduced to the cult of the spectacle and shock, but not merely, as Neil Gabler observes, "in the name of entertainment."[29] The framing mechanism that drives the mainstream media is a shark-like notion of competition that accentuates and accelerates hostility, insults, and the politics of humiliation.

Charles Derber and Yale Magrass are correct in arguing that "capitalism breeds competition and teaches that losers deserve their fate."[30] But it does more. It establishes an unbridled individualism that embodies a pathological disdain for community, produces a cruel indifference to the social contract, disdains the larger social good, and creates a predatory sink-or-swim culture that replaces compassion, sharing, and a concern for the other. As the discourse of cooperation, kindness, and the common good withers, the coercive vocabulary of the bully inflates. Such coercive bullying has only worsened through the violent, insulting, and belittling remarks made daily by Donald Trump. Jessica Lustig captures this organized culture of violence, grudges, and bitterness:

> Trump is a public figure whose ideology, such as it is, essentially amounts to a politics of the personal grudge. It has drawn to him throngs of

disaffected citizens all too glad to reclaim the epithet "deplorable." But beyond these aggrieved
hordes, it can seem at times as if nearly everyone
in the country is nursing wounds, cringing over
slights and embarrassments, inveighing against
enemies and wishing for retribution. Everyone
has someone, or something, to resent.[31]

No one has done more than Donald J. Trump to bring
harassment culture into the mainstream. In doing so, he
has legitimated white nativism and a range of anti-democratic values, sentiments, and desires. Trump and his former strategist "Sloppy" Steve Bannon opened the space
of legitimacy for white nativists, ultra-nationalists, racist
militia types, social media trolls, misogynists, and a variety
of reactionaries who have turned their hate-filled discourse
into a weaponized element of political culture.

This impact was made all the more obvious when
Trump first hired Bannon to join his campaign team.
Bannon was well known for his bigoted views and for
his unwavering support of the political "alt-right." One
of his more controversial headlines on Breitbart News
read, "Would you rather have feminism or cancer?" He
is also considered one of the more prominent advocates
of the right-wing trolling mill which is fiercely loyal to
Trumpism.[32] Jared Keller captures perfectly the essence of
Trump's politics of trolling, which has continued right into
his presidency. He writes:

From the start, the Trump campaign has offered a tsunami of trolling, waves of provocative tweets and soundbites—from "build the wall" to "lock her up"—designed to provoke maximum outrage, followed, when the resulting heat felt a bit too hot, by the classic schoolyard bully's excuse: that it was merely "sarcasm" or a "joke." In a way, it is. It's just a joke with victims and consequences. . . . Trump's behavior has normalized trolling as an accepted staple of daily political discourse. [Quoting Whitney Philips:] "When you have the presidential candidate boasting about committing sexual assault and then saying, 'Oh, it's just locker room banter' . . . it sets such an insidious, sexually violent tone for the election, and the result of that is fearfulness. . . . People are being made to feel like shit."[33]

Another example of this brand of vitriol was noted by Andrew Marantz's profile on Mike Cernovich, a prominent troll. He writes:

His political analysis was nearly as crass as his dating advice ('Misogyny Gets You Laid'). In March, he tweeted, "Hillary's face looks like melting candle wax. Imagine what her brain looks like." Next he tweeted a picture of Clinton winking, which he interpreted as "a mild stroke." By August, he was declaring that she had both a seizure disorder and Parkinson's disease.[34]

In the age of trolls and selfies, politics has dissolved into a pit of narcissism, testament to the distinctive influence of a corporate-driven culture of commercialism and celebrity fawning in the United States that is reconfiguring not just political discourse but the nature of power itself.

In spite of the financial corruption that led to the 2008 Wall Street collapse and the ensuing Great Recession, millions of anxious Americans have turned to the strongman politics of Trumpism. Reinforced by the strange intersection of nationalism, celebrity culture, white supremacy, and obvious *National Enquirer*–level disinformation, their mindset is one that borrows from totalitarian logic but inhabits a new register of resentment that, as Mark Danner points out, takes "the shape of reality television politics."[35] Within such an environment, a personalized notion of resentment drives politics, misdirecting this private form of rage toward issues that reinforce the totalitarian logic of good friend versus evil enemy, atomizing the polity and lobotomizing any collective sense of economic and social justice for all. Under such circumstances, the long-standing forces of nativism and demagoguery emerge in full force to drive American politics, while the truth of events is no longer open to public discussion or informed judgment. All that is left is the empty but dangerous performance of misguided fury wrapped up in the fog of ignorance, the haze of political and moral indifference, and the looming specter of violence. All the more reason to examine the politics of incivility against those historical memories that offer a broader landscape on which to engage the pre-fascist scripts that now blatantly embrace the discourse of performance, political purity, vile stereotypes, tribal hatreds, and vulgarity. Incivility as righteous anger can fuel an emotional connection not to hatred and bigotry, but to a renewed sense of community, compassion, and collective resistance. Hopefully, organizing with indignation, solidarity in diversity, and dedication to the common good will continue to offer meaning, community, and joy to those who work for better in these dark times.

CHAPTER FOUR

THE CULTURE OF CRUELTY
IN TRUMP'S AMERICA

"This is the culture you're raising your kids in.
Don't be surprised if it blows up in your face."
—Marilyn Manson

For the last forty years, the United States has pursued policies that have stripped economic activity from ethical considerations and social costs. One consequence has been the emergence of a culture of cruelty in which the financial elite and big corporations favor policies of intolerance that treat the economically disadvantaged with contempt. Under the Trump regime, the repressive state and market apparatuses that exercised cruel power in the nineteenth century have returned with a vengeance, producing in American society new levels of harsh aggression and daily violence. A culture of cruelty and a politics of disposability have shaped the mood of our times—a specter of insensitivity and lack of kindness hovering over the ruins of a disappearing democracy.

While there is much talk about the influence of

Trumpism, there are few analyses that examine its culture of cruelty and politics of disposability, or the role that culture plays in legitimating intolerance and suffering. The mechanisms of cruelty and disposability reach back to the founding of the United States as a settler-colonial society. How else does one explain a long line of state-sanctioned atrocities—the genocide waged against Native Americans in order to take their land, enslavement and breeding of Black people for profit and labor, forced sterilizations of the mentally ill for much of the first half of the twentieth century, and the passage of the Second Amendment to arm and enforce white supremacy over subordinated populations? The legacies of those roots of U.S. history spike the Kool-Aid of Trumpist propaganda about "Law and Order," "Making America Great Again," and "America First."

More recent instances indicative of the rising culture of bigoted cruelty and mechanisms of erasure in U.S. politics include the racially motivated drug wars, policies that shifted people from welfare to workfare without offering training programs or child care, and morally indefensible tax reforms that will "require huge budget cuts in safety net programs for vulnerable children and adults."[1] As Marian Wright Edelman points out, such actions are particularly alarming and cruel at a time when "Millions of America's children today are suffering from hunger, homelessness and hopelessness. Nearly 13.2 million children are poor—almost one in five. About 70 percent of them are children of color who will be a majority of our children by 2020. More than 1.2 million are homeless. About 14.8 million children struggle against hunger in food insecure households."[2]

In some instances, the culture of cruelty emerges in comments and calls for legislation that pathologically revel in the degradation of others. For instance, in 2015, the Oklahoma Republican party made a "case against food stamps" by comparing the poor to animals who will grow lazy from handouts. It shamefully posted its critique of food stamp programs on its Facebook page in which it appropriated a message from the National Park Service that stated "Please Do Not Feed the Animals" because "the animals will grow dependent on handouts and will not learn to take care of themselves."[3] The "don't feed the animals" meme is common, it seems, among Republican Party politicians. Tara Culp-Ressler reports that "Former House Speaker Newt Gingrich once said that the current welfare system is 'turning children into young animals and they are killing each other.' A Republican congressional candidate in Texas, meanwhile, compared welfare beneficiaries to donkeys."[4] More recently, the Trump administration announced it would rescind protections for hundreds of thousands of Latin Americans now living in the United States, give states the power to force work requirements on Medicare recipients, and put legislation into place that would restrict health care to the most vulnerable. These are savage policies. With the election of Trump and the control of all levers of the government by the Republican Party, impoverishing the poor and developing a punishing state has been accelerated to the point that a culture of cruelty has become a dominant feature of American society. Paul Krugman is on target when he states that "Republicans simply want to hurt people . . . specifically those from poor families."[5]

Some theorists have argued that neoliberalism is dead. Actually, under Trump it is on steroids. Not only has Trump pushed its central organizing principles of deregulation, privatization, anti-intellectualism, and economic benefits for the rich to their limits, he has instituted policies that combine a range of anti-democratic forces with policies that will promote massive suffering and undercut the quality of life for millions of Americans.[6] Millions will lose their health care, and environmental injuries and deaths will increase because regulatory agencies such as the National Academies of Sciences, Engineering, and Medicine have been "ordered to stop studying how pollutants produced by mountaintop-removal mining may lead to increased rates of cancer, birth defects, and respiratory disease."[7] As Ariel Dorfman observes, Trump's policies are about more than a "felonious stupidity."[8] They are death-dealing policies that will have lethal consequences for the elderly, the poor, and vulnerable children. Under such circumstances, a culture of cruelty is the result of a systemic form of domestic terrorism.

Trump's Culture of Cruelty
What is new since the 1980s—and especially evident under Trumpism—is that the culture of cruelty has become more venomous as it has moved to the center of political power. As

Jean Franco explains in a different context, "Neither cruelty nor the exploitation of cruelty is new, but the lifting of the taboo, the acceptance and justification of cruelty and the rationale for cruel acts, have become a feature of modernity."[9]

Further examples of the emboldened culture of cruelty, racism, and violence sweeping over American society can be found in the growing incidents of swastikas being painted on school walls, hate-fueled attacks subjecting people to racial taunts, right-wing attacks on immigrants, and legislation against transgender people. In a blow to civil liberties, the Republicans in eighteen states are introducing laws to curb protesting. Christopher Ingraham reports in the *New York Times*:

> From Virginia to Washington state, legislators have introduced bills that would increase punishments for blocking highways, ban the use of masks during protests, indemnify drivers who strike protesters with their cars and, in at least once case, seize the assets of people involved in protests that later turn violent. The proposals come after a string of mass protest movements in the past few years, covering everything from police shootings of unarmed black men to the Dakota Access Pipeline to the inauguration of Trump.[10]

Emboldened by Trump's attacks on the critical media and his incendiary criticism of immigrants and people of color, Poor Boys and similar groups are "recruiting battalions of mainly young white men for one-off confrontations with "those who stand up to Trump's bigoted policies. What these movements have in common is their defense of Trump's anti-immigration policies, their hatred of what Trump calls political correctness (code for being disallowed to spew racist language), their willingness to battle the so-called "commies," and the embrace of a form of hyper-masculinity with its celebration of confrontation and combat, which has in some cases fueled modes of hatred resulting in murderous acts of violence.[11]

On display here is a culture of cruelty and violence that openly gloats about bullying and intolerance. States of social and literal death have become normalized.[12] How else to explain White House budget chief Mick Mulvaney's defense for drastic budget cuts for the most needy, including the Meals on Wheels program which provides food for the elderly, by arguing "it's probably one of the most compassionate things we can do."[13] What Mulvaney does not mention is that the Trump administration's budget "is shuffling $54 billion from an assortment of spending programs to defense [and] is 'saving' by spending it on Navy ships, F-35 fighter jets, and a border wall with Mexico, while cutting programs that help the old pay for heat during the winter or send low-income kids to after-school programs."[14]

Cruelty is not only hardwired into the U.S. financial system, it is also a fundamental part of the criminal justice system, and with Jeff Sessions as Trump's compromised attorney general, it has become exacerbated. For example, early in his appointment Sessions rescinded a 2013 policy that sought to limit, if not avoid, mandatory sentences. Claiming it was the "moral and just" policy to follow, Sessions "instructed the nation's 2,300 federal prosecutors to pursue the most serious charges in all but exceptional cases."[15] Such sentencing is cruel, unforgiving, and racist. As Nancy Gertner and Chiraag Bains, a federal prosecutor and judge argue:

> Mandatory minimums have swelled the federal prison population and led to scandalous racial disparities. They have caused untold misery at great expense. And they have not made us safer. . . . [Moreover,] they waste human potential. They harm the 5 million children who have or have had a parent in prison—including one in nine black children. And they wreak economic devastation on poor communities.[16]

Focusing on a culture of cruelty as one register of authoritarianism allows us to understand more deeply the conditions under which people are violated and destroyed. Violence is not an abstraction, it is the experience of coercive threat, terror, and suffering. As Brad Evans observes, violence "should never be studied in an objective and unimpassioned way. It points to a politics of the visceral that cannot be divorced from our ethical and political concerns."[17] Acknowledging its pervasive effects on people's lives means understanding how Trump's proposed policies and budget cuts would, for example, reduce funding for programs that provide education, legal assistance, and training for thousands of workers in high-hazard industries. As Judy Conti, a federal advocacy coordinator, notes, this "will mean more illness, injury and death on the job."[18]

The ideological and emotional brutality that fuels such policies will deprive millions of Americans of their health insurance and increase expenses for those who are hurting or suffering the most, as I point out in more detail below. These "savage cuts in benefits for the poor and working class" will be relentlessly pursued when, according to Paul Krugman, they serve "to offset large tax cuts for the rich."[19] Of course, justifying tax cuts for the rich is coded into all right-wing narratives about increasing national economic prosperity. As Lawrence Mishel, president of the Economic Policy Institute argues, it also does not make much sense to believe that "cutting corporate taxes is central to tax policy when corporate profits are near historic highs."[20]

What we do know is that gutting federal spending for programs that help the economically disadvantaged in order to finance a mammoth military buildup and support huge tax breaks for the rich and corporations is part of a political project designed to wage a frontal attack on the welfare state and allow the rich to take over the commanding political, cultural, and economic institutions of American society. What makes the current historical moment unique is that narratives that reinforce such policies are at the heart of the ascendant far-right movement and come bundled with populist authoritarianism, intolerance, and nationalism. Breitbart News delivers such bundles daily and supports characters such as Roy Moore in its attempts to further crystallize such views into policy and law.

This type of political approach is strongly supported by the ultra-rich, including Robert Mercer, billionaire co-CEO of the $50 billion Renaissance Technologies hedge fund group, and former owner of a piece of the Breitbart News operation. Mercer, Goldman Sachs executives, and other members of the financial elite are precisely the kind of people that Donald Trump surrounds himself with most. In fact, the *New York Times* reported that as of May 28, 2017, Trump had met with at least 307 highly paid executives. I am sure their views on militarism, income inequality, privatization, and the common good have little in common with those working-class and lower-middle-class individuals who propelled Trump into office. Trump has not only turned the White House into a private business to expand his own and his family's wealth, he has also morphed into "living proof that the long dreamed of *Pax Republicana* is just another form of war without end on the domestic front."[21] Cruelty now animates the center stage of American political and economic power.

Rather than respond only with a display of moral outrage (however well intended), interrogating a culture of cruelty suggests developing a political and moral lens for thinking through the present convergence of power, politics, and everyday life. It offers the promise of unveiling the way in which a nation demoralizes itself by adopting the position that it has no duty to provide safety nets for its citizens or to care for their well-being, even in a time of misfortune. Politically, it highlights the way structures of domination bear down on American communities and families, and how such constraints function to keep people in a state of existential crisis, if not outright despair.

Democracy withers when people spend most of their time trying to survive and no longer have access to the time, resources, and power that enable them to participate in shaping the conditions and institutions affecting their lives. A culture of cruelty does more than inflict pain and misery, it also undercuts people's sense of agency. However, identifying the concept ethically makes visible how unjust a society has become. It helps us think through how life and death now converge in ways that fundamentally transform how we understand and imagine the act of living—if not simply surviving—in a society that has lost its moral bearings and sense of social responsibility. Within the last forty years, a harsh market fundamentalism has deregulated financial capital, imposed misery and humiliation on the poor through welfare cuts, and ushered in a new style of authoritarianism that preys upon and punishes the most vulnerable Americans.

The culture of cruelty threatens to reach new heights under the Trump regime. What I am arguing here is that we must view this predatory political climate as a central force that has pushed us toward a new form of fascism. Cruelty has become a primary register of the loss of democracy in the United States. The disintegration of democratic commitments offers a perverse index of degradation in a country governed by the rich, big corporations, and rapacious banks through the consolidation of a regime of punishment. This is a country that also reinforces the workings of a corporate-driven media culture whose commercial broadcasts sell audiences to advertisers via entertainment, violence, and intolerance.

Under the Bush-Cheney regime, state-sanctioned torture emerged as a legitimate practice of power during a time of war, and once again torture has been endorsed by a sitting president. It appears that the United States has become a country that celebrates what it should be ashamed of. For instance, under the Trump regime, vast numbers of individuals and communities are relegated to zones of social and economic abandonment, if not terminal exclusion. American capitalism has created a society not just of throwaway goods but also of throwaway populations in which people lose not only their material possessions but also their dignity, self-worth, and bodies. Such unethical grammars of violence find expression in modes of extreme cruelty. For instance, there are repeated reports of hospitals engaging in "patient dumping." That is, hospitals putting people who are sick, mentally ill, and deathly vulnerable out into the street, often wearing nothing but their hospital gowns. Most recently, *CBS* and *60 Minutes* have aired instances of hospitals in Baltimore and Los Angeles that removed patients from their facilities and left them stranded at bus stops and in sections of the downtown area.[22] Such practices have a frightening resonance with policies followed by the Nazis through their secret "OperationT4" program designed to imprison and eventually kill patients considered mentally ill, disabled, or unworthy of life because they "weakened the race . . . and were obstacles to Germany's renewal."[23] Another forgotten and terrifying similarity, one that is often overlooked in the established media, is that Trump like Hitler "mocked disabled people."[24]

Under Trump, the machineries of death have gathered speed so as to accelerate the suffering, exclusion, incarceration, and death of those deemed redundant. In the current climate, state-sanctioned violence seeps into everyday life, while entirely engulfing a U.S. carceral system that embraces the death penalty and produces conditions of incarceration that house many prisoners in solitary confinement—a practice medical professionals consider one of the worst forms of torture. As Jonathan Schell has pointed out:

> Our criminal justice system reeks of cruelty. The death penalty defies standards of decency accepted by all civilized countries. The incarceration of more than 2 million Americans—the highest proportion per capita in the world—is a frightening reflection on a country that seems to know of no remedy for social ills but punishment. The conditions of incarceration are fearful. . . . Prisoners can be held in solitary confinement for years in small, windowless cells in which they are kept for twenty-three hours of every day. Many

prisoners—as well as Senator John McCain, who was a prisoner of war in North Vietnam—have reported that such isolation is more agonizing and destructive than physical torture.[25]

Demolition Budgets of Cruelty

State-inflicted abuse takes many forms. Budget cuts become a matter of life and death. This is particularly true when the vulnerable populations who are sick, homeless, and in dire poverty, including young children, are denied crucial public services. What is distinctive about this historical moment is that the most vital safety nets, social provisions, welfare policies, and health-care reforms are being undermined or are under threat of elimination by right-wing ideologues in the Trump administration. They pursue this course in order to further shore up the power and wealth of the financial elite, and to provide resources for militarism and other repressive state apparatuses that serve as a means of social control and the mode of choice for addressing social problems. For instance, Trump's 2018 budget proposal, much of which was drafted by the ultra-conservative Heritage Foundation, will create a degree of imposed hardship and misery that defies any sense of human decency and moral responsibility.[26] Public policy analyst Robert Reich argues that "the theme that unites all of Trump's [budget] initiatives so far is their unnecessary cruelty."[27] Reich writes:

His new budget comes down especially hard on the poor—imposing unprecedented cuts in low-income housing, job training, food assistance, legal services, help to distressed rural communities, nutrition for new mothers and their infants, funds to keep poor families warm, even "meals on wheels." These cuts come at a time when more American families are in poverty than ever before, including 1 in 5 children. Why is Trump doing this? To pay for the biggest hike in military spending since the 1980s. Yet the U.S. already spends more on its military than the next 7 biggest military budgets put together. His plan to repeal and "replace" the Affordable Care Act will cause 14 million Americans to lose their health insurance next year, and 24 million by 2026. Why is Trump doing this? To bestow $600 billion in tax breaks over the decade to wealthy Americans. This windfall comes at a time when the rich have accumulated more wealth than at any time in the nation's history.[28]

This is a demolition budget that cuts deeply into programs for the poor and would inflict unprecedented cruelty, misery, and hardship on millions of citizens and residents. This is a budget that punishes the most vulnerable and rewards those "wealthiest individuals and corporations who neither need nor deserve massive government support."[29] Julie Hirschfield, a writer for the *New York Times*, rightly observes that this budget, with its massive cuts in entitlement programs, attacks the very people who supported Trump, revealing the hypocrisy underlying his populist rhetoric. Considering the burden of his $4.1 trillion 2018 budget, she writes:

> [This] would hit hardest many of the economically strained voters who propelled the president into office. Over the next decade, it calls for slashing more than $800 billion from Medicaid, the federal health program for the poor, while slicing $192 billion from nutritional assistance and $272 billion overall from welfare programs. And domestic programs outside of military and homeland security whose budgets are determined annually by Congress would also take a hit, their funding falling by $57 billion, or 10.6 percent.[30]

Trump's 2018 federal budget would make life even worse for the rural poor, who would see $2.6 billion cut from infrastructure investments largely used for water and sewage improvements as well as cuts to federal funds used to provide energy assistance so the poor can heat their homes. Roughly $6 billion would be cut from a housing budget that benefits 4.5 million low-income households. Other programs on the chopping block include funds to support Habitat for Humanity, the homeless, legal aid, and a number of anti-poverty programs. Dan Rather argues that this is a budget that is "heartless and cruel" because it punishes the sick, those who need nutritional assistance, and people who rely on Medicaid.[31] One striking example is evident in a budget that proposes to cut more than $72 billion in disability benefits that millions of Americans depend on. Trump's budget appears to be motivated by a desire to annihilate the public good while driving an orgy of excessive investment in weapons of death and destruction.

If Congress accepts Trump's proposal, poor students would be budgeted out of access to higher education as a result of a $3.9 billion cut from the federal Pell grant program, which provides tuition assistance for low-income students entering college. Federal funds for public schools would be redistributed to privately run charter schools, and vouchers would be available for religious schools. Trump's budget cuts $9.2 billion from federal education spending for 2018 alone. Medical research would suffer, thanks to the proposed $6 billion cut to the National Institutes of Health. The curbing of environmental regulations, biomedical research, and other vital public investments will result in the spread of diseases, failure to develop cures for many illnesses, and the specter of major health and environmental disasters that will take an egregious toll on human life, especially for those who are the most vulnerable. What is further abhorrent morally and politically is that the cuts to discretionary programs actually constitute an appallingly small amount of costs in the federal budget.

Trump has also called for the elimination of the National Endowment for the Arts, the National Endowment for the Humanities, the Corporation for Public Broadcasting, and the Institute of Museum and Library Services, making clear that his contempt for education, science, and the arts is part of an aggressive project to eliminate the institutions and public spheres that extend the capacity of people to be imaginative, think critically, and be well informed.[32] Yet, simultaneously, Trump does nothing to lessen or eliminate the corporate control of mainstream media, ensuring instead that it functions largely as a propaganda machine for the financial elite and major corporations.

Trump seeks to impose deep and drastic cuts on the budgets of nineteen agencies designed to help the poor, students, public education, academic research, and the arts. Whatever savings result from these cuts will be used to expand the machineries of war, militarization, and detention. The culture of cruelty is on full display here, as millions would suffer from the lack of loans, federal aid, and basic resources. The winners would be the Departments of Defense and Homeland Security, the private prison industry, and the institutions and personnel needed to expand the police state. What Trump has provided in his 2018 federal budget proposal is a blueprint for eliminating the remnants of the welfare state, while transforming American society into a "war-obsessed, survival-of-the fittest dystopia."[33] Trump's neoliberal austerity policies and priorities are crystal clear not only in the draconian $4.1 trillion cuts he makes to so many vital social programs that benefit the poor, particularly children, but also in the $5 trillion tax benefits for the ultra-rich and big corporations.[34]

War is a central category for understanding Trump's budget proposals in two related ways. First, war functions as an organizing principle for waging an assault against vulnerable populations while expanding the power of the police and punishing state. Second, the ongoing production of the machinery of destruction and death provides enormous profits for the wealthiest individuals and corporations driving the arms, defense, and border security industries. In the first instance, war as an organizing principle of society is particularly evident in the Trump administration's savage cuts to programs that give hope and a small measure of security to the 14.5 million children who live in poverty, lack health care, endure homelessness, and live with disabilities. And these are in addition to the cuts that will come from Trump's obscene cuts as a result of his tax reform policies. Marian Wright Edelman makes this point clear in arguing that Trump's "immoral budget declares war on America's children, our most vulnerable group" and describes some of the more egregious policy cuts in the 2018 budget, which, she says:

> Slashes billions over ten years from Medicaid which nearly 37 million children rely on for a healthy start in life and which pays for nearly half of all births and ensures coverage for 40 percent of our children with special health care needs. . . . Rips $5.7 billion from CHIP (Children's Health Insurance Program), which covers nearly 9 million children in working families ineligible for

Medicaid. . . . Snatches food out of the mouths and stomachs of hungry children by slicing $193 billion over ten years from the Supplemental Nutrition Assistance Program (SNAP), which some still call food stamps. SNAP feeds nearly 46 million people including nearly 20 million children. . . . Whacks $72 billion over ten years from the Supplemental Security Income Program (SSI), which more than 8 million children and adults with the most severe disabilities depend on to keep going.[35]

In the second instance, war as a revenue-producing program is a high priority for the Trump administration, as evident in Trump's proposed budget, which allocates initially $2.6 billion to work on the wall planned for the Mexican border while also increasing the military budget by $54 billion.[36] As Edelman observes:

President Trump's 2018 Budget includes an estimated $5 trillion tax package for the wealthiest individuals and corporations [and] increases base defense spending $54 billion in 2018 alone (and $489 billion over ten years). That's $147,945,205 a day, $6,164,384 an hour and $102,739 a minute. The U.S. military budget is already the largest military budget in the world. We spend more on the military than the next eight countries combined (China, Russia, Saudi Arabia, India,

France, United Kingdom, Japan, and Germany). [The 2018 budget] spends $2.6 billion new dollars on border security including $1.6 billion for a down payment on the President's proposed obscene wall at the Mexican border estimated to cost $10 to $20 billion before completion and after false campaign promises that the Mexican government would pay.[37]

Under Trump, it has also become clear that an increasingly militarized United States is now on a war footing internationally. It is no longer overstating the case—given the nuclear escalations with North Korea—to say that Trump poses a growing threat to the planet itself. On the home front, the war on youth of color is being expanded. For example, under Trump, Americans have witnessed the rapid mobilization of a domestic war against undocumented immigrants, Muslims, people of color, young people, the elderly, public education, science, and democracy. The moral obscenity and reactionary politics that inform Trump's budget were summed up by Bernie Sanders:

> At a time of massive income and wealth inequality, when 43 million Americans are living in poverty and half of older Americans have no retirement savings, we should not slash programs that senior citizens, children, and working people rely on in order to provide a massive increase in spending to the military industrial complex. Trump's

priorities are exactly the opposite of where we should be heading as a nation.[38]

As more and more people find themselves living in a society tilted toward waging war and serving the rich, it becomes difficult for the public to acknowledge or even to understand the everyday hardship and misery that an increasing number of American families and communities will have to endure in the age of Trump. The celebration of human suffering and policies that produce it were on full display in Republicans' relentless campaign to "repeal and replace" the Affordable Care Act.

Attacks on Health Care Are a Threat to National Security

The health-care reform bills proposed by Republicans in the House and Senate have generated heated discussions across a vast ideological and political spectrum. On the right, senators such as Rand Paul and Ted Cruz have endorsed a new level of cruelty—one that has a long history among the radical right—by arguing that the current Senate bill does not cut enough social services and provisions for the poor, children, the elderly, and other vulnerable groups and needs to be even more friendly to corporate interests by providing massive tax cuts for the wealthiest Americans.

The same message is hammered home constantly in right-wing media. For instance, Fox News commentator Lisa Kennedy Montgomery, in a discussion about the Senate bill, stated without apparent irony that rising public concerns over the suffering, misery, and death that would result from this policy bordered on "hysteria," since "we are all going to die anyway."[39] The lack of substance in Montgomery's remarks speaks for itself.

On the other side of the ideological and political divide, liberals such as Robert Reich have described right-wing efforts to destroy the Affordable Care Act as attempts to further enrich the wealthiest at the expense of millions of Americans whose medical security would collapse as a result.[40] In the latest Senate version, tax reductions for the rich have been modified, but that seems inconsequential given the political and economic benefits the rich gain from the bill. Other commentators, such as Laila Lalami of *The Nation*, have reasoned that what we are witnessing with such policies is another example of political contempt for the poorest and most vulnerable on the part of right-wing politicians and pundits.[41] These arguments are only partly right and do not go far enough in their criticisms of the new political dynamics and mode of authoritarianism that have overtaken the United States. Put more bluntly, they suffer from limited political horizons.

What we do know about the proposed Republican Party tax reform, federal budget, and health care policies, in whatever form, is that they will gold-plate the golf carts of the rich before securing affordable health care, college education, or tax relief for average American families. The notion that the government has a responsibility to care for its citizens and that society should be organized around the principles of mutual respect, care, and compassion has been under attack since the 1970s with the advent of the current form of capitalism—neoliberalism. The latest measure of such an attack is evident in various versions of failed Senate bills that would have led to massive reductions in Medicare spending. Medicare covers 20 percent of all Americans, or 15 million people, 49 percent of all births, 60 percent of all children with disabilities, and 64 percent of all nursing home residents, many of whom will be left homeless without this support.

Under the current version of the Senate attempts at gutting Obamacare and proposing a new policy, it has been estimated that a possible 18 to 22 million people will lose their health insurance coverage, accompanied by massive cuts proposed to food-stamp programs that benefit at least 43 million people. Republican health care proposals allow insurance companies to charge more money from the most vulnerable. Such proposals would have cut maternity care and phased out coverage for emergency services. Moreover, as Lalami points out, the first U.S. Senate proposal included "nearly $1 trillion in tax cuts, about half of which will flow to those who make more than $1 million per year."[42] The latter figure is significant when measured against the fact that Medicaid would see a nearly $800 billion cut in the next ten years. This onslaught upon the health of the American people and the savage limits placed on their access to decent health care is compounded by fact that the United States is the wealthiest country in the world and yet, according to the World Health Organization, ranks "37th in overall health care amongst the world's countries."[43]

Under Trump, the culture of cruelty is being pushed to its limits. For instance, not only is he threatening to expel 200,000 Salvadorans and 800,000 Dreamers from the United States, he has allowed states to impose work requirements on Medicaid recipients. Such savagery boggles the mind when one thinks about the harshness of this requirement and the misery and increased suffering it will impose on populations that are already barely able to survive. Writing for the Center for American Progress, Katherine Gallagher Robbins and Rachel West sum up the dire nature of this law well. They write:

> This week, the Trump administration issued policy guidance that effectively ends Medicaid as we know it, allowing states to place punitive work requirements on certain Medicaid recipients—more than 7 in 10 of whom are caregivers or in school. Although these so-called work requirement policies may seem reasonable at first glance, in practice, they're a way to strip away health insurance from struggling unemployed and underemployed workers.[44]

It gets worse. The most recent Senate bill will drastically decrease social services and health care in rural America, and one clear consequence will be rising mortality rates.[45] In addition, Dr. Steffie Woolhandler, co-author of a recent article in the *Annals of Internal Medicine*, has estimated that if health insurance is taken away from 18 to 22 million people, "it raises . . . death rates by between 3 and 29 percent. And the math on that is that if you take health insurance away from 22 million people, about 29,000 of them will die every year, annually, as a result."[46] An earlier study by the *American Journal of Public Health* was more ominous, estimating that "nearly 45,000 annual deaths are associated with lack of health insurance."[47] Given that fact, Republicans' plot to kill the Affordable Care Act can and should be seen as a premeditated right-wing attack with far more destructive power than Timothy McVeigh's Oklahoma attack.

Progressives need new ways to understand and resist the rise of authoritarianism in the United States. Single-issue strategies, whether aimed at regressive tax cuts, police violence, or environmental destruction, are not enough. Nor is the focus on struggles for personal emancipation and minority rights adequate as the basis for a comprehensive politics. Nor is the traditional Marxist discourse of exploitation and accumulation by dispossession adequate for understanding the current historical conjuncture. The problem is not merely one of exploitation but one of exclusion. This politics of exclusion, Slavoj Žižek argues, "is no longer about the old class division between workers and capitalists, but . . . about not allowing some people to participate in public life."[48] Dr. Stephen Grosz calls our collective predicament a "catastrophe of indifference." The disaster of gangster capitalism is that it preys relentlessly upon society looking for wealth to extract and easy targets to extract it from. As it does, increasing social injustice, environmental collapse, and economic despair are normalized, and protest squelched. It is this combination of conditions that has turned everyday life for countless families and communities into an American nightmare.

What does health care, or justice itself, mean in a country dominated by corporations, the military, and the ruling 1 percent? Open attacks on affordable health care make clear that the current problem of corporate capitalism is not only about stealing resources or an intensification of the exploitation of labor, but also about a politics of exclusion, cruelty, and the propagation of forms of social and literal death, through what Zygmunt Bauman described as "the most conspicuous cases of social polarization, of deepening inequality, and of rising volumes of human poverty, misery, and humiliation."[49]

A culture of myopia now propels single-issue analyses detached from broader issues. The current state of progressive politics has collapsed into ideological silos, and feeds "a deeper terror—of helplessness, to which uncertainty is but a contributing factor,"[50] as Bauman put it, which all too often is transformed into a depoliticizing cynicism or a misdirected anger. The fear of disposability has created a new ecology of insecurity and despair that murders dreams, squelches any sense of an alternative future, and cripples the capacity for critical thought and informed agency. Under such circumstances, the habits of oligarchy and authoritarianism saturate everyday life.

Traditional liberal and progressive discourses about our current quagmire are not wrong. They are simply incomplete, and they do not grasp a major shift that has taken place in the United States since the late 1970s. That shift is organized around what Bauman, Stanley Aronowitz, Saskia Sassen, and Brad Evans have called a new kind of politics, one in which entire populations are considered excess and consigned to fend for themselves.

Such expulsions and social homelessness, whether of poor African Americans, Mexican immigrants, Muslims, or Syrian refugees, constitute a new and accelerated level of oppression. Moreover, buttressed by a market-driven appeal to a commercialized individualism, a distrust of all social bonds, a survival-of-the-fittest ethic, and a willingness to view economic activity as separate from social costs, neoliberal policies are now enacted in which public services are underfunded, bad schools become the norm, health care as a social provision is abandoned, child care is seen as an individual responsibility, and social assistance is looked on with disdain. Evil now appears not merely in the overt oppression of the state but as a widespread refusal on the part of many Americans to react to the suffering of others, which is all too often viewed as self-inflicted.

Under this new regime of massive cruelty and disappearance, the social state is gradually defunded and replaced with a carceral one. Resources once used for community development, education, and family social services are used instead for increased surveillance and militarization. Donald Trump's influence further skews the system toward centralized authority and away from egalitarian social justice. The limits of his own authority and power over the U.S. justice and law enforcement systems openly frustrate Trump's desire to dominate adversaries and thwart criminal investigations into him and his staff. "Just this week," reported the *New York Times* on November 3, 2017:

> . . . he denounced the criminal justice system as "a joke" and "a laughingstock." He demanded that the suspect in the New York terrorist attack be executed. He spent Friday berating the Justice Department and FBI for not investigating his political opponents. He then turned to the military justice system and called a court-martial decision "a complete and total disgrace."[51]

Trump's authoritarianism ignores how, in many communities of color, behaviors such as jaywalking, panhandling, and walking or driving while Black, are increasingly targeted, fined, and criminalized. Schools have become feeders into the criminal prison-industrial complex for many young people, especially youth of color. State terrorism bears down with greater intensity on immigrants, minorities of color or religion, and members of the lowest economic class. The official state message is to catch, punish, and imprison excess populations treated as criminals rather than save lives.

The carceral state and a culture of fear have become the foundational elements that drive the new politics of disposability.[52] Trumpism's relentless attacks on the Affordable Care Act openly expose—and even celebrate—a *politics of disposability.* American families who benefit from Obamacare are disparaged as parasites by the alt-right. Republican efforts seek to take federal resources used for health care subsidies and gift them to the wealthiest Americans at tax time instead. The *New York Times* has reported that more than 59,000 Americans died of drug overdoses in 2016, the largest year-over-year increase ever recorded.[53] Despite the crisis, Republican health care proposals attempt to cut funds earmarked for programs that serve Americans who urgently need medical treatment and care.

A politics of disposability and cruelty thrives on distractions—the game show commercialization of U.S. politics—as well as what might be called a politics of disappearance. That is, a politics enforced daily in the mainstream media, which functions as a "disimagination machine" and renders invisible deindustrialized communities, decaying schools, neighborhoods that resemble slums in the developing world, millions of incarcerated people of color, and elderly people locked in understaffed nursing homes.

We live in an age that Brad Evans and I have called an age of multiple expulsions, suggesting that once something is expelled it becomes invisible. In the current age of disposability, the systemic edges of authoritarianism have moved to the center of politics, just as politics is now an extension of state violence. Moreover, in the age of disposability, what was once considered extreme and unfortunate has now become a matter of common sense, whether we are talking about policies that actually kill people or those that strip away the humanity and dignity of millions.

Disposability and cruelty are not new in U.S. history, but their more predatory formations are back in new and more expansive forms. Moreover, what is unique about the contemporary politics of disposability is how it has become official policy, normalized through narratives of national security, economic security, and "Making America Great Again." The moral and social sanctions for greed and avarice that emerged through Reaganism flourish once again under Trumpism.

With the rise of the new authoritarianism coded into slogans of national greatness and law and order, financial elites intensify political pressure for state redirection of resources used for social benefits intended to decrease human suffering, hardship, and early death.

In such a climate, notions of freedom are divorced from social and economic rights and are increasingly redefined to mean decreased government regulation of corporate power, and freedom for the rich to pay less taxes. Freedom from injustice, corruption, and corporate crime simply does not factor in. As Zygmunt Bauman and Leonidas Donskis have observed: "our freedom today becomes localized in the sphere of consumption and self-renewal, but it has lost any connection with the most important thing: believing that you can change something in the world."[54] Countering these trends and winning the battle over resources, institutions, and power requires nothing less than the creation of a new political and economic social order.

Manifestations of domestic terrorism have expanded,

and this more expansive level of repression and intensification of state violence negates and exposes the compromising discourse of neoliberalism, while reproducing new levels of systemic violence. Effective struggle against such repression would combine a democratically energized cultural politics of resistance and hope with a politics aimed at offering all workers a living wage and all citizens a guaranteed standard of living, a politics dedicated to providing decent education, housing, and health care to all residents of the United States. Such struggle also involves refusing to equate capitalism with democracy, and struggling to create a mass movement that embraces a radical democratic future.

CHAPTER FIVE

THE POLITICS OF DISPOSABILITY IN THE AGE OF DISASTERS: FROM DREAMERS AND PUERTO RICO TO VIOLENCE IN LAS VEGAS

"As Black, I am apparently excrement, waste, refuse. That is an attack on my humanity. . . . That is an attack on all Black life. . . . but not beyond the facts of American history and not beyond the pale of the white imaginary to enact forms of grave physical violence."

—George Yancy

Confronting an increasingly authoritarian system means bringing attention to how systemic injustices are lived and experienced, and how iniquitous relations of power impact millions of American families with increased debt, illness, and neglect. The political economy is openly robbing communities of a decent life, dignity, justice, and hope. We live in an age of gangster capitalism, an age where fascism takes new, increasingly corporate, commercialized forms. The lines between self-enrichment and governance blur under the Trump regime. As the Panama and Paradise papers make clear, the global elite park millions in offshore accounts while instructing their political hacks in Congress to lower their taxes. Corporate self-interest, greed, and commercialism now drive politics and everyday life in the United States. Oxfam reports that "eight men own as much as the poorest half of the world," and that "the wealth of 3.5 billion people is the equivalent to the combined net worth" of eight businessmen, six of whom are from the United States.[1] Such gaps in wealth and power turn politics into acts of war and repression.

Instances of politics becoming an extension of war and civic death have been rife during Trump's time in the White House.[2] Such instances include Trump's threat to deport the Dreamers, his refusal to mobilize the government's full resources to aid the people of Puerto Rico in the devastating aftermath of Hurricane Maria, and his silence regarding gun reforms after the mass shooting in Las Vegas. All three of these events are treated as unrelated incidents; examples of life's uncertain twists of fate. The consequences of government's underwhelming response to such crises are further intensified by the neoliberal doctrine that individuals are solely responsible for the ill fortune they experience. This feral ideological assumption is reinforced by undermining any critical attention to the conditions produced by stepped-up systemic lawlessness, state violence, or the harsh consequences of a capricious and cruel head of state.

Progress and dystopia have become synonymous. State-endorsed social provisions and government responsibility are exiled by the neoliberal valorization of freedom construed as the unbridled promotion of self-interest. This narrow celebration of choice ignores constraints and context; it is a wild-eyed emphasis on individual responsibility and its attendant internalization of failure, blind to broader systemic structures and socially produced problems. Existential security no longer rests on collective foundations but on privatized solutions and facile appeals to moral character. Social and economic determinants now disappear in a political backdrop in which social provisions are eliminated, reinforced by the oppressively stupid babble of celebrity culture and self-help talk shows such as Dr. Phil and Oprah Winfrey, all of which appeal to corporate sentiments of total self-reliance and a crippling emphasis on individual responsibility. Mainstream cultural pathways now combine a depoliticizing illiteracy with a spectacle of violence that creates the invisible architecture of social relations, desires, and values through which anti-democratic sentiments gain legitimacy. Under such circumstances, a politics of disposability has merged with an ascendant authoritarianism in the United States in which the government's response to such disparate issues as the DACA crisis, the devastation of Puerto Rico by Hurricane Maria, and the mass shooting in Las Vegas are met uniformly with state-sanctioned violence.

Under Trump, the politics of disposability and the war against democracy have taken on a much harder and crueler edge. In fact, there has been a radical shift in both the investment in government-sponsored violence and the creation of a social order designed to cancel out any promise of a democratic future, especially for young people. Violence is now sown everywhere with an unapologetic and punishing arrogance. The police are being armed with weapons from the battlefields of Afghanistan, young people are being pushed through the school-to-prison pipeline, legislation is used to further disenfranchise African Americans and Latinos, connective forms of justice are dismantled, the police are urged by the president to take the gloves off when dealing with people suspected of crimes, and the attorney general has called for a law-and-order campaign that is steeped in racism.

Today's strain of neoliberal capitalism accelerates the mechanisms by which vulnerable populations are rendered unknowable, undesirable, and unthinkable, considered an excess cost, and stripped of their humanity. Relegated to zones of social abandonment and political exclusion, targeted populations become incomprehensible, civil rights disappear, hardship and suffering are normalized, and human lives are targeted and negated by machineries of violence. For those populations rendered disposable, ethical questions go unasked as the mechanisms of dispossession, forced homelessness, and forms of social death feed corrupt political systems and forms of corporate power removed from any sense of civic and social responsibility. As I stated in the last chapter, the Trump administration is the new face of a politics of disposability that thrives on the energies of the vulnerable and powerless while accelerating what João Biehl calls "the death of the unwanted."[3]

Under such conditions, power is defined by the degree to which it is abstracted from any sense of responsibility or critical analysis.

Evidence of this type of disposability is especially visible under the influence of Trump. Not only is it obvious in his discourse of humiliation, bigotry, and objectification, but also in policies designed to punish those populations who are the most vulnerable. These include the victims in Puerto Rico of Hurricane Maria, and illegal immigrant children no longer protected by DACA; a state-sanctioned culture of violence has become the driving force for expanding the armed forces and para-militarizing local police forces throughout the country as part of a race-based law and order policy. Trumpism is fomenting a war culture in which state-sanctioned violence is becoming the baseline for creating a society soaked in fear, manufactured ignorance, and pervasive loathing of those typecast as weak, parasitic, disloyal, or not contributing to making America great again.[4]

Fear no longer prompts the U.S. government to address real dangers, now posed as inescapable. On the contrary, fear now "evokes an insomnia full of nightmares,"[5] and is framed mostly within a discourse of threats to personal safety, serving to increase the criminalization of a wide range of everyday behaviors while buttressing the current administration's call for "law and order." Fear has become a petri dish for racism and state-sanctioned dogmatism, and has spurred the increased development of gated communities, a mass incarceration state, schools modeled after prisons, and the call for walls and sealed borders. Such fears further reinforce a punishing state wedded to the growth of a militarized culture, state violence, and expanding authoritarianism. America has reached a political and ethical low point, and has become a society saturated in acute violence, ethical indifference, and impunity.

Under such circumstances, America's fascist drift not only produces harsh and dire political changes but also a failure to address a continuous series of economic, ecological, and social crises. At the same time, the machinery of disposability and death rolls on in both punishing entire populations and making them disappear, conferring upon them the status of the living dead and catapulting them out of a moral universe that acknowledges what it means to live with dignity, but also what it means to be human. The death-dealing logic of disposability has been updated and now parades in the name of freedom, choice, efficiency, security, progress, and, ironically, democracy. Disposability has become so normalized that it is difficult to recognize it as a distinctive if not overriding organizing principle of the new American authoritarianism. As a result, it becomes difficult, as Judith Butler argues, to recognize that some lives are not grievable. She notes that

> certain lives are not considered lives at all, they cannot be humanized, that they fit no dominant frame for the human, and that their dehumanization occurs first, at this level, and that this level then gives rise to a physical violence that

in some sense delivers the message of dehuman-
ization that is already at work in the culture. . . .
Violence renews itself in the face of the apparent
inexhaustibility of its object.[6]

While the politics of disposability has a long legacy in
the United States, Trump has given it a new and powerful
impetus, and it differs from the past both in terms of an
unapologetic embrace of the ideology of white supremacy and its willingness to expand state-sanctioned violence
and death as part of a wider project of America's drift from
authoritarianism to fascism. Running through these events
is a governmental response that has abandoned a social
contract designed, however tepidly, to prevent hardship,
suffering, and death. Relentless right-wing attacks on the
Affordable Care Act and the elderly and infirm whose lives
depend on it, demonstrate this abandonment in the stark-
est terms. In fact, at work here is the haunting specter of a
politics of disposability in which people are catapulted out
of the moral universe of human beings for whom the government has any responsibility. Such populations, inclusive
of such disparate groups as the residents of Puerto Rico and
the Dreamers, are left to fend for themselves in the face
of natural or man-made disasters—considered collateral
damage in the construction of a neoliberal order in which
those marginalized by race and class become the objects of
a violent form of social engineering relegating its victims
to what Richard Sennett has termed a "specter of useless-
ness," whose outcomes are both tragic and devastating.

Puerto Rico as a Zone of Social and Political Abandonment

On September 20, 2017, Hurricane Maria, a Category 5 storm with 155-mile-an-hour winds slammed into and devastated the island of Puerto Rico. In the aftermath of a slow government response, conditions in Puerto Rico reached unprecedented and unacceptable levels of misery, hardship, and suffering. As of October 19, over one million people were without drinking water, 80 percent of the island lacked electricity, and ongoing reports by medical staff, nurses, and other respondents indicated that increasing numbers of people were dying.[7] Thousands were living in shelters, lacked phone service, and had to bear the burden of a health-care system in shambles.

Such social immiseration is complicated by the fact that the island is home to twenty-one hazardous Superfund sites, places of severe contamination and toxicity that pose serious risks to human health and the environment. Families that had lost everything found themselves facing the further horror that their source of drinking water had been contaminated by the flooding.[8] Lois Marie Gibbs ominously reported that waterborne illnesses were spreading just as hospitals were running low on medicines. Caitlin Dickerson observed that the water shortages were so severe that people were in desperation:

> [It was] a perpetual game of cat and mouse, scouring the city for any hints of places with water to sell. People are so desperate that . . . the

Environmental Protection Agency cited reports of residents trying to obtain drinking water from wells at hazardous Superfund sites. These are wells that were once sealed to avoid exposure to deadly toxins. [9]

The governor of Puerto Rico, Ricardo Rossello, warned that a number of people have died from Leptospirosis, a bacterial disease spread by animal urine.[10]

The Trump regime's response has been unforgivably slow, with conditions worsening. Given the accelerating crisis, the mayor of San Juan, Carmen Yulín Cruz, made a direct appeal to President Trump for aid, stating with an acute sense of urgency: "We are dying."[11] Trump responded by lashing out at her personally, telling her to stop complaining. While meeting with Jon Lee Anderson, a reporter from *The New Yorker,* Cruz became emotional when referring to elderly and ill victims of Maria whom she could not reach and who were "still at great risk in places where relief supplies and medical help had yet to arrive."[12] Cruz said the situation for many of these people was "like a slow death."[13]

Stories began to emerge in the press that validated Cruz's concerns. Many seriously ill dialysis patients either had their much-needed treatments reduced or could not get access to health-care facilities.[14] Because of the lack of electricity, Harry Figueroa, a 58-year-old teacher "went a week without the oxygen that helped him breathe," and eventually died. "His body went unrefrigerated for so long that the funeral director could not embalm his badly decomposed corpse."[15]

Scholar Lauren Berlant has used the term "slow death" in her own work to refer "to the physical wearing out of a population and the deterioration of people in that population that is very nearly a defining condition of their experience and historical existence."[16] Slow death captures the colonial backdrop and structural oppression deeply etched in Puerto Rico's history. The scale of suffering and devastation was so great that Robert P. Kadlec, the assistant secretary of Health and Human Services for Preparedness and Response, stated: "The devastation I saw, I thought was equivalent to a nuclear detonation."[17]

Puerto Rico's tragic and ruinous problems brought on by Hurricane Maria are amplified both by its crippling $74 billion debt burden, an unending economic crisis, and by the legacy of its colonial status and continuous lack of political power in representing its sovereign and economic rights in Washington. With no federal representation and lacking the power to vote in presidential elections, it is difficult for Puerto Ricans to get their voices heard, secure the same rights as U.S. citizens, and politically advocate and lobby on their own behalf.[18] Prior to the storm, people in Puerto Rico suffered a poverty rate of 46 percent, a depressing household median income of $19,350 (compared to the U.S. median of $55,775), and a crippling debt. In fact, the debt burden is so overwhelming that "pre-Maria Puerto Rico was spending more on debt service than on education, health, or security. Results included the shuttering of 150 schools, the gutting of health care, increased taxes, splitting of families between the island and the mainland, and increased food insecurity."[19] Amy Davidson Sorkin was right in arguing that "the crisis in Puerto Rico is a case study of what happens when people with little political capital need the help of their government."[20]

Not only did Trump allow three long weeks to saunter by before asking Congress to provide financial aid to the island, but his request reeked of indifference. Instead of asking for grants, he asked for loans, which, as Paul Krugman points out, "is mind-boggling when you bear in mind that the territory is effectively bankrupt."[21] Throughout the crisis, Trump released a series of tweets in which he suggested that the plight of the Puerto Rican people was their own fault and threatened to cut off aid from services proclaiming that the federal government "cannot keep FEMA, the Military & the First Responders . . . in P.R. forever."[22] Adding insult to injury, he also said that they were "throwing the government's budget out of whack because we've spent a lot of money on Puerto Rico."[23] He lambasted local officials for not doing enough, "scolded them for their alleged profligacy and indolence," and shamelessly stated that they should do more to help themselves rather than rely on aid from the federal government.[24]

Trump also suggested that the crisis in Puerto Rico was not a real crisis when compared to Katrina, because the latter had a much higher body count. Trump's view of Puerto Ricans as second-class citizens was exposed repeatedly in an ongoing range of tweets and comments that extended from the insulting notion that "they want everything to be done for them" to the visual image of Trump throwing rolls of paper towel into a crowd as if he were on a public relations tour. Throughout the crisis, Trump has repeatedly congratulated himself on the government response to Puerto Rico, falsely stating that everybody thinks we are doing "an amazing job."[25] A month after the crisis, Trump insisted, without irony or a shred of self-reflection, that he would give himself a "perfect ten."

These responses suggest more than a callous expression of narcissistic self-delusion and sociopathic indifference to the suffering of others. Trump's callous misrecognition of the magnitude of the crisis in Puerto Rico and extent of the islanders' misery and suffering, coupled with his insults and demeaning tweets, demonstrate the convergence of race and class divisions in his governance. There is more being put into place here than a disconnection from the poor, there is also a white supremacist ideology that registers race as a central part of both his politics and a wider politics of disposability. It is difficult to miss the racist logic of malign neglect and reckless disregard for the safety and lives of Puerto Rican citizens, bordering on criminal negligence, that simmers just beneath the surface of Trump's rhetoric and actions. Hurricane Maria revealed more than an island unprepared for a natural disaster, it exposed a long history of racism and a stupefying lack of sympathy for people of color who are in need, impoverished, elderly, or ill. The inadequate government response to Hurricane Maria makes visible the hidden face of a politics of disposability and death-dealing racism.

Trump not only embodies the shortcomings of a neoliberal power structure that fails to protect its citizens but also reveals the full spectrum of mechanisms to further enrich the wealthy at the expense of everyone else. Trump's utterly failed response to the disaster in Puerto Rico reinforces Ta-Nehisi Coates's claim that the spectacle of bigotry that shapes Trump's presidency has "moved racism from the euphemistic and plausibly deniable to the overt and freely claimed."[26] What has happened in Puerto Rico not only exposes the great class and racial animus that drives Trump's policies, it also reveals the frightening marker of a politics of disposability in which any appeal to democracy loses its claim and becomes hard to imagine, let alone enact, without the threat of violent retaliation.

Revoking DACA and the Killing of the Dream

Trump's penchant for cruelty in the face of great hardship and human suffering is evident not only in his slow response to the devastation Puerto Rico suffered after Hurricane Maria. It is also strikingly visible in the racial bigotry that has shaped his cancellation of the DACA program [Deferred Action for Childhood Arrivals], instituted in 2012 by former President Obama. Under the program, over 800,000 undocumented immigrants brought to the country as children or teens before 2007 had been allowed to live, study, and work in the United States without fear of deportation. The program permitted these young people, known as Dreamers, to have access to Social Security cards and drivers' licenses, and to advance their education, start small businesses, and become fully integrated into the fabric of American society. Seventy-six percent of Americans believe that Dreamers should be granted resident status or citizenship. In revoking the program, Trump has made clear his willingness to deport individuals who came to the United States as children through no actions of their own, and for whom the United States is their only home. Trump's actions are both cruel and racist, given that 78 percent of DACA residents are from Mexico: these are the same people Trump once labeled as rapists, drug addicts, and criminals.

Attorney General Jeff Sessions, one of the more visible symbols of Trump's white supremacist commitment, was called upon to be the front man in announcing the cancellation of DACA. In barely concealed racist tones, Sessions argued that DACA had to end because "the effect of this unilateral executive amnesty, among other things, contributed to a surge of unaccompanied minors on the southern border that yielded terrible humanitarian consequences . . . denied jobs to hundreds of thousands of Americans by allowing those same jobs to go to illegal aliens" and had to be rescinded because "failure to enforce the laws in the past has put our nation at risk of crime, violence and even terrorism."[27] None of these charges were true.

According to Juan Cole, "Dreamers are 14 percent less like to be incarcerated than the general population . . . are from unusually educated families and are themselves disproportionately well educated . . . and 91percent of Dreamers are employed."[28] As William Finnegan has observed, "Connecting Dreamers, moreover, to crime, violence, and terrorism is both absurd—anyone convicted of a serious crime is ineligible—and a tactic drawn straight from the nativist-demagogue playbook."[29] Rather than taking jobs from U.S. workers, Dreamers add an enormous economic benefit to the economy and "it is estimated that the loss of the Dreamers' output will reduce the G.D.P. by several hundred billion dollars over a decade."[30] Sessions' claim that DACA contributed to a surge of unaccompanied minors at the border is simply an outright lie given that the surge began in 2008, four years before DACA was announced, and was largely due, as Mark Joseph Stern points out, "to escalating gang violence in Central America, as well as drug cartels' willingness to target and recruit children in Mexico. . . . [A] study published in International Migration . . . found that DACA was not one of these factors."[31]

Trump's move to snuff DACA was politically indefensible and heartless. Only 12 percent of Americans want the Dreamers deported, and this support is drawn mostly from Trump's following of ideological extremists, religious conservatives, ultra-nationalists, and angry white males. This would include Steve Bannon, still an advocate for Trumpism, who helped bring white supremacist and ultranationalist ideology from the fringes of society into national politics.[32] On a segment of *60 Minutes*, Bannon told Charlie Rose that the DACA program shouldn't be codified, adding, "As the work permits run out, they self-deport. . . . There's no path to citizenship, no path to a green card and no amnesty. Amnesty is nonnegotiable." Bannon's comments are cruel but predictable, given his support for the uniformly bigoted policies Trump has pushed before and after his election.

Since revoking DACA, Trump has wavered between attempts to work with Democrats to renew the program and flatly stating that without the latter's support for building a wall on the Mexico-U.S. border, he will not approve of a policy saving DACA. That demand appeared to effectively kill any hope of a political solution to the problem. After the government shutdown, Trump equivocated again claiming he was in favor of eventually giving citizenship to Dreamers if he could reach a deal with the Democratic Party. Senator Schumer was right when he said "Negotiating with this White House is like negotiating with Jell-O."[33] Things took another turn in January 2018 when a federal judge ordered the Trump administration to restart DACA, which would prevent "young, undocumented immigrants from deportation."[34] On the downside, the judge stated that the "government will not be required to accept new applications from immigrants who had not previously submitted one. The judge also said the administration could continue to prevent DACA recipients from returning to the United States if they leave the country."[35] Trump responded by attacking the U.S. court system as unfair.

The call to end DACA is part of a broader racist anti-immigration policy aimed at making America white again, a throwback to the Jim Crow era in which white supremacy was socially, culturally, and legally overt. The current push against people of color and immigrants not only reminds us of our own racist national history, but also resonates with the varieties of social intolerance experienced under the totalitarian regimes that emerged in Germany in the 1930s and Latin America in the 1970s.

Las Vegas and the Politics of Violence

On Sunday, October 1, 2017, Stephen Paddock, a lone gunman, ensconced on the thirty-second floor of the Mandalay Bay Resort and Casino Hotel in Las Vegas, opened fire on a crowd of country and western concertgoers below, killing fifty-eight people and wounding more than five hundred. While the venues for such shootings differ, the results are always predictable. People die or are wounded, and society weighs in on the cause of the violence. If the assailants are people of color or Muslim, they are labeled terrorists, but if they are white, they are often labeled mentally disturbed or even racist, as was the case with Dylann Roof, an admitted white supremacist who was sentenced to death after killing nine members of an African American church. Paddock was immediately branded by President Trump a "sick" and "deranged man" who had committed an act of "radical evil."

Trump's characterization of the shooting as an act of radical evil is more mystifying than assuring, and it did little to explain how such an egregious act of brutality fits into a broader pattern of civic decline, cultural decay, political corruption, and systemic violence. Or, as Jeffrey St. Clair observes, how "state-sponsored violence propagates violence within the state."[36] Connecting the dots appears to be one of great absences from corporate media that trade in isolated spectacles. Rarely is there a connection made in the mainstream media, for instance, between the fact that the United States is the largest arms manufacturer with the biggest military budget in the world and the almost unimaginable fact that there are more than 300 million guns in the United States, which amounts to "112 guns per 100 people."[37] While the Trump administration is not directly responsible for the bloodbath in Las Vegas, it does feed a culture of violence in the United States, and in doing so has contributed to priming "the mind which did and made accessible the machinery of death."[38]

Many Republicans, including Senate Majority Leader Mitch McConnell, reinforced the lack of civic and ethical courage that emerged in the aftermath of the Las Vegas massacre by arguing that it was "particularly inappropriate" to talk about gun reform or politics in general after a mass shooting. When the issue of politics is eliminated from the discussion, the power of gun manufacturers to flood the country with guns disappears, as does the power of lobbyists to ensure that gun-safety measures do not become part of a wider national conversation. Excluding politics from the Las Vegas mass shooting makes it easier to erase the conditions that made it possible for Paddock to amass forty-nine guns with various killing capacities, including a bump-stock that allowed him to turn rifles into automatic weapons and massively increase the amount of carnage. This depoliticizing logic also enabled most discussion about Paddock to center on him as an aberration—a person whose "wires are screwed up," according to Trump.

The corporate press, with few exceptions, was unwilling to address how and why mass shootings have become routine in the United States, and how everyday violence benefits a broader cultural commercialization of violence.[39] There was no reference to how young children are groomed for violence by educational programs sponsored by the gun industries, how military recruiting and training have moved into public schools, how video games and other aspects of a militarized culture are used to teach youth to be insensitive to the horrors of real-life violence, how the military-industrial complex "makes a living from killing through defense contracts, weapons manufacturing and endless wars."[40] Or, how war propaganda provided by the Pentagon influences not only pro-sports events and Hollywood blockbuster movies but also reality TV shows such as *American Idol* and *The X-Factor*. John W. Whitehead puts the militarizing of American culture in perspective. He writes:

> U.S. military intelligence agencies (including the NSA) have influenced over 1,800 movies and TV shows. And then there are the growing number of video games, a number of which are engineered by or created for the military, which have accustomed players to interactive war play through

> military simulations and first-person shooter sce-
> narios. This is how you acclimate a population
> to war. This is how you cultivate loyalty to a war
> machine.[41]

In this instance, the culture of violence cannot be separated from the business of violence. Similarly, popular culture does more than sanitize killing, it also creates conditions for what Cornelius Castoriadis once termed "the shameful degradation of the critical function" and a flight from responsibility, and allows people to view themselves as exempt from the realm of moral responsibility and evaluation.[42] In the event of mass shootings, the hidden structures of violence disappear in the narratives of personal sorrow, the call for prayers, and the insipid argument that such events should not be subject to political analysis. Trump's dismissive comments on the Las Vegas massacre as an act of evil misses the fact that what is evil is the pervasive presence of violence throughout U.S. history, and the how commonplace extreme violence and mass shootings have become on college campuses, in elementary schools, at concerts, in workplaces. Mass shootings are now perpetrated daily in the United States, but the deeper issue is the fact that such violence has become a normal and routine aspect of the American experience.

Militant Neoliberalism in Armed America

American dreams have turned into nightmares, white supremacy has become normalized at the highest levels of power, and militarized responses have become the primary medium for addressing, if not the solution to solving, all social problems, rendering critical thought less and less probable, less and less relevant. Science and evidence are under siege, a resurgent nationalism has produced what Wendy Brown calls an "apocalyptic populism,"[43] and willful ignorance has gained its most powerful and toxic expression in President Trump, who as Ariel Dorfman argues, exhibits "a toxic mix of ignorance and mendacity [as well as a] lack of intellectual curiosity and disregard for rigorous analysis."[44] This lethal mix of anti-intellectualism, ideological fundamentalism, and retreat from the ethical imagination become a perfect storm for what can be labeled a war culture, one that trades democratic values for a machinery of social abandonment, misery, and death.

American society is armed and radiates violence. War as an extension of politics fuels a spectacle of violence that has overtaken popular culture while normalizing concrete acts of gun violence that kill ninety-three Americans every day.[45] Traumatic events such as the termination of DACA, impacting grown young people, or the refusal on the part of the government to quickly and effectively respond to the hardships experienced by the people of Puerto Rico, no longer appear to represent an ethical dilemma to those in power. Instead, these groups represent disposable populations who inhabit frontier zones whose borders are shaped by racism and economic inequality.

In America's new space of disposability, a liminal purgatory of social homelessness is experienced by those who are deemed excess, and marked for terminal exclusion. Fueled by a retreat from any sense of ethical responsibility and accelerated by a punitive culture of lawlessness and state-legitimated violence, the politics of disposability has intensified and seeped into everyday life with a vengeance. What is distinctive about the politics of disposability, especially when coupled with the transformation of governance into a legitimation of violence and cruelty under Trump, is that it has both expanded a culture of extreme violence and has become a defining feature of American life. Chris Hedges has argued convincingly that "violence is the habitual response by the state to every dilemma."[46] This insight has taken on a more ominous register as the state, corporations, and individuals choose violence as a primary mode of engagement. For people immersed in a "death culture" such choices imprison rather than educate. They legitimate the militarizing of every major public institution from schools to airports. The carceral state now provides the template for interacting with others in a society addicted to persistent rituals of violence both as entertainment and in real life.

Under a global regime of neoliberalism, the political and ethical vigor that historically has driven social movements to embrace the promise of a radical democracy has given way to the vitalities of the living dead and what Adorno once called "authoritarian irrationality," the dark and menacing underside of a racist, anti-democratic and totalitarian politics and psychology. The flirtation with elements of totalitarianism haunts existing notions of ideology, power, and politics, spreading across much of Europe and the United States. All these modes of authoritarianism undermine democracy and feed on fear and uncertainty. Uncertain possibilities now abound in the age of extreme privatization and commodification, accompanied by a new sense of meaninglessness that produces the widespread social atomization endemic to neoliberal capitalism. As Josep R. Llobera has observed, Darwin's expression "'survival of the fittest' [has been] transformed into an ideological component that incorporate[s] racial inequality and struggle for existence."[47] It also gives rise to monstrous forms of barbarism in which brutality becomes more "rational" and fascist ideas more normalized. One consequence, in terms of state action, is that the boundaries between the acceptable and forbidden collapse.

Democracy is becoming all the more irrelevant in the United States under the Trump administration, especially in light of what Robert Weissmann, president of the watchdog group Public Citizens, calls "a total corporate takeover of the U.S. government on a scale we have never seen in American history."[48] Corporate governance and economic sovereignty has replaced state sovereignty. Democratic values and civic culture are under attack by a class of political extremists who embrace without reservation the cynical instrumental reason of the market, while producing on a global level widespread mayhem, suffering, and violence. How else to explain the fact that over 70 percent of Trump's picks for top administration jobs have corporate ties or work for major corporations? Almost all of these people represent interests diametrically opposed to the agencies for whom they now lead and are against almost any notion of the public good. Hence, under the Trump regime, we have witnessed a slew of rollbacks and deregulations, and a shift on toxic chemicals that will result in an increase of pollution, thus putting at risk children, the elderly, and others who might be exposed to hazardous toxins. The *New York Times* has reported that one E.P.A. appointee, Nancy Beck, a former executive at the American Chemistry Council, has initiated changes to make it more difficult to track and regulate the chemical perfluorooctanoic acid, which has been linked to "kidney cancer, birth defects, immune system disorders and other serious health problems."[49]

The link between violence and authoritarianism increasingly finds expression not only in endless government and populist assaults on immigrants, Blacks, and other vulnerable groups, but also in a popular culture that turns representations of extreme violence into entertainment. In addition, a powerful and unaccountable gun culture now feeds what Hedges calls "vigilante violence" against those protesting white supremacy, as well as the rise of neo-fascism and populist racist delusions aimed at ridding the country of Muslims and Mexican immigrants, however lawless the actions might be.[50]

America has become a society organized both for the production of violence and the creation of a culture brimming with fear, paranoia, and social atomization. Under such circumstances, the murderous aggression associated with authoritarian states becomes more common in the United States and is increasingly mirrored in the everyday actions of citizens. Mass shootings in the United States have become as ubiquitous as they are now mundane, with chances of gun control more remote than ever, even as an incomplete reform. If the government response to crisis that enveloped DACA and Puerto Rico points to a culture of state-sanctioned violence and cruelty, the mass shooting in Las Vegas represents the endpoint of a culture newly aligned with the rise of authoritarianism.

The shooting in Las Vegas does more than point to a record-setting death toll for vigilante violence, it also provides a signpost about a terrifying new political and cultural horizon in the relationship between violence and everyday life. The Las Vegas massacre represents more than another act of senseless violence, it also points to an expression of absolute lawlessness that has become all too common in the United States. At the same time, such lawlessness and its accompanying culture of cruelty point to increasingly dark expressions of individual brutality that push the boundaries of violence to levels that heretofore seemed unimaginable. What is difficult, yet crucial, to comprehend is the connection between the state-sanctioned violence at work in ending DACA, the inadequate government response to the disaster in Puerto Rico, and the mass shooting in Las Vegas. All of these incidents must be understood as a surface manifestation of a much larger set of issues endemic to the rise of authoritarianism in the United States.

These indices of violence offer pointed and alarming

examples of how inequality, systemic exclusion, and a culture of cruelty define American society, even, and especially, as they destroy it. Each offers an individual snapshot of how war culture and violence merge, and are experienced and distributed across different sites. As part of a broader category indicting the rise of authoritarianism in the United States, they make visible the pervasiveness of violence as an organizing principle of American life. While it is easy to condemn the violence at work in each of these specific examples, it is crucial to address the underlying economic, political, and structural forces that create these conditions.

In the face of this epidemic of violence, there is an urgent need for a broader awareness of the scope, range, and effects of violence in America as well as the relationship between politics and disposability, one that offers a warning against limiting such criticism to isolated issues of brutality and aggression. Only then will America be able to address the need for a radical restructuring of its politics, economics, institutions, and a refashioning of its citizens. Violence in the United States has to be understood as part of a wide-scale epidemic that is an outgrowth of a crisis in politics and culture defined by meaninglessness, helplessness, neglect, and commercial disposability. Historically, expressions of violence created moral outrage, but such outrage is less visible today and less effective. Today, resistance to such violence should also produce widespread thoughtful, informed, and collective action over the fate of civilian society itself. This suggests the need for a shared vision of economic justice, class, race, and gender—one that offers the promise of a new understanding of politics and the need for creating a powerful coalition among existing social movements, youth groups, workers, intellectuals, teachers, and other progressives.

Under Trump, a mounting attitude of scorn is developing toward the increasing number of people caught in the web of marginalization and misfortune. This scorn is fueled by right-wing influence operations that endlessly spew out rhetoric of intolerance. These conditions pose a serious challenge to U.S. society, especially since they are openly fostered by the president himself. There will, no doubt, continue to be an increase of repression under Trump. The conditions required for countering such repression will require not only understanding the roots of authoritarianism in the United States, but also eliminating the economic, political, and cultural forces that have produced its long history and ascendancy, one that, as the renowned historian Robert O. Paxton points out, began with the emergence of the Klu Klux Klan in the United States.[51] Addressing these forces will be more complicated than simply getting rid of Trump. We must resist efforts that equate corporate commercialism with democracy. The same goes for U.S. acts of aggression and military interventions abroad. We must stand in solidarity, not just against Trumpism but against a two-party system that seems to consistently prioritize corporate power and financial interests over social injustice and the common good.

CHAPTER SIX

STATE VIOLENCE AND THE SCOURGE OF WHITE NATIONALISM

"Hatred, which could destroy so much, never failed to destroy the man who hated, and this was an immutable law."

—James Baldwin

The militarization of U.S. culture meshes seamlessly with the machineries of war that enable the United States to ring the world with its military bases, maintain vast stockpiles of weapons, deploy thousands of troops all over the globe, and retain the shameful title of "the world's preeminent exporter of arms, [controlling] more than 50 percent of the global weaponry market."[1] Forces of militarization and war provide an array of platforms with the capacity to produce spectacles of violence, a culture of fear, ultra-masculine ideologies, and armed policies that give violence legitimacy. Under such circumstances, the pretense of national security enables authorities to redirect resources away from institutions dedicated to the public interest and the common good.

Under the Trump regime, armed power is being elevated as the preeminent measure of national greatness. While soldiers and war have long been central to Americana, militarized culture is now being sutured into the very tissue of everyday life in the United States. Trump's celebration of militarization as the highest of America's ideals was evident in his speech to a joint session of Congress when he stated: "To those allies who wonder what kind of friend America will be, look no further than the heroes who wear our uniform."[2] The irony here lies in the gesture of a helping hand that hides the investment in and threat of an aggressive militarism. Needless to say, such militarism is on full display as Trump undermines the sophisticated work of statecraft in favor of taunting his enemies with public threats to "totally destroy" them.

Police brutality and impunity seem to rouse little ethical and moral concern among much of the American public. Under Trump, such behavior appears to be officially condoned. How else to explain Trump's comment, without irony or remorse, during a campaign rally in Iowa that he "could stand in the middle of Fifth Avenue and shoot someone and not lose any voters"? How else to explain his July 2017 instructions to law enforcement officers not to be "too nice" to criminal suspects? Trump's remarks immediately prompted the acting head of the Drug Enforcement Administration, Chuck Rosenberg, to send a memo to all DEA agents and officers *not to mistreat suspects.* Disgusted with Trump, Rosenberg then announced his resignation.[3]

Falsehood and retribution appear to be key strategies

in Trump's only-winning-matters approach to politics and his bumper-sticker promise to "Make America Great Again." Taken with his distorted call for "law and order"—a code for a strengthening of the police state—it limns the outline of a militant authoritarian regime taking shape.[4] David Leonhardt, writing for the *New York Times*, has argued that "Democracy is not possible without the rule of law" and that Trump appears to have nothing but contempt for the principle.[5]

As president of the United States, Trump has attempted to politicize law enforcement by undermining the protected space between the Department of Justice and the White House. For Trump, unmitigated loyalty appears to be the only important factor in shaping his relationship with other branches of government. Such actions are well established among fascist dictators. Trump's emphasis on loyalty was particularly evident in the ways Trump pressured FBI director James Comey to back off his investigations into Michael Flynn and other members of Trump's inner circle, and in Trump's subsequent dismissal of Comey. As Jennifer Rubin has noted: "Trump's insistence on personal loyalty bolsters Comey's claim that Trump demanded the same of him. It also reveals an intent to remove or interfere with the Justice Department's actions, as if it were his personal law firm. The idea that the Justice Department should be protecting him and not the country goes to the essence of abuse of power."[6]

Trump has publicly slandered almost every judge who has disagreed with him. He has publicly criticized Jeff

Sessions, his attorney general, for recusing himself from the federal investigation into Russian covert operations and for appointing former FBI director Robert Mueller as special counsel for supervising the investigation.[7] According to Trump, Sessions was partly criticized for not passing the loyalty test. As I have mentioned earlier, in Trump's dysfunctional notion of governance, anyone who does not commit to a notion of total loyalty incurs his wrath. Loyalty in Trump's regime simply means deference and subordination to go along with whatever the bossman says, even if it's unethical, unconstitutional, or illegal.

Among Trump's most flagrant expressions of his disregard for the law are his constant reference to a list of political enemies and his "openly calling for the Department of Justice, which he controls, to put his political opponents in jail," a demand targeting Hillary Clinton, Huma Abedin, and James Comey, among others.[8]

In a blatant act of interference with a federal inquiry—what many consider an obstruction of justice—Trump has publicly criticized Mueller and his team, suggesting they should not investigate him, his family, or their intricate web of global financial holdings. In addition, Trump brazenly courts foreign businesses and governments "to speed up [Trump's] trademark applications" while a ranking "senior administration official urges people to buy Ivanka Trump's clothing."[9] And his violations of ethics laws appear to increase daily. Marjorie Cohn, the former president of the National Lawyers Guild, has gone so far as to claim that Trump is not only negligent in enforcing the law but has become a serial lawbreaker in his ongoing efforts to obstruct justice. She writes:

> Six months after taking office, Donald Trump has demonstrated contempt for the rule of law. He has not only refused to enforce certain laws; he has become a serial lawbreaker himself and counseled others to violate the law. Trump is undermining Obamacare, which is currently the law of the land. He is advocating police brutality. Plus, he has illegally bombed Syria, killed large numbers of civilians in Iraq and Syria, instituted an unconstitutional Muslim Ban, violated the Emoluments Clause and obstructed justice.[10]

Taken as whole, Trump's conduct signals not only the undermining of democracy, but the emergence of a quasi-fascist form of power. Trumpism is, as I stress throughout this book, the symptom of the long legacy of pro-corporate authoritarianism in the United States that waged its first frontal assault under Ronald Reagan in the 1980s, was embraced by the Third Way politics of the Democratic Party, and then solidified its power under the anti-democratic policies of the Bush-Cheney and Obama administrations. During this period, democracy was further undermined by bankers and big corporations, with power concentrated in the hands of a financial elite determined to ignore mechanisms of social justice achieved through the New Deal and the civil rights and education struggles of the 1960s. In the face of Trump's bald authoritarianism, Democratic Party members and the liberal elite are trying to place themselves at the forefront of organized resistance. But it is difficult not to see their gestures of defiance as hypocritical in light of the role they have played during the last forty years in subverting democracy and throwing communities of color under the bus.

Consider who Trump has installed around him: elite billionaires such as Rex Tillerson (since fired), the former ExxonMobil CEO, as secretary of state; Steven Mnuchin, a banker and hedge fund manager, as his treasury secretary; Wilbur Ross, a billionaire investor, to head the Commerce Department and Amway heiress Betsy DeVos as secretary of education. Those worth millions include Ben Carson as secretary of Housing and Urban Development, Elaine Chao as secretary of Transportation, David Shulkin (since fired) as secretary of Veterans Affairs, and the list goes on. Such political curation makes clear that Trump intends to allow former managers of big banks, private corporations, and other major financial institutions to run the country's economy. As Cornel West points out, these appointments serve to "reinforce corporate interest, big bank interest, and to keep track of those of who are cast as other—peoples of color, women, Jews, Arabs, Muslims, Mexicans, and so forth. . . . So this is one of the most frightening moments in the history of this very fragile empire and fragile republic."[11] On the other hand, Trump has filled a number of other high-level appointments with former military generals such as John Kelly as White House chief of staff, James

Mattis (since fired) as secretary of defense, and H.R. Mc-Master as his national security advisor, all of them known as "warrior thinkers."

Trump's strongman posturing has become a vehicle for producing the kind of shallow sensationalism and self-promotion once used to market his commercial television program. With Trump, the truth is simply irrelevant. Under such circumstances, it is extremely difficult to grasp what he actually understands about complex situations. He steals words and discards their meaning, refusing to own up to them ethically, politically, and socially. There is a recklessness in Trump's written and spoken utterances that pushes far beyond the bounds of rationality, potentially inciting the everyday fears and moral anxiety characteristic of an earlier period of fascism.

How else to explain his persistent claims that Barack Obama was not born in the United States, that climate change is a hoax, that terrorist attacks have taken place that no one knows about because they are covered up by the press, and that U.S. intelligence agencies are no different than the Nazis? Such conduct emulates the totalitarian claim not just to power, but to reality itself. With Trump, such claims are further coded with affirmations of white supremacy, ultra-nationalism, anti-intellectualism, and nuclear militancy. The American nightmare we are witnessing is the emergence of fascism in a new hybrid form.

The militarization of culture serves to connect the wars abroad with the ones being waged at home. This is an action-oriented mode of fascist ideology in which all thoughtfulness, critical thinking, and dissent are subordinated, if not cancelled out, by the pleasure quotient and commercialized sensationalism. Trump's discourse feeds the cultural formation of a right-wing populism that weighs in on the side of a militant racism and a racist militarism. For instance, the only moments of clarity in Trump's discourse occur when he uses the toxic vocabulary of hate, xenophobia, racism, and misogyny to target those he believes refuse to "Make America Great Again" or are critical of his use of historically fascist-tinged slogans such as "America First." Trump's racism has been on display for quite some time, and in January 2018 it emerged once again, provoking condemnation across the globe, when he referred to Haiti, El Salvador, and certain nations in Africa as "shithole countries."[12] These racist stabs followed earlier comments in which Trump said that Haitian immigrants "all have AIDS" and that Nigerian immigrants living in the United States would never "go back to their huts" in Africa.[13] He went on to say that the United States should be accepting people from countries like Norway. These statements are reminiscent of those of fascist dictators in the 1930s. His remarks about accepting people from Norway are thinly veiled appeals to racial purity. This is a racist and white supremacist discourse that feeds off upheaval, political uncertainty, and economic precarity through an appeal to authoritarian ideals and policies that offer a fraudulent sense of reassurance and certainty that does little to mitigate doubts, feelings of exclusion, anger, and anxieties.[14] This is language in the service of a racist police state.

Unapologetic Racism and Military Mania

As Trump's presidency unfolds, it appears that Americans are entering a period in which civic formations and public spheres will be modeled after a state of perpetual warfare. More militant U.S. foreign policy can be expected abroad, while an intensification of economic warfare can be expected at home. Corporations will seek to deregulate, militarize, and privatize everything they can, and Trump will be there to help them irrespective of the consequences.

Trump's open intolerance, which has targeted American citizens in addition to immigrants and refugees from foreign countries, has been accompanied by affirmations of white supremacy at home. As Chauncey DeVega points out in *Salon*,

> Since the election of Donald Trump in November, there have been almost 1,000 reported hate crimes targeting Muslims, Arabs, African-Americans, Latinos and other people of color. At this same moment, there have been terrorist threats against Jewish synagogues and community centers as well as the vandalizing of Jewish cemeteries. These hate crimes have also resulted in physical harm and even death: An Indian immigrant was shot and killed by a white man in Kansas who reportedly told him, "Get out of my country." [A] white man shot a Sikh man in Washington State after making a similar comment.[15]

Heidi Beirich, director of the Intelligence Project at the Southern Poverty Law Center, has stated that the increase in hate crimes in the United States corresponded with Trump's endless hate-filled discourse during the presidential primary, which included "xenophobic remarks, anti-immigrant remarks, anti-Muslim remarks, racist remarks, trading in anti-Semitic imagery and misogynist comments. Let's not forget that during the campaign there were hate crimes committed—very severe ones—in Trump's name."[16] Such violence and coded bigotry coincides with Trump's symbolic embrace of the Andrew Jackson presidency. For African Americans and Native Americans, few periods of U.S. history were more miserable and violent than that of Trump's great hero, President Andrew Jackson.

What is urgent to recognize is that Americans are entering a historical conjuncture under President Trump in which racism will be a major force used to rouse support and impose social control. As mentioned in previous chapters, not only did Trump make "law and order" a central motif of his presidential campaign, he also amplified its meaning in his attacks on the Black Lives Matter movement and his depiction of Black neighborhoods as cauldrons of criminal behavior, suggesting that the families who lived there be treated as enemies and criminals.

An especially disturbing sign can be found in the hiring a number of intolerant and racist ideologues to top White House posts. Some of the most egregious thus far have been the appointment of Jeff Sessions as attorney general, Betsy DeVos as secretary of education, Mike

Pompeo to head the CIA, and Tom Price as secretary of Health and Human Services (who has now resigned after reports surfaced of him spending $1 million in taxpayer money for personal travel on private and military jets), all of whom promote policies that will further increase the misery, suffering, and policing of the vulnerable, ill, and impoverished Americans. Price's appointment, given his abysmal record on women's issues, left little doubt as to the war on women's reproductive rights will worsen under Trump. As Sasha Bruce, senior vice president of NARAL Pro-Choice America, observed:

> With the selection of Tom Price as secretary of Health and Human Services, Donald Trump is sending a clear signal that he intends to punish women who seek abortion care. Tom Price is someone who has made clear throughout his career that . . . he wants to punish us for the choices we make for our bodies, our futures, and our families.[17]

The racially repressive state will be intensified and expanded, especially under the ideological and political influence of Jeff Sessions. Sessions is a strong advocate of mass incarceration and the death penalty, and is considered a leading spokesperson for the Old South. *The Nation*'s Ari Berman observes that Sessions is a "white-nationalist sympathizer . . . the fiercest opponent in the Senate of immigration reform, a centerpiece of Trump's agenda, and has a long history of opposition to civil rights, dating back to his days as a U.S. Attorney in Alabama in the 1980s."[18] Sessions' extensive legacy of using racist language, insults, and practices includes speaking out against the Voting Rights Act and addressing a Black lawyer as "boy."[19] He was denied a federal judgeship in the 1980s because his colleagues claimed that he made, on a number of occasions, racist remarks. Sessions has also called organizations such as the ACLU, the NAACP, and the National Council of Churches "un-American" because of their emphasis on civil rights, which he believed were being shoved down the throats of the American public. He was also accused of falsely prosecuting Black political activists in Alabama for voting fraud. Not only does Sessions share Trump's bigoted views of minority and foreign-born residents as "America's chief internal threat," he will also use the power of the Justice Department to issue orders "to strengthen the grip of law enforcement, raise barriers to voting and significantly reduce all forms of immigration, promoting what seems to be a long-standing desire to reassert the country's European and Christian heritage."[20]

Sessions' racism often merges with his religious fundamentalism. As Miranda Blue observes, he has "dismissed immigration reform as 'ethnic politics' and warned that allowing too many immigrants would create 'cultural problems' in the country. Earlier this year, he cherry-picked a couple of Bible verses to claim that the position of his opponents on the immigration issue is 'not biblical.'"[21]

As Andrew Kaczynski points out, Sessions made his

religiously inspired racist principles clear while appearing in 2016 on the *Matt & Aunie* talk radio show. While on the program, Sessions praised Trump's stance on capital punishment by pointing to Trump's "1989 newspaper ads advocating the death penalty for five young men of color accused of raping a jogger in Central Park."[22] Sessions made these comments knowing full well that the Central Park Five were not only exonerated by DNA evidence after serving many years in jail, but were also awarded a wrongful conviction settlement that ran into millions of dollars. In doing so, Sessions would have been aware that Trump had later criticized the settlement, calling it a disgrace, while suggesting the Central Park Five were guilty of a crime for which they should not have been acquitted, in spite of the testimony of convicted felon Matias Reyes, who confessed to raping and attacking the victim, and the DNA evidence proving their innocence.

The ramifications of Sessions' and Trump's shared racism were made evident when Sessions stated in the same interview that Trump "believes in law and order and he has the strength and will to make this country safer. . . . The biggest benefits from that, really, are [for] poor people in the neighborhoods that are most dangerous where most of the crime is occurring."[23] Sessions' statements barely conceal a full-on bigoted notion designating disadvantaged communities, mostly inhabited by people of color, as rife with crime.

Under Sessions, a racist militarism can be expected to proliferate as an organizing principle to stoke the fear of crime in order to increase the militarized presence of police in the inner cities. This is one part of a larger agenda that aims to reshape the country in alignment with the Jacksonian national security vision advanced by Trumpism. Another part of this reactionary agenda is to establish ways to restrict the voting rights of minorities. Trump's tweets that falsely allege voter fraud in order to defend the ludicrous claim that he won the popular vote are ominous, because they suggest that in the future he will allow Sessions to make it more difficult for poor minorities to vote. As the rhetoric of lawlessness and war is applied to inner cities, it provides a rationale for redirecting funds toward policing and denying these communities much-needed economic and social reforms. Far from receiving benefits to aid the "poor," these neighborhoods will be transformed into gun-filled, violence-ridden outposts and war zones subject to military solutions and forms of racial sorting and cleansing. How else to explain Trump's call to deport millions of undocumented Mexican immigrants as a "military operation"?

Within the Trump regime, Sessions is far from an anomaly and only one of a number of prominent officials appointed by Trump who are overtly racist. These newly appointed Trumpists argue for everything from a Muslim registry and suppressing voter rights to producing social and economic policies that target immigrants and low-income communities of color. Of all Trump's appointments, his initial choice of Stephen Bannon as senior counselor and chief strategist was possibly the most disturbing.

Bannon is a devious and incendiary figure whom critics as politically diverse as Glenn Beck and Senator Bernie Sanders of Vermont have accused of being racist, sexist, and anti-Semitic. When he was the head of Breitbart News, Bannon openly courted white nationalists, neo-Nazi groups, and other right-wing extremists. In doing so, he not only provided a platform for the "alt-right," but helped to rebrand "white supremacy [and] white nationalism for the digital age."[24] Bannon was fired by Breitbart because of remarks he made about the Trumps to Michael Wolff, the author of Fire and Fury.

Bannon is on record stating that only property owners should vote, saying to his ex-wife that he "did not want his twin daughters to go to school with Jews," calling conservative commentator Bill Kristol a "Republican spoiler, renegade Jew," and publishing inflammatory headlines on Breitbart such as "Birth control makes women unattractive and crazy."[25] Richard Cohen, the president of the Southern Poverty Law Center, states that Trump's racist overtones during the election campaign were confirmed with Bannon's appointment.[26] And, of course, they became crystal clear after Trump's remarks provided moral support for the neo-Nazis who marched through the streets of Charlottesville, claiming some of them were "very fine people." What we see in Trump and his advisors and appointees is an America that embraces white supremacy's fears, intolerance, and adulation of authoritarianism. With Trump in office, the menace of authoritarianism is taking on a visible and hideous shape, "exploding in our face, through racist attacks on schoolchildren, the proliferation of swastikas around the country, name-calling, death threats, and a general atmosphere of hate."[27]

Trump's simultaneous appointment of both aggressively racist individuals and warmongering right-wing military personnel to top government positions, along with his ongoing bombast suggesting the need for a vast expansion of the military-industrial complex, signal that conditions are set in place for an imminent intensification of America's war culture. Following Trump's election victory, *Forbes* published an article with the headline: "For the Defence Industry, Trump's Win Means Happy Days Are Here Again."[28] William D. Hartung makes the point clear by citing a speech Trump gave in Philadelphia before the election:

> [Trump] called for tens of thousands of additional troops, a Navy of 350 ships (the current goal is 308), a significantly larger Air Force, an anti-missile, space-based Star Wars–style program of Reaganesque proportions, and an acceleration of the Pentagon's $1 trillion "modernization" for the nuclear arsenal, [all of which] could add more than $900 billion to the Pentagon's budget over the next decade.[29]

Evidence of Trump's mission to foster an updated and expansive war culture was also visible in Trump's willingness to consider including in his administration a cabal of racist neoconservatives such as John Bolton and James Woolsey—both of whom believe that "Islam and the Arab world are the enemy of Western civilization" and are strong advocates of a war with Iran.[30] Trump has welcomed disgraced military leaders such as David H. Petraeus, former four-star U.S. Army general and director of the Central Intelligence Agency, and has appointed as secretary of defense retired U.S. Marine Corps General James Mattis (since fired), who opposed both closing Guantánamo and Obama's nuclear treaty with Iran. Mattis was brusquely fired by the Obama administration as head of Central Command.

Trump's first choice of Lieutenant General Michael Flynn as national security advisor was particularly telling. Flynn had already been fired by President Obama for abusive behavior and had been accused of mishandling classified information, but was a firm supporter of Trump's pro-torture policies.[31] The *New York Times* reported that Flynn's occupation of "one of the most powerful roles in shaping military and foreign policy" suggested Trump's alignment with Flynn's outspoken belief that "Islamist militancy poses an existential threat on a global scale, and the Muslim faith itself is the source of the problem. . . . [He describes] it as a political ideology, not a religion."[32] In other words, Flynn believed that 1.3 billion Muslims are the enemy of Western civilization. He had also claimed that "Sharia, or Islamic law, is spreading in the United States (it is not). His dubious assertions are so common that when he ran the Defense Intelligence Agency, subordinates came up with a name for the phenomenon: They called them 'Flynn facts.'"[33] A mere twenty-four days after taking up his position as National Security Advisor, it was revealed that Flynn had lied about conversations he had with the Russian ambassador, Sergey Kislyak, while Obama was still in office, talks he had not revealed to the FBI, White House spokesman Sean Spicer, and the vice president, Mike Pence.[34] Flynn resigned in disgrace once it was discovered that he had covered up his conversations with the Russian ambassador. In December 2017, Flynn pleaded guilty to lying to about the contacts and agreed to cooperate with Mueller's investigative team.

The deeper message underlying Flynn's short-lived appointment is that Trump evidently plans to do nothing to alter a dishonorable foreign policy trajectory that has propelled the United States into a permanent war status "for virtually the entire twenty-first century," and since the latter part of 2001 has resulted in approximately "370,000 combatants and non-combatants [being] killed in the various theaters of operations where U.S. forces have been active."[35] This is how democracy comes to an end. What is more, Trump's early decisions in office and professed love of the military suggest that he's not interested in a holding pattern, but will expand America's investment in and infatuation with its wars. Unsurprisingly, Trump has asked Congress to provide an additional $54 billion to expand an already obese military budget.

Landscapes of a War Culture

Under Trump's influence, war culture will spread, and incitements and retaliations to aggression and state violence will intensify. This means growing incidents of the suppression of dissent, similar to the police violence used against those protesting the Dakota Access Pipeline in Standing Rock, North Dakota, which included police arrests of several journalists covering the movement. It is reasonable to assume that under Trump there will be an intensification of the harassment of journalists similar to what happened to the renowned Canadian photojournalist Ed Ou, who has worked for a number of media sources including the *New York Times* and *Time* magazine. Ou, who was traveling from Canada to the United States to report on the growing protest at Standing Rock, was detained by U.S. Border Patrol authorities. According to Hugh Handeyside, "Ou was detained for more than six hours and subjected . . . to multiple rounds of intrusive interrogation. [The border officers] questioned him at length about his work as a journalist, his prior professional travel in the Middle East, and dissidents or 'extremists' he had encountered or interviewed as a journalist. They photocopied his personal papers, including pages from his handwritten personal diary."[36] In the end, he was denied entry into the United States.

But the harassment of individuals is only one register of Trump's escalating suppression of dissent. He constantly derides all media who are critical of him and his policies as "fake news" and labels them as part of the opposition. Trump's attack on the press is about more than discrediting traditional sources of facts and analysis, or collapsing the distinction between the truth and lies—it is also about undermining the public's grip on evidence, facts, and informed judgment. Such intimidation tactics serve only to stifle the freedom of the press. The result is the purposeful destruction of public spheres that make dissent possible, and the simultaneous infantilizing of the American public to a mob mentality. Given Trump's further insistence that protesters who burn the American flag should be jailed or suffer the loss of citizenship, his hostile criticism of the Black Lives Matter movement, and his ongoing legacy of stoking white violence against anti-racism activists and protesters, it is not unreasonable to assume that his future domestic policies will legitimate a wave of repression and violence waged against dissidents and the institutions that support them. For instance, his public threats regarding the burning of the American flag can be read as code for green-lighting repression of protesters. How else to explain the motive behind his consideration of Milwaukee sheriff David Clarke as a potential candidate for secretary of the Department of Homeland Security? Clarke has referred to the Black Lives Matter movement as "Black Lies Matter" and has compared them to ISIS.

> [Clarke has] proposed that terrorist and ISIS sympathizers in America need to be rounded up and shipped off to Guantánamo, and has stated that "It is time to suspend habeas corpus like Abraham Lincoln did during the civil war." . . .

He guessed that about several hundred thousand or even a million sympathizers were in the United States and needed to be imprisoned.[37]

It is difficult to believe that this type of call for repressive state violence, and what amounts to an egregious disregard for the U.S. Constitution, garners one favor rather than disqualification for a high-ranking government office.

Expanding what might be called his Twitter battles, Trump has made a number of scornful remarks regarding what he views as criticism of either himself or staff whom he favors. For instance, when Brandon Victor Dixon, an actor in the Broadway play *Hamilton*, addressed vice president–elect Mike Pence after the curtain call, stating, in part, "We are diverse Americans who are alarmed and anxious that your new administration will not protect us, our planet, our children, our parents, or defend us and uphold our inalienable rights," Trump tweeted that Pence was harassed by the actor and that he should apologize. Trump also took aim at the *Saturday Night Live* episode in which Alec Baldwin satirized a post-election Trump in the process of trying to figure out what the responsibilities of the presidency entail. Trump tweeted that he had watched *Saturday Night Live* and declared, "It is a totally one-sided, biased show—nothing funny at all. Equal time for us?"

Trump has taken to Twitter to launch caustic tirades not only against the cast of the play *Hamilton* and *Saturday Night Live*, but also against Chuck Jones, president of United Steelworkers Local 1999. Trump's verbal takedown of the union chief was the result of Jones accusing Trump of lying about the number of Indiana jobs he saved from being shipped to Mexico by Carrier Corporation. Actually, since 350 jobs were slated to stay in the United States before Trump's intervention, the number of jobs saved by Trump was 850 rather than 1,100. To some this may seem like a trivial matter, but Trump's weaponization of Twitter against his perceived detractors and political opponents not only functions to produce a chilling effect on critical expression, but gives legitimacy to those willing to suppress dissent through various modes of harassment and even the threat of violence.

Frank Sesno, the director of the School of Media and Public Affairs at George Washington University, is right in stating, "Anybody who goes on air or goes public and calls out the president has to then live in fear that he is going to seek retribution in the public sphere. That could discourage people from speaking out."[38] Such actions could also threaten their lives, as Chuck Jones found out. After the President attacked him on Twitter, he received an endless stream of harassing phone calls and online insults, some even threatening him and his children. According to Jones, "Nothing that says they're gonna kill me, but, you know, you better keep your eye on your kids. . . . We know what car you drive. Things along those lines."[39]

Many of Trump's tweets have come back to haunt him by drawing unfavorable attention to his own morally reprehensible actions. For instance, he has mocked then-Senator Al Franken for a photo that shows him pretending to grope

Leeann Tweeden, a former model, while refusing to comment on the numerous sexual harassment charges lodged against failed Republican Senate candidate Roy Moore. Moore has been "accused of initiating a sexual encounter with a 14-year-old girl when he was in his 30s, sexually assaulting a 16-year-old waitress and pursuing relationships with at least five other teenagers who were much younger than he."[40] Trump's empty moralism regarding Franken and his cowardly silence regarding Moore, along with his defense of serial sex offenders such as former Fox News chief executive Roger Ailes and Fox News commentator Bill O' Reilly, has not only drawn attention to his blatant acts of hypocrisy but has also prompted the charge that he is diverting attention away from his own history of sexual misconduct and harassment.

Moreover, in addition to exposing his confused and dangerous state of mind, Trump's tweets reveal his willingness to use half-baked conspiracy theories, ultra-nationalist views, and white supremacist ideology to continually trigger support from his followers. For instance, on November 29, 2017, Trump retweeted three inflammatory anti-Muslim videos posted by Jayda Fransen, the leader of the far-right extremist group Britain First. Fransen had been previously "convicted of religiously aggravated harassment in November 2016 after abusing a woman wearing a hijab."[41] She was also arrested in Belfast after making a racist and inflammatory speech. The videos were taken out of historical context and misleading, in one case falsely identifying the participants as Muslims. The presidential tweets were not only condemned in the mainstream press, but also by British prime minister Theresa May, who called them "hateful narratives."[42] Republican Senator Lindsay Graham, who increasingly has come to support Trump, flatly admitted that "Mr. Trump was 'legitimizing religious bigotry' with the Twitter posts."[43] *New York Times* columnist Charles Blow went further, noting that Trump's use of a racial slur in a White House ceremony honoring Navajo veterans of World War II, his stating once again that Obama was not born in the United States, and his endorsement of unverified anti-Muslim videos—all in one week, no less:

> [Trump is] unfit to be the president of the United States [with] his lack of impulse control to conceal his [open hostility] to people of color. . . . Not satisfied with his implicit (though obvious) endorsement of white supremacy here in America, Trump has now explicitly endorsed white supremacy in another country. . . . The Trump Doctrine is White Supremacy. Yes, he is also diplomatically inept, overwhelmed by avarice, thoroughly corrupt and a pathological liar, but it is to white supremacy and to hostility for everyone not white that he always returns.[44]

Trump did get some support for posting the videos to his tens of millions of followers. One notable endorsement came from David Duke, a former Klu Klux Klan leader, who tweeted "Thank God for Trump! That is why we love him."[45] When White House spokesperson Sarah Huckabee Sanders was confronted with evidence that the videos posted by Trump were racist, misleading, and un-verified, she replied: "Whether it's a real video, the threat is real, and that is what the President is talking about."[46] The irony of yet another Team Trump official covering for the possibility that the president is issuing false informa-tion speaks volumes. Sanders once again proves that she is willing to work full time as paid defender of an unhinged liar who incites racial discord as a way of appealing to his fascist and anti-Islamic followers.

Donald Trump's Twitter feed currently has approxi-mately 42.2 million followers; this platform alone grants his remarks considerable audience and reach. His ongoing exchange and battle with former Fox News host Megyn Kelly, especially after her questioning of Trump in the first Republican primary debate, provides a vivid example of the way he has weaponized his Twitter account. After Trump started attacking her on Twitter, she told Terry Gross, the host of NPR's radio show *Fresh Air*, that "every tweet he unleashes against you . . . creates such a crescendo of an-ger." She then went on to spell out the living hell she found herself as a result of being a target of Trump's humiliation and derision:

> The c-word was in thousands of tweets directed at me—lots of threats to beat the hell out of me, to rape me, honestly the ugliest things you can imagine. But most of this stuff I was able to just

dismiss as angry people who are trying to scare me, you know. However, there were so many that rose to the level of "OK, that one we need to pay attention to," that it did become alarming. It wasn't like I walked down the street in constant fear of someone trying to take my life, but I was very aware of it. The thing I was most worried about was that I have a 7- and a 5- and a 3-year-old, and I was worried I'd be walking down the street with my kids and somebody would do something to me in front of them; they would see me get punched in the face or get hurt.[47]

Between Twitter, Instagram, and Facebook, Trump has direct communication with tens of millions of people. I am not convinced that these tweets are simply the impetuous outbursts of an adult who has the temperament of a spoiled 12-year-old. It seems more probable that his alt-right advisors view such tweet attacks as an effective way to manipulate allies and diminish rivals, especially since they are waging an all-out online assault on Trump's critics.[48] Trump is at war with democracy, and his online threats and belittlement are consistent with the culture of violence and aggression he projects at home and abroad.

Frank Rich likewise detects more operating behind Trump's tweets than one might see at first glance. On the surface, Trump's attacks seem as trivial as they are thoughtless, given the actual issues that Trump should be considering. But, as Rich suggests, the tweets not only amount to an attack on the First Amendment, they likely form part of a strategy, first originated by Bannon, designed to promote a culture war that incites Trump's "base and retains its loyalty should he fail, say, to deliver on other promises, like reviving the coal industry."[49] These multiple functions performed by Trump's online attacks aggravate a culture war that represses dissent and diverts the public from more serious issues. Referring to the Dixon incident, Rich writes:

> It's possible that much of [Trump's] base previously knew little or nothing about *Hamilton*, but thanks to Pence's visit, it would soon learn in even the briefest news accounts that the show is everything that base despises: a multi-cultural-ethnic-racial reclamation of "white" American history with a ticket price that can soar into four digits—in other words, a virtual monument to the supposedly politically correct "elites" that Trump, Bannon, and their wrecking crew found great political profit in deriding throughout the campaign. Pence's visit to *Hamilton* was a sure-fire political victory for Trump even without the added value of a perfectly legitimate and respectful curtain speech that he could trash-tweet to further rouse his culture-war storm troopers. The kind of political theater that Trump and Bannon fomented around *Hamilton* is likely to be revived routinely in the Trump era.[50]

How concentrated a form of authoritarianism Trump might manage to wield is difficult to predict, though the words of some of his high-level appointees offer a glimpse. For example, soon after Trump's trip to Saudi Arabia, one of the most repressive regimes in the world, Commerce Secretary Wilbur Ross gave an interview on CNBC in which he said that "[the] thing that was fascinating to me was there was not a single hint of a protester anywhere there during the whole time we were there. Not one guy with a bad placard. . . . "[51] When CNBC host Becky Quick pointed out that the Saudi Arabian government squelches dissent, Ross replied that "In theory, that could be true. . . . But boy there was not a single effort at any incursion. There wasn't anything. The mood was a genuinely good mood."[52] Maybe Ross should talk to the thousands of protesters and activists who have vanished into Saudi Arabian prisons.

Ross is either ignorantly unaware or morally irresponsible in refusing to acknowledge that protesting in Saudi Arabia is punishable by death. In fact, soon after Ross left Saudi Arabia, the government sentenced to death Munir al-Adam, a disabled man who was arrested after he attended a protest meeting. *The Independent* in London reported that Mr. Adam lost his hearing in one ear as a result of being tortured and was forced to sign a confession.[53] With no other evidence presented, Mr. Adam was sentenced to death by beheading. Ross's remarks about how happy he was over the lack of protest in Saudi Arabia and his refusal to speak out against the government's human rights abuses send the clear and chilling message that the Trump regime has little tolerance for dissent or human rights. Even more puzzling is Trump's willingness to heap praise on a number of the world's most ruthless dictatorships while openly criticizing and undermining his relations with long-term allies such as Germany and Australia.

Trump's rhetoric of violence was on full display in July 2017 when he addressed police chiefs across the country in Brentwood, New York. In a speech about law enforcement that focused on the notorious MS-13 gang, Trump openly endorsed brutality in dealing with alleged gang suspects. Trump called alleged suspects "animals" and once again stoked the flames of fear in low-income communities while disparaging the more productive use of building police-community relations. Among Trump's incendiary comments:

> And when you see these towns and when you see these thugs being thrown into the back of a paddy wagon—you just see them thrown in, rough—I said, "Please don't be too nice." Like when you guys put somebody in the car, and you're protecting their head, you know, the way you put the hand over? Like, don't hit their head, and they've just killed somebody, don't hit their head. I said, "You can take the hand away, OK?"[54]

Trump's advocacy for police aggression is particularly shameful in light of the post-Ferguson racial justice movement that demands police be held more accountable for perpetrating unnecessary violence. Moreover, Trump's comments reinforce his support "for an attorney general for the Department of Justice who takes the position that institutional reform at police departments is not going to be the fundamental agenda of the Department of Justice."[55]

This dangerous and brazen retreat from the rule of law, however shocking, will not only undermine the memories of democratic struggles and possibility—it will also lead to increased state violence and further the criminalization of targeted groups in a variety of sites such as schools and the streets of underserved neighborhoods. It will surely escalate, for example, the arrest of students for trivial behaviors in schools, the transformation of local police forces into SWAT teams, and police targeting of communities of color through entrenched policies of racial profiling.[56] And with racists such as Jeff Sessions and Bannon, in spite of being derided by the president, actively serving Trump inside and out of his administration, the fantasy of turning America back into a whites-only public sphere will continue to degrade democracy and incite followers to follow suit.

CHAPTER SEVEN

NEO-NAZIS IN CHARLOTTESVILLE

"Our lives begin to end the day we become silent about the things that matter."
—Martin Luther King Jr.

When hundreds of white supremacists, neo-Nazis, and other right-wing extremists marched across the University of Virginia campus during the summer of 2017, it offered a glimpse of the growing danger of authoritarian movements both in the United States and across the globe. The image of throngs of fascist thugs chanting anti-Semitic, racist, and white nationalist slogans such as "Heil Trump" and later attacking peaceful anti-racist counter-demonstrators makes clear that right-wing groups that have been on the margins of American society for decades are now comfortable operating openly in public. They appear especially emboldened to come out of the shadows because elements of their neo-fascist ideology have found a comfortable if not supportive political climate under the influence of Trump and his servile political acolytes.

As is well-known, Trump has not only supported the

presence and backing of white nationalists and white supremacists, but has refused to denounce their Nazi slogans
and violence in strong political and ethical terms, suggesting his own complicity with such movements. It should
surprise no one that David Duke, a former imperial wiz-
ard of the Klu Klux Klan, told reporters that the Unite
the Right followers were "going to fulfill the promises of
Donald Trump . . . to take our country back." Nor should
it surprise anyone that Trump initially refused to condemn
the fascist groups behind the shocking images and violence
that took place in Charlottesville. His silence was music to
the ears of the far right. For instance, The Daily Stormer, a
white supremacist website, issued the following statement:
"Refused to answer a question about White Nationalists
supporting him. No condemnation at all. When asked to
condemn, he just walked out of the room. Really, really
good. God bless him."[1]

It appears that the presence of Nazi and Confeder-
ate flags, along with the horrible history of millions lost
to the Holocaust, slavery, lynchings, church bombings,
and assassinations of Black leaders such as Medgar Evans
and Martin Luther King Jr., did little to move Trump to
a serious understanding or repudiation of the poisonous
historical forces that surfaced in Charlottesville. As Jelani
Cobb, a writer for *The New Yorker*, observes, this was a telling moment:

> When he did speak about the crisis, he de-
> nounced bigotry and violence "on many sides,"

in a statement that was bizarrely punctuated by references to efforts to reform trade relationships and better conditions for veterans. We have seen a great number of false equivalencies in the past two years, and the most recent Presidential election was defined by them. Yet it remains striking to hear Trump imply that Nazis and the inter-racial group of demonstrators who gathered to oppose them were, in essence, equally wrong.[2]

While Trump did eventually deliver a speech in which he asserted that "racism is evil" and that "the KKK, neo-Nazis, white supremacists, and other hate groups . . . are repugnant to everything we hold dear as Americans," the days-long delay between the racist attacks in Char-lottesville and the statement was telling.[3] Unable to con-tain his white supremacist views, Trump later reverted to his initial assertion of "blame on both sides," equating neo-Nazis with anti-racist counter-protesters (whom he labeled the "alt-left") and speaking of "very fine people" among the crowd of bigoted extremists who chanted rac-ist and anti-Semitic slogans in public.[4] Trump's defense of neo-Nazis, white supremacists, and Klu Klux Klan members—arms stretched out in a Nazi salute, marching through the streets of Charlottesville shouting, "Blood and Soil" and brandishing banners stating "Jews will not re-place us"—further clarified his support for race-based ex-tremism and his divorce from any sense of moral respon-sibility. By placing neo-Nazis and their hate-filled racism on the same plane as those who opposed them, Trump clarified that white supremacy remains at the heart of U.S. history and contemporary power relations. Jeffrey St. Clair captures this sentiment perfectly:

> Trump pulled back the curtains on the cesspool of American politics for the inspection of all but the most timid. Trump speaks the forbidden words that many other Americans secretly think. Trump utters these heresies self-righteously and without shame. . . . Trump's rapacity and bigotry strike too close to home. He reminds us that we haven't buried the worst of our past. . . . Now middlebrow America is getting a glimpse of itself through the mirror of its own bombastic, vindictive and racist leader. He has fractured the rituals and conventions that desensitized most Americans from what our system is really all about. The elites fear Trump because he gives the game away. He personifies the reality they've been working for decades to conceal. The role of most presidents has been to comfort the nation when it recoils at a sudden view of its own depravity, from the My Lai massacre to Abu Ghraib, assuring the citizenry that the system isn't as malign as it appears. Trump pours acid on the wounds, as when he impertinently reminded the country that its two most revered founders were big time slave-owners.[5]

The violence in Charlottesville was but one register of domestic terrorism and populist manifestations of fascism that have been appearing in the United States. Trump's response to Charlottesville should surprise no one, given the history of racism in the United States in general, and in the Republican Party in particular, from Nixon's Southern strategy and George W. Bush's treatment of the Black victims of Hurricane Katrina, to current Republican efforts at voter suppression. Trump not only embraces white supremacy, he elevates it. How else to explain his administration's announcement that it would no longer "investigate white nationalists, who have been responsible for a large share of violent hate crimes in the Unites States?"[6] How else to explain Trump's willingness to lift restrictions imposed by the Obama administration on local police departments' acquisition of military surplus equipment such as armed vehicles, bulletproof vests, and grenade launchers?[7] Clearly, such measures deliver on Trump's Jacksonian approach to law and order, escalate racial tensions in cities that are often treated like combat zones, and reinforce notions of militarism over community among police officers.

Trump's presidential pardon of Joe Arpaio, the notorious white supremacist and disgraced former sheriff of Maricopa County, Arizona, also speaks volumes. Not only did Arpaio engage in racial profiling, despite being ordered by a court to decease, he also had a notorious reputation for abusing prisoners in his Tent City. These inmates were subjected to blistering heat and forced to work on chain gangs, wear pink underwear, and dress in demeaning striped uniforms, among other indignities.[8]

Such actions do more than reinforce Trump's endorsement of white nationalism; they send a clear message of support for a culture of violence, amounting to acts of domestic terrorism. Moreover, we see clear contempt for the rule of law, and an endorsement not just of racist ideology but also of institutional racism and the primacy of the racially based incarceration state. In addition, there is the chilling implication that Trump would be willing to pardon those who might be found guilty in any upcoming investigations involving Trump and his administration. Trump's law-and-order regime represents a form of domestic terrorism because it is a policy of state violence designed to intimidate, threaten, harm, and instill fear in a particular community.

By pardoning Arpaio, Trump signals an official position regarding racialized state violence against immigrants, especially Latin Americans. In addition, Trump's conduct emboldens right-wing extremists, giving them the green light to support profoundly intolerant legislation and ideologies. This is evident in attempts on the part of many states to criminalize dissent, overtly decry the benefits of higher education, and openly assert that Republicans would support postponing the 2020 election if Trump proposed it.[9]

The demonstration held in Charlottesville by militant torch-bearing groups of Nazi sympathizers, Klu Klux Klan members, and white nationalists represents a historical moment that re-introduce elements of a past that led to some of the worst atrocities in modern history. The crucial lesson to be learned, if we are to avoid falling prey to historical amnesia, is that the ideology, values, and institutions of a multicultural democracy are once again under assault by those who oppose openness, equality, justice. As historian Timothy Snyder has observed, it is crucial to remember that the success of authoritarian regimes in Germany and other places succeeded, in part, because they were not stopped in the early stages of their development.[10] Authoritarian regimes consolidate their power by normalizing intolerance and bigotry, which we have witnessed under the Trump regime. This process evolves further when right-wing groups begin developing their own militias and paramilitary forces.

Charlottesville provides a glimpse of the social consequences of authoritarianism in the United States. The horrors of the past are real. The challenge of historical memory, civic courage, and moral responsibility are to address and overcome the possibility that such horrors could further consolidate and spread.

In *Selections from the Prison Notebooks*, the great Italian Marxist philosopher Antonio Gramsci identified one measure of a time of crisis:

> The great masses . . . become detached from their traditional ideologies and no longer believe what they used to believe previously. The crisis consists precisely in the fact that the old is dying

and the new cannot be born; in this interregnum
a great variety of morbid symptoms appear.[11]

While Gramsci was characterizing a different historical period, his words are as relevant today as they were
when he wrote them in the 1930s. All over the globe,
multicultural democracy is under attack. As institutions
that once provided public vision and proactive spaces are
stripped of their sovereignty, new modes of authoritarian
populism are displaying an intolerance for social diversity and a willingness to feed off the nationalist anger and
rage of those who have suffered under punishing austerity
measures imposed by corporate power and the wealthiest
1 percent.[12]

In the midst of a massive global attack on the welfare
state and social provisions set in place by neoliberal policies, the social contract central to liberal democracies has
been shredded, and with it any viable notion of solidarity, economic justice, and the common good. Progress has
been turned into its opposite, registering more inequality,
suffering, and violence. The older language of collective
rights has given way to the discourse of individual rights,
and the vocabulary of collaboration and compassion has
been uprooted by a discourse of radical individualism and
a harsh, survival-of-the fittest ethos. Freedom has mor-
phed into a synonym for unbridled self-interest and a
rationale for abdicating any sense of moral and political
responsibility. Under global neoliberalism, the future is
viewed as more of a curse than a blessing, and has lost

its value as what Zygmunt Bauman calls "the safest and most promising location for investing [one's] hopes."[13] In contrast, as Bauman observes, the future has now become the space for projecting our most dreaded anxieties. He writes that such fears and apprehensions are now driven by a number of elements that have come to characterize neoliberal societies:

> the growing scarcity of jobs, of falling incomes reducing our and our children's life chances, of the yet greater frailty of our social positions and the temporality of our life achievements, of the increasingly widening gap between the tools, resources, and skills at our disposal and the momentousness of the challenges facing us. Above all, we feel our control over our own lives slipping from our hands, reducing us to the status of pawns moved to and fro in a chess game played by unknown players indifferent to our needs, if not downright hostile and cruel, and all too ready to sacrifice us in pursuit of their own objectives. Not so long ago associated with more comfort and less inconvenience, what the thought of the future tends nowadays to bring to mind most often is the gruesome menace of being identified or classified as inept and unfit for the task, denied value and dignity, and for that reason marginalized, excluded, and outcast.[14]

The dream of democracy has turned into a nightmare as more and more people are considered expendable and subject to the dictates of a plutocratic political economy rigged to benefit the wealthy. The promise of social mobility, equal opportunity, employment, and privatized dream worlds has given way to regressive taxation, offshoring, deindustrialization, the slashing of social provisions, the dismantling of public services, and the rise of a proto-fascist populism. Desperation, isolation, and a sense of abandonment coupled with the collapse of democratic institutions and public spheres have produced a new collective fatalism all over the globe.

The increasing failure of establishment politics has produced conditions in which more and more people are inclined to express support for authoritarian alternatives rather than address the structural roots of economic, cultural, and social injustice. Viktor Orban, the Hungarian prime minister, spoke for many when he proclaimed that societies founded on liberal principles will not be able to compete successfully in a global market and that there is no reason for democracies to be liberal in order to be successful. According to Orban, the state is not defined by democratic values, but by its economic and cultural interests, interests that cohere among a growing number of far-right regimes. He writes:

> The new state that we are building is an illiberal state, a non-liberal state. It does not deny foundational values of liberalism, as freedom, etc. But

it does not make this ideology a central element of state organization, but applies a specific, national, particular approach in its stead. . . . We are searching for (and we are doing our best to find, ways of parting with Western European dogmas, making ourselves independent from them) the form of organizing a community, that is capable of making us competitive in this great world-race.[15]

This worldwide slide toward authoritarianism takes place upon a landscape of massive instability, inequality, fear, and insecurity driven by an economic-political system that can neither "fulfil its own promise of general prosperity [nor conceal] its contempt for the democratic principle of equality."[16] In the face of failed states and broken economies there has been a retreat into promises offered by the rise of the security state, racial criminalization, economic nationalism, xenophobia, suppression of dissent, and a growing militarization of local law enforcement. Heinrich Geiselberger called this "the great regression," an apt metaphor for the growing collapse of public discourse, values, democratic institutions, and public spheres.[17]

The political earthquakes shaking the foundations of liberal democracy reveal more than the pent-up collective energies of despair, rage, and insecurity. They also speak to the growing mechanisms of exclusion and ideologies of racist contempt that have returned with a vengeance all over Europe and in the United States. Dressed up in the discourse of trickle-down economic prosperity, the crises haunting democracies across the globe have provided fodder for right-wing demagogues to promote nationalistic policies. They denounce democratic values in the name of a popular will, the will of people who are both resentful for what the political establishment has done to them and comfortable with political leaders who are "typically xenophobic, authoritarian, and patriarchal."[18] The growing presence of right-wing political formations in France, Greece, Italy, and a number of other countries accompanies the rise of authoritarian states in Russia, India, Turkey, Hungary, Egypt, the Philippines, and the United States, among others.

The authoritarian nightmare is shared by many other societies around the world. Under Recep Tayyip Erdogan, for example, Turkey has seen a return to the traditions and grandeur of an Ottoman past. In India, the right-wing ideologue Narendra Modi has resurrected the ideology of Hindu nationalism. In a similar vein, President Trump has fueled a culture of fear, racism, and demonization as part of his efforts to resuscitate a culture of white Christian nationalism. As Paul Mason points out:

> If we analyse Trump through his actions, rather than his garbled words, it is political illiberalism that has won out during the first seven months of his presidency. When a judge blocked his Muslim immigration ban, he attacked the judiciary's constitutional role. When the press revealed

malfeasance, he labelled them "enemies of the American people." When James Comey refused Trump's appeals for "loyalty," he was sacked.[19]

White resentment and white nationalism have come to symbolize Trump's politics, beginning with his egregious false claim that Barack Obama was not born in the United States, and continued through his appointment of white nationalists to the highest levels of government. Such measures have bolstered his credibility with white militias, neo-Nazis, and other white nationalist groups.[20] Carol Anderson correctly states that "the guiding principle in Mr. Trump's government is to turn the politics of white resentment into the policies of white rage—that calculated mechanism of executive orders, laws, and agency directives that undermines and punishes minority achievement and aspiration."[21]

Arjun Appadurai argues that what Trump and similar authoritarian leaders have in common is a hatred of democracy, because it stands in the way of their monomaniacal efforts to seize political power. He writes:

> The leaders hate democracy because it is an obstacle to their monomaniacal pursuit of power. The followers are victims of democracy fatigue who see electoral politics as the best way to exit democracy itself. This hatred and this exhaustion find their natural common ground in the space of cultural sovereignty, enacted in scripts of racial

victory for resentful majorities, national ethnic purity, and global resurgence through the promises of soft power. This common cultural ground inevitably hides the deep contradictions between the neoliberal economic policies and well-documented crony capitalism of most of these authoritarian leaders and the genuine economic suffering and anxiety of the bulk of their mass followings. It is also the terrain of a new politics of exclusion, whose targets are either migrants or internal ethnic minorities or both.[22]

It is against this wider historical and social context, marked by a mounting embrace of illiberal democracy, that the authoritarian populism of Donald Trump and other demagogues can be both interrogated and challenged, especially when the political interests that partly bear responsibility for producing a "neoliberal economics turned punitive and illiberal" now claim to be the only force capable of resisting Trump's authoritarianism.[23] Rather than separate matters of race and economics, it is crucial to examine the racialized moral panic produced by Trumpism against the emerging landscape of obscene inequality that is being produced under the global influence of corporate capitalism. It is also against this worldwide embrace of illiberal democracy that a debate must begin over rethinking politics outside of the discourse of capitalism.

The Politics of Distraction

Trumpism spreads through a politics of resentment, one that suppresses the theoretical and political tools to assess the conditions for free-floating anger and despair in the first place. Put differently, the political crisis posed by the rise of authoritarianism in the United States has not been matched by a crisis of ideas. That is, the issue of how everyday problems and hardships are connected to wider economic and political structures remains unanswered for most Americans. Instead, the politics of resentment has become part of a threefold failed project of politics.

First, the politics of resentment is used by alt-right Republicans to serve as part of a politics of authoritarianism. Second, resentment politics has produced highly restricted forms of resistance on the part of many liberals, those whose focus is on Trump the man rather than on the economic conditions and ideological movements that produced him. Third, the expressions of resentment and the authoritarian politics they produce become a new form of entertainment through which the commercial media can capture and sell larger audiences to advertisers. Trump's tweets are sensational, and sensationalism sells. Trump weaponizes the media limelight, using fabrication and ridicule to manipulate reality and to dominate allies and rivals with ridicule and belittlement.

Understanding the surge of demagoguery in the United States and Europe begins with interrogating the changing nature of neoliberal ideology and its transformation from a free-market utopia to a normalized dystopian reality. At stake here is a post-neoliberal narrative in which democratic ideals can be defended apart from the terms of corporate globalization. The rise of authoritarianism is based, in part, on convincing populations that democracy should not be defended because it weakens economic and political security. The bold new authoritarian strategy is to convince populations that they are choosing benign trickle-down plutocracy over welfare-state democracy. In reality, such choices are being made for them, as in the recent Senate move to "strike down a sweeping new rule that would have allowed millions of Americans to band together in class-action lawsuits against financial institutions."[24]

No longer able to hide the massive misery, inequality, and hardship that free-market financial institutions have produced across the globe, the new authoritarians rely on a politics of distraction, such as an appeal to cultural nationalism and the longing for the re-establishment of a mythic past. Trump has appropriated this politics of distraction and given it a unique configuration, one that reinforces the domination of financial elites while obscuring the underlying structures of predatory economic and political power that have consolidated further still under his family's influence. Of course, this is not meant to confuse elements of his popular racist, fascistic, and white nationalist followers. Rather, it is meant to distract those politicians, pundits, and anti-public intellectuals who have no interest in fighting for progressive change and who prefer the sensationalism and pageantry associated with Trump's tweets rather than engaging in a serious debate about the bankruptcy of the political-economic system. This diversion has been successful in delaying the debate about how the crisis of democracy is largely connected to the crisis of the global financial system, militarism, and the confluence of authoritarian forms of top-down governance, corporate self-interest, commercial media, and social support.

While demagogues across Europe and in places like Turkey, China, Russia, and Egypt maintain control through the outright suppression of dissent and the dismantling of civil liberties, Trump has taken a different route. Trump's policies benefit not only the financial master class but also the establishment politicians and intellectuals who still champion globalization, assuming the role of his most serious opposition and posturing as the vanguard of resistance against his accelerating authoritarianism. Trump inverts the rules of ideology by denying its very premises, thus introducing a form of depoliticization and manufactured ignorance that eliminates the affective and educational foundations of a liberal democracy. Trump's endless lies, impetuous outbursts, and regressive policies—such as stepping up deportations of undocumented immigrants, rolling back affirmative action, and banning transgender troops from serving in the military—are largely engineered to satisfy his network of followers.[25] But there is more going on here than simply creating subterfuge for political ends, justifying such deceitfulness as part of a militaristic reactionary strategy of making politics an extension of the art of war.[26] The latter has become an industry, one that it has a long history in U.S. politics. Trump's mendacity should be viewed as part of a staged politics of distraction that provides cover for the brutal neoliberal policies that he both ruthlessly supports and egregiously symbolizes. After all, it was partly the debris of economic policies that brought Trump to power, a wreckage he relentlessly exploited.

It is obvious that Trumpism is racist, nationalist, sexist, and militant. But most of all Trumpism is greedy, self-serving, and callous, emblematic of a corporate elite that will continue to do everything possible to increase its wealth and financial power irrespective of the consequences to other people or the planet. Donald Trump's sensationalism signals the need to divert attention away from the economic, political, and structural forces that have laid the groundwork for the popular appeal of proto-fascist forms of authoritarianism in the United States. Such sensationalism serves as a suitable matador's cape for those Trump supporters who may not be triggered by white supremacist codes but who want pro-corporate financial advantages imposed without obstruction or fanfare. The sensationalism distracts the underclass to act against their own economic interests.

What Trumpist strategists such as the vile Stephen Miller are well aware of is that the struggle over power is not only about the struggle over language and beliefs, but also about the destruction of intellectual and institutional forces that enable the capacity for informed judgment, ethical commitment, and integrity. Hence, *The Economist* reported that "When YouGov asked whether courts should be allowed to 'shut down news media outlets for publishing or broadcasting stories that are biased and inaccurate,' 45% of Republicans were in favor, compared with 20% who opposed the measure. More than half thought it acceptable to fine an offending news outlet (and 40% thought it would not violate the First Amendment to do so)."[27] More than dissent is on the chopping block. A 2017 poll found that "about half of Republicans say they would support postponing the 2020 presidential election" in order to fix nonexistent electoral fraud. The erosion of democracy on display here merges almost seamlessly with the rampant racism and anti-Semitism on display in Charlottesville.[28] Rules of impartiality in law, justice, the social contract, and democracy itself are clearly under assault.

The politics of distraction has been in overdrive since Trump took the political stage, and its racial undertones have been difficult to ignore. Commercial media and corporatized culture are potent forces for depoliticization and play major self-interested roles in diverting public attention from issues of corporate influence, accountability, power, and corruption. Such a politics devolves into near-propaganda as it merges spectacle with the suppression of dissent and overt forms of race baiting. For instance, Team Trump ordered Mike Pence to stage a phony protest against mostly Black football players who had been kneeling to protest police brutality against people of color. Pence walked out of a game between the Indianapolis Colts and the San Francisco 49ers, the latter being "the former team of blacklisted quarterback Colin Kaepernick."[29] Soon after Pence left the game, the vice president stated that he did so because he "will not dignify any event that disrespects our soldiers, our flag, or our national anthem," none of which were at issue in the protest. The travel expense for Pence to pull off this stunt set taxpayers back around $200,000. The incident also made it clear, once again, that the Trump regime will invest time and resources to push back against dissent. Trump made this point abundantly clear when he later stated at a campaign rally in September, "Wouldn't you love to see one of these NFL owners, when somebody disrespects our flag, to say, 'Get that son of a bitch off the field right now. Out! He's fired." That Trump did not express similar outrage at the neo-Nazis who marched in Charlottesville speaks volumes.

The blight of celebrity culture, engineered ignorance, the destruction of vital public spheres, the rise of the surveillance state, the militarization of the police, and the war on terrorism all contribute to a collective paranoia that produces social isolation, a heightened sense of rootlessness, the privatization of everything, and the conflation of citizenship with a dreary ethos of consumerism, all of which produce susceptibility to a politics of distraction in large numbers of the American public. Trapped in their own private orbits, they are unable to address the systemic conditions that destroy the ties connecting them to others, leaving the body uprooted from any sense of community and the existential need for belonging. The spectacle offers one of the few places for people to find emotional satisfaction and a sense of belonging. As George Orwell, Hannah Arendt, Zygmunt Bauman, and other prominent intellectuals have predicted, such isolation kills the imagination and finds symbolic compensation in the ideological appeals of authoritarian leaders who promise communities organized around hate, violence, and exclusion. All of this amounts to a swindle of fulfillment and a rejection of liberal democracy.

Trump clearly despises democracy and the institutions that support it. He has dispensed with the fiction of democracy because he believes that in the interest of hegemonic power both people and the planet are disposable, excess to be plundered and discarded. As part of an effort to normalize this pathology, he systematically employs a politics of diversion to prevent the public from addressing the underlying neoliberal forces and conditions that sold democracy to the bankers, hedge fund managers, and other surrogates of finance. Under Trump, democracy is not being thinned out, it is being replaced by a regime hostile to its existence, intent on maintaining the economic conditions that have allowed the United States to slide into a unique brand of fascism.

CHAPTER EIGHT

THE DEATH OF THE DEMOCRATIC PARTY

"The Democrats are unable to defend the United States of America from the most vicious, ignorant, corporate-indentured, militaristic, anti-union, anti-consumer, anti-environment, anti-posterity [Republican Party] in history."

—Ralph Nader

There is a certain level of duplicity in the Democratic Party's attempt to remake itself as the enemy of the corporate establishment and a leader in resistance to Trump's authoritarian regime. Democrats such as Ted Lieu, Maxine Waters, and Elizabeth Warren represent one minority faction of the party that rails against Trump. Meanwhile, less progressive types who actually control the party, such as Chuck Schumer and Nancy Pelosi, claim they have heard the cry of angry workers and are in the forefront of developing an opposition party that will reverse many of the policies that benefited the financial elite. Both views are part of the Democratic Party's attempt to rebrand itself. Pushing its new and more liberal brand, it has embraced some of the principles of FDR's New Deal. Yet it says little about developing a multicultural democratic vision and economic and social policies that would allow the Democratic Party to do for communities of color, the economically disadvantaged, and young people what they have done for the corporate sector. Most Democrats' anti-Trump rhetoric rings hollow. For Democratic Party leaders, the rebranding of the party rests on the assumption that resistance to Trump merely entails embracing the needs of those who are the economic losers of neoliberalism and globalization. What they forget is that authoritarianism thrives on more than economic discontent, as the recent white supremacist violence in Charlottesville, Virginia, made clear. Authoritarianism also thrives on political intolerance, racism, ultra-nationalism, exclusion, expulsion, and the deeming of certain subgroups as "disposable"—a script that the "new" Democratic Party has little to say about.

David Broder has recently argued that being anti-Trump is not a sufficient political position, because it ignores a myriad of ongoing policies that have impoverished the working class, destroyed the welfare state, polluted the environment, created massive inequities, expanded the reach of surveillance state, and increased conflict and militarization at home and abroad.[1] Even though such policies were produced by both Republicans and liberal Democrats, this message appears to have been taken up, at least partly, by the Democrats in a focused attempt to rebrand themselves as the guardians of working-class interests.

The pro-corporate political economy of the United

States over the last several decades, especially under Clinton and Obama, accelerated conditions for Trump to come to power in the first place. Trump's rise to power represents not merely the triumph of authoritarianism but also the natural result of a deregulated finance sector that benefited investment bankers, Wall Street, lawyers, hedge fund managers, and other members of the financial elite who promoted free trade, financial deregulation, cutthroat competition, and the commercialization of everything as the highest articulation of freedom. Trump is not simply the result of a surprising voter turnout by an angry, disgruntled working class (along with large segments of the white suburban middle class), he is also the endpoint of a brutal economic and political system that celebrates the market as the template for governing society while embracing a narrative of greed, self-interest, and corporate power. The establishment's mantra of deregulation, privatization, tax cuts for the rich, the financialization of everything, and the massive migration of wealth to the upper 1 percent, has, for many, turned the promise of the American Dream into a nightmare. The promise of social and economic mobility, racial justice, and a responsible welfare state has given way to an explosion of racialized resentment, fear, anger, militant authoritarianism, and shattered dreams. Too many people found themselves victims of gutted wages, lost jobs, growing insecurity, and a future of bottomless debt. Under such circumstances, Trump was able to breathe new life into a reactionary discourse that bundled white supremacy with market fundamentalism.[2] Trump sold the American public a live reality show, one that sensationalized the demise of a civil society based on democracy, justice, community, openness, and what Cornel West calls ethical and socially responsible "non-market values."

A History of Betrayal by Both Political Parties

The tyranny of the current moment bespeaks a long history of betrayal by a financial and political class that inhabits both major parties. It is no secret that the Republican Party has been laying the groundwork for authoritarianism since the 1970s by aggressively pushing for massive tax handouts for the rich, privatizing public goods, promoting a culture of fear, crushing trade unions, outsourcing public services, and eliminating restrictions designed to protect workers, women, and the environment. But they have not been the only party beholden to the financial interests of their rich donors.

It was the Democratic Party, especially under President Clinton, that prepared the groundwork for the financial crisis of 2007 by loosening corporate and banking regulations while at the same time slashing welfare provisions and creating the conditions for the intensification of the mass incarceration state. The Clinton administration did more than court Wall Street, it played a decisive role in expanding the neoliberal gains that took place three decades before he was elected. Nancy Fraser insightfully sums this up in the following commentary:

> Neoliberalism developed in the United States roughly over the last three decades and was

ratified with Bill Clinton's election in 1992. . . . Turning the U.S. economy over to Goldman Sachs, it deregulated the banking system and negotiated the free-trade agreements that accelerated deindustrialization. . . . Continued by his successors, including Barack Obama, Clinton's policies degraded the living conditions of all working people, but especially those employed in industrial production. In short, Clintonism bears a heavy share of responsibility for the weakening of unions, the decline of real wages, the increasing precarity of work, and the rise of the "two-earner family" in place of the defunct family wage.[3]

The Obama administration continued this abandonment of democratic values by bailing out the bankers who victimized the millions of American families who lost their homes to predatory loans, bad mortgages, and criminal foreclosures. It was the Obama administration that added a kill list to its foreign policy and matched it domestically with educational policies based on massive testing and accountability schemes that collapsed education into vocational training and undermined it as a moral and democratizing public good. Obama mixed neoliberalism's claim to unbridled economic and political power with an educational reform program that undermined the social imagination and the critical capacities that make democracy possible. Promoting charter schools and mind-numbing accountability schemes, Obama and the Democratic Party paved the way for the appointment of the hapless reactionary billionaire Betsy DeVos as Trump's secretary of education. And it was the Obama administration that enlarged the surveillance state while allowing CIA operatives who tortured and maimed people in the name of American exceptionalism and militarism to go free.

The growing disregard for public goods such as schools and health care, the weakening of union power, the erosion of citizenship to an act of consumption, the emptying out of political participation, and the widening of social and economic inequality are products of a form of ideological extremism and market fundamentalism embraced not only by Republicans. The Democratic Party also has a long legacy of incorporating the malicious policies of financial deregulation in their party platforms in order to curry favor with the rich and powerful.

Neoliberalism stands for the death of democracy, and the established political parties have functioned as accomplices. Both political parties, to different degrees, have imposed massive misery and suffering on the American people and condemned many to what David Graeber has described as "an apparatus of hopelessness, designed to squelch any sense of an alternative future."[4] While Trump and the Republican Party leadership display no shame over their strong embrace of neoliberalism, the allegedly reform-minded Democratic Party covers up its complicity with Wall Street and uses its alleged opposition to Trump to erase its history with the crimes of economic mass destruction that plunged millions of American families into foreclosure, poverty, and despair. With Republican majorities, mainstream Democrats share an unwillingness to detach themselves from an ideology that challenges the substance of a viable democracy and the public spheres and formative cultures that make it possible.

Chris Hedges has laid bare both the complicity of the Democratic Party in neoliberal and authoritarian politics, as well as the hypocrisy behind its claim to be the only political alternative to challenge Trump's illiberalism. He is worth quoting at length:

> The liberal elites, who bear significant responsibility for the death of our democracy, now hold themselves up as the saviors of the republic. They have embarked, despite their own corruption and their complicity in neoliberalism and the crimes of empire, on a self-righteous moral crusade to topple Donald Trump. It is quite a show. . . . Where was this moral outrage when our privacy was taken from us by the security and surveillance state, the criminals on Wall Street were bailed out, we were stripped of our civil liberties, and 2.3 million men and women were packed into our prisons, most of them poor people of color? Why did they not thunder with indignation as money replaced the vote and elected officials and corporate lobbyists instituted our system of legalized bribery? Where were the impassioned critiques of the absurd idea of allowing a nation

to be governed by the dictates of corporations, banks and hedge fund managers? Why did they cater to the foibles and utterings of fellow elites, all the while blacklisting critics of the corporate state and ignoring the misery of the poor and the working class? Where was their moral righteousness when the United States committed war crimes in the Middle East and our militarized police carried out murderous rampages?[5]

According to Katie Sanders, writing in PunditFact, under the Obama presidency, the Democrats "lost 11 governorships, 13 U.S. Senate seats, 69 House seats, and 913 state legislative seats and 30 state legislative chambers."[6] And the losses and humiliations got worse in the 2016 elections. It is no secret that the Democratic Party is a political formation of diminished power and hopes. Yet, in the face of Trump's authoritarianism, it has attempted to reinvent itself as the party of reform by updating its worn-out economic policies and ideological scripts. As proof of its reincarnation, it has proposed a work-in-progress platform titled "A Better Deal,"[7] signaling a populist turn in economic policy. A number of its proposals would certainly help benefit low-income communities. These include an increase of the minimum wage to $15, tax credits to encourage job training and hiring, regulations to lower drug costs, stronger anti-trust laws, and a $1 trillion infrastructure plan. The platform, however, does not support universal health care, and it says nothing about providing free higher education, reducing military spending, or reversing the huge growth in inequality.

As Anthony DiMaggio points out, the plan "doesn't even reach a Bernie Sanders level of liberalism, and it is a far cry from the kind of progressive populist policies introduced in FDR's New Deal and Johnson's Great Society/War on Poverty."[8] Eric Cheyfitz adds to this argument by insisting that the plan does nothing to challenge the rapacious system of unfettered capitalism the Democrats and Republicans have supported since the 1970s.[9] Both parties are politically and morally bankrupt and represent two sides of a political establishment that appears clueless in the face of a revolt by the disenfranchised and disgruntled. Historian Andrew Bacevich comments on the forces and crisis that led to Trump's rise to power:

> The response of the political establishment to this extraordinary repudiation testifies to the extent of its bankruptcy. The Republican Party still clings to the notion that reducing taxes, cutting government red tape, restricting abortion, curbing immigration, prohibiting flag-burning, and increasing military spending will alleviate all that ails the country. Meanwhile, to judge by the promises contained in their recently unveiled (and instantly forgotten) program for a "Better Deal," Democrats believe that raising the minimum wage, capping the cost of prescription drugs, and creating apprenticeship programs for

the unemployed will return their party to the good graces of the American electorate.[10]

Any reform policy worth its name would directly address income inequality and the power of the military-industrial complex, while fighting for single-payer health care and a redistribution of wealth and income. There will have to be a massive refiguring of power and restructuring and reallocation of wealth to address the health care crisis, poverty, climate change, inadequacies in education, and the plague of mass incarceration—problems not addressed in the Better Deal. It is reasonable to assume that such vexing challenges cannot be addressed within a two-party system that supports the foundational elements of a predatory economic system.

In spite of the horrendous policies driving the Democratic Party, various Democrats and progressives cannot bring themselves to denounce either big business as the bane of democracy nor its suffocating hold on reform efforts. They appear thunderstruck when asked to denounce a corrupt two-party system and develop a social movement and political apparatus that support democratic socialism. For instance, unrepentant centrist liberals such as Mark Penn and Andrew Stein have castigated progressives within the party while unapologetically embracing neoliberalism as a reform strategy. They believe that the Democratic Party has lost its base because it rushed to defend "identity politics" and leftist ideas, and that workers felt abandoned by the party's "shift away from moderate positions on trade and immigration, from backing police and tough anti-crime measures."[11] Instead, they claim that the Democratic Party needs "to reject socialist ideas and adopt an agenda of renewed growth, greater protection for American workers . . . [and a] return to fiscal responsibility, and give up on . . . defending sanctuary cities."[12] This sounds like a script written by a Trump policy advisor. It gets worse. Others, such as Leonard Steinhorn, have argued that the real challenge facing the Democratic Party is to change not their actual policies but their brand and messaging techniques.[13] This argument suggests that the Democrats lost their base because they failed to win the messaging battle, rather than placing the blame on their move to the right and alignment with corporate and moneyed interests.

Suffering from an acute loss of historical memory, Jonathan Chait argues, incredibly, that the Democratic Party never embraced the policies of neoliberalism and has in its recent incarnations actually moved to the left, upholding the principles of the New Deal and Great Society.[14] Leah Hung-Hendrix observes:

> One need not be anti-capitalist to understand that the Democratic [Party] . . . allowed for policies that deregulated the finance sector (under President Bill Clinton), allowed for the privatization of many public goods (including the weakening of the public education system through the promotion of charter schools), and bailed

out Wall Street banks without taking measures to truly address the needs of struggling working Americans.[15]

Chait seems to have overlooked the fact that Trump and Sanders have proved conclusively that the working class no longer belongs to the Democratic Party or that the Democratic Party under Clinton and Obama became the vanguard of unfettered corporate capitalism. He goes even further, arguing implausibly that neoliberalism is simply an epithet used by the left to discredit liberals and progressive Democrats.[16] Chait appears oblivious to the fact that the Democratic Party has become an adjunct of the rich and corporate elite.[17] Is Chait unaware of Clinton's elimination of the Glass-Steagall Act, his gutting of the welfare system, and his love affair with Wall Street, among his many missteps? How did he miss Obama's bailout of Goldman-Sachs, his abandonment of education as a public good, his attack on whistleblowers, or the Democrats' assault on organized labor via NAFTA? Did he not know that, in a White House interview given to Noticias Univision 23, Obama admitted that his "policies are so mainstream that if I had set the same policies that I had back in the 1980s, I would be considered a moderate Republican"?[18] Such admissions document the steady drift of the U.S. political-economic system to the surreal nightmare we find ourselves in today.

In the end, Chait is most concerned about what he calls an attempt on the part of the left to engage in the trick of bracketing "the center-left with the right as 'neoliberal' and force progressives to choose between that and social-ism."[19] He goes on to say that "the 'neoliberal' accusation is a synecdoche for the American left's renewed offensive against the center-left and a touchstone in the struggle to define progressivism after Barack Obama [and] is an attempt to win an argument with an epithet."[20] Because of his fear of democratic socialism, Chait is like many other centrists in the Democratic Party who are oblivious to the damaging effects of the policies adopted under the Clinton and Obama administrations.

Other progressive spokespersons such as John Nichols and Leah Hunt-Hendrix, and groups such as "Our Revolution" and the "Incorruptibles" want to rebuild the Democratic Party from the base up by running candidates with progressive values "for local offices: in statehouses, city councils, planning commissions, select boards and more."[21] The emphasis here would be for activists to revitalize and take over the Democratic Party by turning it to the left so that it will stand up for the economically disadvantaged and politically underprivileged. Tom Gallagher adds to this reform strategy by arguing that Bernie Sanders should join the Democratic Party—forgetting that when he supported Hilary Clinton in the presidential election, Sanders presented himself as a member of the party in all but name.

Many of the strategies that have been proposed to move the Democratic Party away from its history of centrism and the violence of neoliberalism are noble. If they were enacted at the level of policies and power relations, they would certainly make life easier for the poor, vulnerable, and excluded. Progressives are right to be motivated and inspired by Sanders' courage and policies. Sanders' campaign against a rigged economy, coupled with his critique of the fixed political system that serves neoliberalism, has provided a new language that has the potential to be visionary and comprehensive. But there is a difference between calling for reform and offering a new and compelling vision with an emphasis on a radical transformation of the political and economic systems.[22] At the same time, calls for a new vision and supporting values for radical democratic change do not mean abandoning attempts at reforming the Democratic Party. Rather, they view such attempts as part of a broader strategy designed to make immediate progressive gains on a number of fronts. The assumption here is that such a strategy will make clear that the Democratic Party is incapable of being transformed radically, and as such should not be expected to be on the forefront of radical democratic change.

Political and ideological centrism is endemic to the Democratic Party. It has never called for restructuring a system that is corrupt to the core. As a result, it has ignored, in the words of Nancy Fraser, that the antidote to authoritarianism is "a left project that redirects the rage and the pain of the dispossessed towards a deep societal restructuring and a democratic political 'revolution'"[23] The power of a left-progressive presence in the United States will, in part, depend on developing a comprehensive and accessible narrative that is able, as Fraser observes, to "articulate the legitimate grievances of Trump supporters with a fulsome critique of financialization on the one hand, and with an anti-racist, anti-sexist and anti-hierarchical vision of emancipation on the other."[24] The left needs a community-level populism with a social conscience, one that allows young people, workers, the middle class, and others to see how their futures might develop in a way that speaks to their needs and a more just and equitable life, one in which the utopian possibilities of a radical democracy appear possible.

Looking Beyond the Democratic Party

A new vision for change cannot be built on the legacy of the Democratic Party. What is needed is a concerted attempt to figure how democratic socialism can secure justice, political sovereignty, and economic stability for all sectors of American society. This suggests a rethinking of the meaning of politics, one that can rekindle the social imagination. Central to such a struggle is the role education must play in creating the formative culture that can produce critical and engaged citizens. Politics must move beyond short-lived protests while recalibrating itself to create the public spheres that enable progressives to think what long-term movements, organizations, and institutions. How can these be aligned to create new political formations willing to confront neoliberal capitalism and other forms of oppression not simply as symptoms of a distorted democracy but as part of a more radical project unwilling to compromise on identifying root causes?

Michelle Alexander is right in warning us that it would be a tragedy to waste this growing resistance against Trump and for greater unity "by settling for any Democrat the next time around."[25] We must instead struggle for a radical restructuring of society, one that gives meaning to a substantive democracy. Resistance cannot be defensive or ephemeral, reduced to either a narrow criticism of Trump's policies or to short-lived expressions of protest. As Michael Lerner has pointed out, protests are moments, and however pedagogically and politically valuable, do not constitute a movement.[26] They function as "an explosion of political subjectivity" and generally tell us what people are against, but not what they want.[27] In addition to a new vision, moral language, and democratic values, the left and other progressives need a platform for thinking beyond neoliberal capitalism.[28]

As David Harvey observes, the problems Americans face are too intractable and extensive to resolve without a strong anti-capitalist movement.[29] This resolution can only take place if progressives move beyond the fragmenting nature of single-issue politics and create a broad-based social movement that aligns struggles at the local, state, and national level with democratic movements at the global level. The peripheral demands of single-issue movements cannot be abandoned, but they must translate into wider opportunities for social change. There should be no contradiction between the call for educational reform, women's rights, and ecological change and what Katrina Forrester calls an alternative economic and political vision for America.[30]

What is needed is a narrative that brings together struggles for minority rights and personal emancipation with struggles for social justice and social equality. At the same time, it is a mistake for progressives to look at society only in terms of the call for justice in economic structures and issues. A mass-based movement to challenge neoliberalism and authoritarianism cannot be constructed unless it also commits to combating the many forms of oppression extending from sexism and racism to xenophobia and transphobia. Only a movement that unifies these diverse struggles will lead us toward a radically open and culturally diverse democracy. Struggles to counter the war on immigrants, women, people of color, protesters, low-income families, workers, educators, and the environment must be joined with efforts to defend targeted communities, defeat fascist movements, resist police violence, rebuild the labor movement, abolish the carceral state, fight white supremacy, and make education central to politics. Together, they must find a common ground in building a mass movement for a socialist democracy.[31]

Politics becomes radical when it translates society's troubles into broader systemic issues and challenges the commanding institutional and educational structures. To be effective, it must do so in a language that speaks to people's needs, enabling them to identify and invest in narratives in which they can recognize themselves and the conditions that produce the suffering they experience. For this reason, the call for institutional change is inextricably connected to the politics of social and economic transformation. Such transformation must propel us toward an international movement to build a society that embraces the beauty of universal emancipation and the promise of a radical democracy. At a time in history when the stakes for democracy are so acutely threatened and life on the planet itself so imperiled, collective action is the only way out of the age of authoritarian power. It is time to go for broke.

CHAPTER NINE

TOWARD A POLITICS OF UNGOVERNABILITY

"In this country we are menaced—intolerably menaced—by a lack of vision. . . . "
                                        —James Baldwin

Martin Luther King Jr., in his speech at the Riverside Church, spoke eloquently about what it meant to use nonviolent direct action as part of a broader struggle to connect racism, militarism, and war. His call to address a "society gone mad on war" and the need to "address the fierce urgency of now" was rooted in an intersectional politics, one that recognized a comprehensive view of oppression, struggle, and politics itself.[1] Racism, poverty, and disposability could not be abstracted from the issue of militarism and how these modes of oppression informed each other. This was particularly clear in the program put forth by the Black Panther Party, which called for "equality in education, housing, employment and civil rights" and produced a 10 Point Plan to achieve its political goals.[2] A more recent example of a comprehensive engagement with politics can be found in the Black Lives Matter movement's call to connect racially motivated police violence to wider forms of state violence, allowing such a strategy to progress from a single-issue protest movement to a full-fledged social movement.[3]

Such struggles at best should be about both educating people and creating broad-based social movements dedicated not merely to reforms but to transforming the ideological, economic, and political structures of the existing society. Social transformation has to be reconnected with institutional change.[4] This means rejecting the notion that global capitalism can be challenged successfully at any one of these levels alone, especially if such resistance, however crucial, is not connected to a comprehensive understanding of the reach of global power. Lacino Hamilton is right in arguing that "institutional patterns and practices will not change unless protesters go beyond rallying, marching, and what usually amounts to empty slogans. The function of activists is to translate protest into organized action, which has the chance to develop and to transcend immediate needs and aspirations toward a radical reconstruction of society."[5]

Resistance to the impending reality of neo-fascist domination is more urgent than ever and necessitates challenging not only the commanding structures of economic power but also those powerful cultural apparatuses that trade in the currency of ideas. An effective resistance movement must work hard to create a formative culture that empowers and brings together the most vulnerable along

with those whose activism is currently limited to single issues. For many progressives, their political landscape lacks
connections to a variety of single-issue movements such as
resistance to police violence, militarism, denying abortion
rights, climate change, right-wing school reform, and the
rejection of decent health care for all. All of these issues are
crucial, but they exist in a fractured political environment
that impedes a broader ethical and radical movement from
harnessing the energies of progressives, liberals, and left-
ists under one political tent and fighting for a comprehensive politics in the name of a radical democracy or form of
democratic socialism. While there has been an increase in
the number of resistance movements—close to 5,000 individual groups—since Trump's election, "there is no common indivisible national agenda, nor is there a common
organization to set a coherent strategic direction."[6]

The power of such a broad-based movements could
draw inspiration from the historically relevant anti-war,
anti-racist, and civil rights movements of the past, including the Black freedom movement of the 1960s and the
ACT UP movement of the late 1980s. The theoretical and
political agenda for such movements has a long history and
is available in the writings of Martin Luther King Jr., Vaclav Havel's well-documented resistance to Soviet tyranny,
the history of the Black Panther Party, and Gene Sharp's
conceptual framework for liberation in *From Dictatorship to
Democracy*, to name just a few sources.[7] At the same time,
current social movements such as Podemos in Spain also
offer the possibility of creating new political formations

that are anti-fascist and fiercely determined to both challenge authoritarian regimes such as Trump's and dismantle the economic, ideological, and cultural structures that produce them. What all of these movements reveal is that diverse, interlocked forms of oppression, ranging from the war abroad to the racist and homophobic wars at home, are symptomatic of a more profound illness and deeper malady that demand a new understanding of theory, politics, and oppression.

There is certainly something to be learned from older, proven tactics including using education to create a revolution in consciousness and values, and using broad-based alliances to create the conditions for mass disruptions such as a general strike.[8] These tactics combine theory, consciousness, and practice as part of a strategy to dismantle the complex workings of the death-dealing machinery of casino capitalism and its recent intensification under the Trump administration. Certainly, one of the most powerful tools of oppression is convincing people that the oppressive conditions they experience are normal and cannot be changed. The ideology of normalization functions to prevent any understanding of the larger systemic forces of oppression by insisting that all problems are individually based and ultimately a matter of individual character and responsibility. Despite all evidence to the contrary, the message spread through a range of cultural apparatuses extending from the schools to the mainstream media continues to be that there are no structures of domination, only flawed individuals, and the system of capitalism as a whole is organized for our own good. The 1960s produced a range of critical thinkers who already recognized and challenged this oppressive neoliberal narrative as it emerged, including Herbert Marcuse, Malcolm X, James Baldwin, Robin Morgan, Stanley Aronowitz, Mary Daly, Louis Althusser, Pierre Bourdieu, Zygmunt Bauman, and many others. For them, structures of domination were rooted in subjectivity itself, as well as in larger economic apparatuses. Learning from this past resistance means remembering what was at stake for society then, and considering what is at stake for all of us now. Memory can be a powerful force for change, because it provides us with a critical perspective and a much fuller understanding of the times in which we live, and in doing so inspires us to take risks to ensure a better future, one that does not merely repeat history but struggles to transform it.

Restoring Historical Memory
The great Spanish novelist Javier Marías captures in a 2016 interview why memory matters, especially as a resource for understanding the present through the lens of history. He writes:

> I do not know what I might say to an American young person after Trump's election. Probably that, according to my experience with a dictatorship—I was 24 when Franco died—you can always survive bad times more than you think you can when they start. . . . Though the predictions

are terrible, I suppose we must all wait and see what Trump does, once he is in office. It looks ominous, indeed. And [Vice President Mike] Pence does not seem better, perhaps even worse. It is hard to understand that voters in the United States have gone against their own interests and have decided to believe unbelievable things. One of the most ludicrous interpretations of Trump's victory is that he represents the poor, the oppressed, the people "left behind." A multi-millionaire, and a very ostentatious one to boot? A man who surrounds himself with gilded stuff? A guy whose favorite sentence is, "You're fired!"? A bloke who has scorned blacks, Mexicans, women, and of course, Muslims in general? He *is* the elite that he is supposed to fight. Indeed, it is a big problem that nowadays too many people (not only Americans, I'm afraid) don't know anything about history, and therefore cannot recognize dangers that are obvious for the elder ones (those with some knowledge of history, of course, be it first- or second-hand).[9]

As Marías suggests, historical legacies of racist oppression and dangerous memories can be troublesome for the authoritarians now governing American society. This was made clear in the backlash to Ben Carson's claim that slaves were immigrants; Trump's insistence that all Black communities are crime-ridden, impoverished hellholes;

and Education Secretary Betsy DeVos's assertion that historically Black colleges and universities were "pioneers of school choice."[10] Memories become dangerous when exposing this type of ideological ignorance aimed at rewriting history so as to eliminate its oppressive and poisonous legacies. This is particularly true of the genocidal brutality waged against Native Americans and Black slaves in the United States and its connection to the atrocity of Nazi genocide in Europe and the disappearance of critics of fascism in Argentina and Chile in the 1970s.

Dangerous memories are eliminated by today's political reactionaries in order to erase the ugliness of the past and to legitimate America's shopworn legacy of exceptionalism with its deadening ideology of "habitual optimism," one that substitutes a cheery, empty, Disney-like dreamscape for any viable notion of utopian possibility.[11] The Disney dreamscape evacuates hope of any substantive meaning. It attempts to undercut a radical utopian element in the conceptual apparatus of hope that speaks to the possibility of a democratic future very different from the authoritarian past or present. Jelani Cobb is right in insisting that "the habitual tendency to excise the most tragic elements of history creates a void in our collective understanding of what has happened in the past and, therefore, our understanding of the potential for tragedy in the present."[12] The revival of historical memory as a central political strategy is crucial today, given that Trump's white supremacist policies not only echo elements of a fascist past but also point to the need to recognize, as Paul Gilroy has observed, "how elements of fascism appear in new forms," especially as "the living memory of the fascist period fades."[13] What historical memory discloses is that subjectivity and agency are the material of politics and offer the possibility of creating spaces in which "the domestic machinery of inscriptions and invisibility" can be challenged.[14] Catherine Clément argues correctly that "somewhere every culture has an imaginary zone for what it excludes, and it is that zone we must try to remember today."[15] The historical and dangerous memories relegated to that zone in the contemporary social order must be recovered. Historical memory is crucial to keeping the American public attuned to what elements in the national landscape signal the emergence of updated elements of fascism. Memory in this sense functions as a critical guidepost that help us to recognize and analyze "where and how totalitarian practices might emerge." For instance, Trump's insistence that there is "no truth" in politics or that the critical media is a form of "fake news" provides a clear signal from the past of how fascism works.[16]

While it would be irresponsible to underestimate Trump's skulking proximity to neo-fascist ideology and policies, he is not solely answerable for the long legacy of authoritarianism that became a frontal assault with the election of Ronald Reagan in 1980, the emergence of the Tea Party, and the rise of Sarah Palin as a national voice for the new extremism. This neoliberal attack was later embraced in the Third Way politics of the Democratic Party, expanded through the growth of a mass incarceration state, and solidified under the anti-democratic "war on terror" and permanent war policies of the Bush-Cheney and Obama administrations. During this period, democracy was sold to the bankers and big corporations. Whistleblowers were sent to prison. The financial elite and CIA torturers were given the green light by the Obama administration to commit the gravest of crimes with impunity. This surge of repression was made possible mostly through the emergence of a savage neoliberalism, a ruthless concentration of power by the ruling classes, and an aggressive ideological and cultural war aimed at undoing the social contract and the democratic, political, and personal freedoms gained in the New Deal and culminating in the civil rights and education struggles of the 1960s.

As mentioned previously, Trump's unapologetic authoritarianism has prompted Democratic Party members and the liberal elite to position themselves as the only model of organized resistance. It is difficult not to see their alleged moral outrage and faux resistance as both comedic and hypocritical in light of the role these centrist liberals have played in the last forty years—subverting democracy and throwing the working class and people of color under the bus. As Jeffrey St. Clair observes, "Trump's nominal opponents," the Democrats, are "encased in the fatal amber of their neoliberalism."[17] They are part of the problem and not the solution. Rather than face up to a sordid history of ignoring the needs of workers, young people, and minorities of class and color, the Democratic Party acts as if its embrace of a variety of neoliberal political and economic policies along with its support of a perpetual war machine had nothing to do with paving the way for Donald Trump's election. Focusing only on how Trump represents the transformation of politics into a reality TV show misses the point. Underlying Trump's rise is the ruling-class conviction that U.S. Presidential candidates should be judged in terms of how much value they generate as an advertisement for casino capitalism.[18]

Dangerous memories and critical knowledge, and the genuinely democratic formative cultures they enable, must be at the forefront of resisting the armed ignorance of the Trump disimagination machine. While a critical consciousness is the precondition of struggle, it is only the starting point for effective resistance. What is also needed is a bold strategy and a social movement capable of shutting down the authoritarian political machine at all levels of government through general strikes, constant occupation of the political spaces and public spheres controlled by the new authoritarians, and the creation of an endless groundswell of educational strategies and demonstrations that make clear and hold accountable the different ideological, material, psychological, and economic registers of authoritarianism at work in U.S. society. This is a time to study, engage in critical dialogues, develop new educational sites, support and expand the alternative media, and counter force with reason and a resurgence of the collective will. It will not be easy to turn the tide, but it *can happen*, and there are historical precedents.

Shutting Down American-style Authoritarianism

Effective strategies to support social change and political agency have to focus, in part, on the young and those most vulnerable to the advancing wave of authoritarianism. Young people, workers, and those now considered disposable, especially, are the driving force of the future, and we have to learn from them, support them, contribute where possible, and join in their struggles. At the same time, as Robin D.G. Kelley argues:

> We cannot build a sustainable movement without a paradigm shift. Stopgap, utilitarian alliances to stop Trump aren't enough. . . . So where do we go from here? If we really care about the world, our country, and our future, we have no choice but to resist.[19]

This would also suggest building up unions again and putting their control in the hands of workers, fostering the conditions for the creation of a massive student movement, and working to build sanctuary cities and institutions that will protect those considered the enemies of white supremacy—immigrants, Muslims, Blacks, and others considered disposable. Democratic politics must be revived at the local and state levels, especially given the control of 56 percent of state legislatures by right-wing Republicans.[20] Education must be made central to the formation and expansion of study groups throughout the country, and a public pedagogy of justice and democracy must be furthered through the alternative media and when possible in the mainstream media. Central to the latter task is expanding the range of dialogues regarding how oppression works to focus not merely on economic structures but also on the way it functions ideologically, psychologically (as Wilhelm Reich once argued), and spiritually, as Michael Lerner has pointed out.[21] It is not enough for progressives to examine the objective forces and conditions that have pushed so many people to give up on politics, have undercut acts of solidarity, and have dismantled any viable notion of hope in the future. It is also crucial to understand the devastating emotional forces and psychological narratives that harm them from the inside out.[22]

A successful resistance struggle must be comprehensive, and at the same time embrace a vision that is unified, democratic, and equitable. While talking about youth in the age of precarity, Jennifer Silva makes an important point about the need for this comprehensive vision of politics. She writes, "I find that without a broad, shared vision of economic justice, race, class and gender become sites of resentment and division rather than a coalition among the working class."[23] Instead of simply reacting to the horrors and misery produced by capitalism, it is crucial to call for its end, while supporting the formation of a democratic socialism that gives voice to and unifies the needs and actions of those who have been left out of the discourse of democracy under the financial elite. The need here is for a language of both critique and possibility, a rigorous analysis of the diverse forces of oppression and a discourse of educated hope.

Such a task is both political and pedagogical. Not only must existing relations of power be called into question and their authority to govern society be denied, but notions of neoliberal "common-sense" learning must be disconnected from democratic forms of political agency and civic literacy. As Michael Lerner insightfully observes, rather than engage in a politics of shaming, progressives have to produce a discourse in which people can recognize their problems and the actual conditions that produce them.[24] As I have stressed throughout this book, this is not just a political but a pedagogical challenge in which education becomes central to any viable mode of resistance. Making education central to politics means the left will have to remove itself from the discourse of meritocracy that is often used to dismiss and write off those who hold conservative, if not reactionary, views. Not doing so only results in a discourse of blaming others and a self-indulgent congratulatory stance on the part of those who occupy progressive political positions. The hard political and pedagogical work of changing consciousness, producing new kinds of identity, desires, and values conducive to a democracy, doesn't stop with the moral high ground often taken by liberals and other progressives.

The right wing knows how to address matters of self-reproach and anger head on, often through a racism-inflected diversion, whereas the left and progressives continue to shy away from the pedagogical challenges posed by those vulnerable groups caught in the magical thinking of reactionary ideologies.[25] So while it is crucial to address the dramatic shifts economically and politically that have produced growing poverty and unemployment along with enormous anger and frustration in American society, it is also important to address the accompanying existential crisis that has destroyed the self-esteem, identity, and hopes of those considered disposable, and those whom Hillary Clinton shamelessly called a "basket of deplorables." The ideological mix of untrammeled self-interest, unchecked individualism, unrestrained self-reliance, a culture of fear, and a war-against-all ethic has produced a profound sense of precarity and hopelessness, not only among immigrants and poor people of color, but among working-class whites who feel crushed by the economy, threatened by those deemed other, and demeaned by so-called elites.

Resistance on each of these several fronts will not be easy, but it has to happen, and it has to happen in a way that connects these multiple fronts through a shared politics and pedagogy. It must at the same time open the public's eyes to an understanding of how a new class of financial scavengers operates in the free flow of a global space with no national allegiances, no respect for the social contract, and a degree of power unparalleled in its ability to exploit people, produce massive inequality, destroy the planet, and accelerate human suffering across and within national boundaries. Clearly, a broad social movement must create a shared common agenda that rejects the notion that capitalism is synonymous with democracy. Such a movement must grow out of shared spaces, alternative public spheres, and what I call democracies in exile. There must be a space for dialogue, for educational work aimed at developing a comprehensive understanding of oppression and not just a critique of Wall Street. Most important, there is a need to create a radical vision of what a democratic socialism would look like, how such a vision can be conveyed to the American public, and what sort of educational spheres and institutions would be vital to such a task. Such a vision may be impossible without a new language for theorizing politics, culture, power, and collective resistance.

Trump's speech has a history that must be acknowledged, made known for the suffering it imposes, and challenged with an alternative critical and hope-producing narrative. No form of oppression, however hideous, can be overlooked. And along with that critical gaze there must emerge a critical language, a new narrative and a different story about what a socialist democracy will look like in the United States.

At the same time, there is a need to strengthen and expand the reach and power of established public spheres as sites of critical learning. There is also a need to encourage artists, intellectuals, academics and other cultural workers to talk, educate, and challenge the normalizing discourses of casino capitalism, white supremacy, and fascism. There is no room here for a language shaped by political purity or limited to a politics of outrage. A truly democratic vision has a more capacious overview of the project of struggle and transformation.

Language is not simply an instrument of fear, violence, and intimidation; it is also a vehicle for critique, civic courage, resistance, and informed agency. We live at a time when the language of democracy has been pillaged, stripped of its promises and hopes. If fascism is to be defeated, the first step is to acknowledge that fascism begins with words, and in response there is a need to develop a language of critique and possibility that exposes and unravels falsehoods, systems of oppression, and corrupt relations of power while making clear that an alternative future is possible. A critical language can guide us in our thinking about the relationship between older elements of fascism and how such practices are emerging today in new forms. The use of such a language can also reinforce and accelerate the creation of alternative public spaces in which critical dialogue, exchange, and a new understanding of politics can emerge. Focusing on language as a strategic element of political struggle is not only about meaning, critique, and the search for the truth. It is also about power: understanding how it works and using it as part of ongoing struggles that merge the language of critique and possibility, theory and action.

Without a faith in intelligence, critical education, and the power to transform, humanity will be powerless to challenge the threat that fascism poses to the world. All forms of fascism aim at destroying standards of truth, openness, accountability, empathy, informed reason, and the institutions that make them possible. The current struggle against a nascent fascism in the United States is not only a struggle over economic structures or the commanding heights of corporate power. It is also a struggle over visions, ideas, consciousness, and the power to shift the culture itself.

Progressives need to formulate a new language, alternative cultural spheres, and fresh narratives about community, collective welfare, social justice, environmental sustainability, empathy, solidarity, and the promise of a real socialist democracy. We need a new vision that refuses to equate capitalism and democracy, normalize greed and excessive competition, and accept self-interest as the highest form of motivation. We need a language, vision, and understanding of power to enable the conditions in which education is linked to social change and the capacity to promote human agency through the registers of cooperation, compassion, care, love, equality, and respect for difference.

Resistance is no longer an option: it is now a matter of life or death. The lights are going out on democracy across the globe, and the time to wake up from this nightmare is now. There are no guarantees in politics, but this is not a cause for retreat. No politics that matters is without hope—a hope forged in an educated awareness of history and the possibilities for real intervention and social change. This is not simply a call for a third political party. Progressives need to create a new politics and new social and political formations. The time for mounting resistance through a range of single-issue movements is over. Nothing is more important now than to bring such movements together as part of a broad-based political formation.

Those who believe in a radical democracy must find a way to make this nation ungovernable by the powers that currently claim governing authority. Small-scale defiance and local actions are important, but there is a more urgent need to educate and mobilize through a comprehensive vision and politics that is capable of generating massive teach-ins all over the United States so as to enable a collective struggle aimed at producing powerful events such as a nationwide boycott, sit-ins, and a general strike in order to bring the country to a halt. The promise of such resistance must be rooted in the creation of a new political movement of democratic socialists, one whose power is grounded in the organization of novel political formations, unions, educators, workers, young people, religious groups, and others who constitute a popular progressive base. There will be no resistance without a vision of a new society and new mechanisms of resistance. In this instance, effective resistance involves cutting off power to the financial elite, religious fundamentalists, and neoconservative warmongers. In doing so, it gives birth to a social wakefulness and a politics of ungovernability. Hopefully, in that wakefulness, a resurgent act of witnessing and moral outrage will grow and provide the basis for a new kind of politics, a fierce wind of resistance, and a struggle too powerful to be defeated: democracy in exile.

DEMOCRACY IN EXILE

"We don't live in the best of all possible worlds. This is a Kafkaesque time. . . . Yet somehow the old discredited values and longings persist . . . We still believe that we can save ourselves and our damaged earth—an indescribably difficult task. . . . But we keep on trying, because there is nothing else to do."

—Annie Proulx

While Trumpism attempts to expand its alt-right social base under its authoritarian hierarchy, forces of grassroots resistance are mobilizing around a renewed sense of ethical courage, social solidarity, and a revival of the political imagination.[1] We see this happening in the increasing number of mass demonstrations in which individuals are putting their bodies on the line, refusing the fascist machinery of misogyny, nativism, and white supremacy. Airports are being occupied, people are demonstrating in the streets of major cities, town halls have become sites of resistance, campuses are being transformed into sanctuaries to protect undocumented students, scientists are marching en masse against climate change deniers, and progressive cultural workers, public intellectuals, and politicians are speaking out against the emerging authoritarianism. In a number of red states, middle-aged women are engaged in the "grinding scutwork of grassroots organizing" while addressing big issues such as "health care and gerrymandering, followed by dark money in politics, education, and the environment."[2] Democracy may be in exile in the United States, and imperiled in Europe and other parts of the globe, but the spirit that animates it remains resilient. Once again the public memory of an educated and prophetic hope is in the air, echoing Martin Luther King Jr.'s call "to make real the promise of democracy."

In today's historical moment, such a promise finds sanctuary in the notion of "democracy in exile." This concept is meant as a counterforce and remedy to the Jacksonian intolerance, violence, expulsion, and racism of Donald Trump, Stephen Miller, and Trumpism as a nationalist movement drifting in plain sight from plutocracy and authoritarian nepotism to fascism. Democracy in exile is the space in which people, families, networks, and communities fight back. It unites the promise of insurrectional political engagement with the creation of expansive new manifestations of justice—social, economic, environmental. The concept speaks to the rise of innumerable marches, protests, and acts of political resistance that form a growing challenge to existing power relations and the expanding forces of authoritarianism and tyranny consolidated under

Trump's rule. It argues for a model of critical consciousness and an "ethical space where we encounter the pain of others and truly reflect on its significance to a shared human community."³ Such sanctuaries function as alternative spheres of a democracy in exile and do more than offer refugees protection and services such "as emergency shelters, recreation, public transit, libraries, food banks, and police and fire services without asking questions about their status."⁴ They also point toward and beyond the identification of structures of domination and repression in search of new understanding and imaginative response to the need to live well together in diverse communities. In part, this means responding to the ominous forces at work in U.S. society, now marked by a collapse of civic culture, shared literacy, and meaningful citizenship. Such spaces call for new apparatuses enabling people to learn together, to engage in extended dialogue, and to develop new social formations in the service of advancing political, economic, and environmental justice and transformation. As democracy cannot survive without informed and socially responsible citizens, such spaces are driven by community-centered education, culture, and family.

What might it mean for educators to create sanctuaries that preserve the ideals, values, and experiences of an insurrectional democracy? What might it mean to imagine a landscape of resistance in which the metaphor of *democracy in exile* inspires and energizes young people, educators, workers, artists, and others to engage in political and pedagogical forms of resistance that are disruptive, transformative, resilient, and emancipatory? What might it mean to create multiple protective spaces of resistance that would allow us to think critically, ask troubling questions, take risks, transgress established norms, and fill the spaces of everyday life with ongoing acts of nonviolent organizing resistance? What might it mean to create cities, states, and other public spheres defined as sanctuaries for a democracy in exile? Cities such as Boston and Hamilton, Ontario, have declared themselves sanctuaries, or what I am calling democracies in exile. Brit McCandless recently reported that "more than 800 places of worship have volunteered to shelter undocumented immigrants who face deportation and their families—double the number since the 2016 election. They join the more than 600 cities and counties that have declared themselves sanctuaries—ordering their police not to detain people solely because of their immigration status."[5]

These cities and counties have not only refused to comply with Trump's repressive policies on climate change and travel bans, but they have also defined themselves, in part, as public spaces designed to protect those who fear expulsion and state terrorism. In many respects, cities have become front lines in the fight against Trump's repressive immigration policies and disastrous attack on climate change reform. As of February 2017, more than sixty-eight mayors have signed an open letter protesting Trump's opposition to limiting greenhouse gases.[6] Cities such as Seattle and Burlington, Vermont, are on the cutting edge, enacting radical legislation while promoting broad-based progressive political formations heavily indebted to the values and policies of democratic socialism. In fact, an avowed socialist, Kshama Sawant, sits on the city council in Seattle, one of America's most insurgent cities.[7]

In the face of Trump's January 25, 2017, executive order in which he called for stripping federal funds from cities that defy his border enforcement and immigration policies, many cities have chosen to resist Trump anyway, because of his attacks on environmental protections and public schools. In the face of such attacks, new coalitions are emerging between labor groups, young people, immigrant rights groups, evangelicals, church groups, and others that Adriana Cadena, coordinator for Reform Immigration for Texas Alliance, points to as a reservoir of "untapped voices."[8] At the same time, such struggles will not be easy. Not only is the threat of repression by the federal government a looming reality, but a similar threat is posed by Republican-controlled state legislatures, which now number thirty-two. Yet many progressive states such as California are finding new ways to pass laws "that grant undocumented immigrants access to state driver's licenses, in-state tuition, financial aid, health care and professional licenses, and that shield them by limiting state participation in enforcing federal law."[9]

Such cities and counties, and a host of diverse public spheres, function as parallel structures that create alternative modes of communication, social relations, education, health care, and cultural work, including popular music, social media, the performing arts, and literature. These spaces are what Vaclav Benda has called a "parallel polis,"[10] which brings pressure on official structures, implements new modes of pedagogical resistance, and provides the basis for organizing larger day-to-day protests and more organized and sustainable social movements. Just as dissidents in Eastern Europe developed the concept of a parallel polis, there is a need in the current historical moment to create new modes of organizing, community, and resistance: democracies in exile.[11]

The concept of democracy in exile is grounded in community building, economic justice, and a discourse of critique, hope, social justice, and self-reflection. As a mode of critique, it models the call for diverse forms of resistance, critical dialogue, collaboration, and a rethinking of political processes and the kinds of public spaces where they can take place. As a discourse of hope, it offers the possibility of organizing new forms of social networking designed to dismantle proto-fascist formations from consolidating further. As a model for a new progressive politics, democracies in exile are open communities and collectivities joined in the spirit of mutual aid and justice; they mark the antithesis of Trumpism's falsehoods, walls, guns, white supremacy, and menacing intolerance. These models for democracy signal a mode of witnessing and organized resistance inspired by a renewed commitment to justice and equality. This is a spirit of redemption matched by mass protests such as the "Day Without Immigrants" strike, the 4.2 million people who took to the streets in protest on Trump's second day in office, and the thousands of scientists and their supporters who participated in the 2017 March for Science. In all of these cases, the aim was "to demonstrate the productive power of the people" in the struggle to take back democracy.[12]

Democracy in exile offers the opportunity to fuse popular movements and reinvigorate educational spheres that include traditional sites of struggle such as unions, churches, and synagogues. For example, churches throughout the United States are using private homes in their parishes as shelters while at the same time "creating a modern-day underground railroad to ferry undocumented immigrants from house to house or into Canada."[13] Hiding and housing immigrants is but one important register of political resistance that such sanctuaries can provide. Organizations such as the Protective Leadership Institute and the State Innovation Exchange are fighting back against conservative state legislation by modeling progressive legislation, putting ongoing pressure on politicians, educating people on issues and how to develop the skills for disruptive political strategies, and building "a progressive power base in the states."[14] In addition, cities such as New York have proclaimed themselves sanctuary cities, and students in "as many as 100 colleges and universities across the country" have held protests "demanding their schools become sanctuary campuses."[15]

The concept of democracy in exile offers a new rhetorical approach to understanding such resistance and the new stage of authoritarianism that has made it necessary. Such outposts of exile offer new models of collaboration, united by a perpetual striving for a more just society. As such, they join in solidarity and in their differences, mediated by a respect for the common good, human dignity, and decency. Together they offer a new map for resisting a demagogue and his coterie of reactionaries who harbor a rapacious desire for concentrating power in the hands of a financial elite and the economic, political, and religious fundamentalists who seek to amass wealth and power by any means necessary. This call for a new mode of opposition connects the educational challenge of raising individual and collective consciousness with mobilizing against the suffocating ideologies, worldviews, and policies that are driving the new species of authoritarianism. These alternative spaces and new public spheres reflect what Sara Evans and Harry Boyte have called "free spaces," which welcome the challenge of ongoing community engagement designed to revitalize civic education and civic courage.[16]

The language of exile also projects a threat to pro-fascist nationalist networks, for it signals the rival mobilization of emancipatory social forces organizing against political intolerance, white supremacy, economic oppression, police violence, and the constant fabrications that serve to normalize and enforce them. The creation of new spaces for community resistance asserts the right to reject all such formations of domination, impunity, and abuse.

Rethinking the possibility for social movements and a new form of politics can begin by reconceptualizing what might it mean to create public spheres and institutions that represent models of a democracy in exile—sanctuaries that preserve the ideals, values, and experiences of a radical democracy. What will it take to create communities whose diverse institutions function as sanctuaries for those who fear expulsion and state terror? How might we together generate a multi-pronged resistance that revives and defends the ideals of an already fragile and wounded democracy—one that cultivates educated hope and actions that safeguard our future? Such a society would foster "the eradication of all forms of racial, gender, class, and sexual hierarchy"[17] and would be based on a call not for reform but for a radical restructuring, a substantive socialist democracy that rejects the notion that capitalism and democracy are synonymous.

This certainly raises further questions about what proactive roles educational institutions can take to counter the creeping influence and further normalization of authoritarianism in all its forms. One of the challenges confronting the current generation of educators, students, progressives, and other concerned citizens is the need to address the role they might play in any resistance effort. What can and should education accomplish in a democracy under siege? What work must educators do to create the economic, political, and ethical conditions necessary to endow young people and the general public with the capacities to think, question, doubt, imagine the unimaginable, and defend education as essential for inspiring an informed, thoughtful citizenry integral to the existence of a robust democracy? In a world witnessing an increasing abandonment of egalitarian and democratic impulses and the erasure of historical memory, what will it take to educate young people and the broader polity to learn from the past and understand the present in order to challenge rabid, unbridled authority and hold power accountable?

Many of the resources are already available. In his book *On Tyranny*, historian Timothy Snyder provides a list of suggestions that range from not being afraid to disobey, to defending democratic institutions.[18] Michael Lerner has produced a number of invaluable proposals that include what he calls a global Marshall Plan and a strategy for U.S. progressives to take seriously matters of education, subjectivity, compassion, and care in any political struggle.[19] George Lakoff has provided a number of useful suggestions for engaging in the individual and collective practice of resistance, including the call to re-examine the nature of power and to focus on substance not sideshows in the realm of criticism.[20] Bill Quigley has offered a number of substantive points on how to engage in direct action to stop government raids.[21] Reverend William J. Barber II has written extensively on the need to create broad-based alliances, especially among the religious left, and in doing so has infused the call for resistance with an energizing sense of moral and political outrage.[22] In *The American Prospect*, Theo Anderson has provided an insightful commentary on how the left's long march of resistance must include direct action at the state level.[23] Robin D.G. Kelley has written a series of brilliant articles on the need to develop emancipatory strategies in the university that call for students and faculty to move beyond framing grievances in the discourse of victimhood and personal travail.[24] *Harper's Magazine* engaged a number of intellectuals to talk about what the ecology of resistance under a Trump regime might look like.[25] These are only a few of the many valuable sources that can be studied, talked about, and potentially used to advance networks and movements for democracies in exile.

Universities have an essential role to play in midwifing democracies in exile. In addition to creating safe spaces for undocumented immigrants and others deemed vulnerable or disposable, universities can also equip people with the knowledge, skills, experiences, and values they need to organize, litigate, and achieve higher levels of justice, openness, and accountability. For many universities, this would mean renouncing their instrumental approach to knowledge, creating the conditions for faculty to connect their work with important social issues, refusing to treat students as customers, and choosing administrative leaders who have a vision rooted in the imperatives of justice, ethics, social responsibility, and democratic values.[26] The culture of business has produced the business of education, and to be frank, it has corrupted the mission of too many universities. It is necessary for students, faculty, and others to reverse this trend at a time when the dark shadows of authoritarianism and fascism threaten both the spaces for critical inquiry and democracy itself.

We must also ask what role education, historical memory, and critical pedagogy might have in the larger society, where the social has been individualized, political life has collapsed, and education has been reduced to either a private affair or a kind of algorithmic mode of regulation in which everything is narrowly focused on achieving a desired empirical outcome? What role could a resuscitated critical education play in challenging the deadly neoliberal claim that all problems are individual, when the roots of such problems lie in larger systemic forces? What role might universities fulfill in preserving and scrutinizing cultural memory in order to ensure our current generation and the next are on the right side of history? What might it mean to return to and rethink critically the ideals of the 1960s and 1970s, when university life was defined by students and faculty? What will it take to give power back to faculty and students so they can play a major role in the governing of higher education? How might faculty and students best collaborate in order to eliminate the tsunami of exploitative part-time labor that has been employed by the corporatized university to de-skill and punish faculty since the 1970s?[27]

At the very least, students and others need the historical knowledge, critical tools, and analytical skills to be able to understand the underlying factors and forces that gave rise to Trump's ascendency to the presidency of the United States. Understanding how "the possible triumph in America of a fascist-tinged authoritarian regime" is poised to destroy "a fragile liberal democracy" is the first step toward a viable and sustained resistance.[28] It is crucial to repeat that this authoritarian regime draws on a fascist legacy that not only decreed the death of the civic imagination but also unleashed nothing short of a mass-scale terror and violence.

Historical memory is too easily subverted by manu-factured ignorance. The corporate-controlled media and entertainment industries make it easy to forget that Trump is more than the product of the deep-seated racism, attacks on the welfare state, and corporate-centered priorities that have characterized the Republican Party since the 1980s. He is also the result of a Democratic Party that has sepa-rated itself from the needs of working people, minorities of color, and young people by becoming nothing more than the party of the financial elite. There is a certain dreadful irony in the fact that the neoliberal wing of the Democratic Party has been quick to condemn Trump and his coterie as demagogic and authoritarian. What cannot be forgotten is that this is the same ruling elite who gave us the sur-veillance state, bailed out Wall Street, ushered in the mass incarceration state, and punished whistleblowers. Chris Hedges is right in arguing that the Democratic Party is an "appendage of the consumer society" and its embrace of "neoliberalism and [refusal] to challenge the imperial wars empowered the economic and political structures that destroyed our democracy and gave rise to Trump."[29] The only answer the Democratic Party has to Trump is to strike back when he overreaches and make a case for the good old days when they were in power. What they refuse to acknowledge is that their policies helped render Trump's victory possible and that what they share with Trump is a mutual support for bankers, the rule of big corporations, neoliberalism, and the erroneous and fatal assumption that capitalism is democracy, and vice versa. What is needed is a new understanding of the political, a new democratic socialist party, and a radical restructuring of politics itself.

At the same time, any confrontation with the current historical moment has to be infused with hope, possibility, and new forms of political practice. While many countries have been transformed into what Stanley Aronowitz calls a repressive "national security state,"[30] there are signs that authoritarianism in its various versions is currently being challenged, especially by young people, and that the radical imagination is still alive. Marine Le Pen's National Front Party lost the presidential election in France; Jeremy Corbyn's Labor Party just dealt a blow in the United Kingdom to Theresa May and the conservatives in the 2016 election; and young people under thirty across the globe are marching for a radical democracy. No society is without resistance, and hope can never be reduced to a mere abstraction. Hope has to be informed, militant, and concrete.

Nothing will change unless people begin to take seriously the deeply rooted structural, cultural, and subjective underpinnings of oppression in the United States and what it might require to make such issues meaningful, in both personal and collective ways, in order to make them critical and transformative. This is fundamentally a pedagogical as well as a political concern. As Charles Derber has explained, knowing "how to express possibilities and convey them authentically and persuasively seems crucially important"[31] if any viable form of resistance is to take shape. Trumpism normalizes official falsehoods, intolerance, violence, and pro-fascist social manifestations. Taken as a whole, these conditions do not simply repress independent thought, but constitute their own mode of indoctrinated perceptions that are reinforced through a diverse set of cultural apparatuses ranging from local gun clubs and hate groups to corporate media such as Fox News and online commercial operations like Infowars and Breitbart News.

The dark clouds of an American-style fascism are brewing on the horizon and can be seen in a countless number of Trump's statements and orders, including his instructions to the Department of Homeland Security to draw up a list of "Muslim organizations and individuals that, in the language of the executive action, have been 'radicalized.'"[32] Given Trump's intolerance of criticism and dissent, it is plausible that this list could be expanded to target Black Lives Matter activists, investigative journalists, feminists, community organizers, university professors, and other outspoken left-wing intellectuals. One indication that the Trump regime is compiling a larger list of alleged wrongdoers was the Trump transition team's request that the Energy Department deliver a list of the names of individuals who had worked on climate change. Under public pressure, the Trump regime later rescinded this request.[33] Couple these political interventions with the unprecedented attack on the media and the barring of the *New York Times*, CNN, and other alleged "fake news" media outlets from press conferences, and what becomes clear is that the professional institutions that make democracy possible are not only under siege but face the threat of being abolished. Trumpists' constant cry of "fake news" to discredit critical media outlets is part of a massive disinformation campaign designed to undermine investigative journalism, eyewitness news, fact-based analysis, reason, evidence, and any knowledge-based standard of judgment.

Despite everything, optimism and resistance are in the air, and the urgency of mass action has a renewed relevance. Workers, young people, environmental activists, demonstrations against the massive tax cuts for the rich posing as health-care reform, along with numerous expressions of protest against Trump's draconian policies are popping up all over the United States and symbolize an emerging collective opposition to pro-fascist tendencies.[34] As I pointed out earlier, thousands of scientists have rallied against the assaults being waged on scientific inquiry, the veracity of catastrophic climate change, and other forms of evidence-based research, and are planning further marches in the future.[35] Mass protests movements at the local level are coming into play, as seen in the Moral Monday movement and the anti-pipeline campaigns. In addition, a number of big city mayors are refusing to obey Trump's orders; demonstrations are taking place every day throughout the country; students are mobilizing on campuses; and all over the globe women are marching for their rights. Many people entering politics for the first time are demonstrating for affordable health care, a social wage, and a jobs program, especially for young people. Some individuals and groups are working hard to build a mass movement organized against militarism, inequality, racism, the increasing possibility of nuclear war, and the ecological destabilization of the planet.

We are witnessing the imminent emergence of new forms of resistance willing to support broad-based struggles intent on producing ongoing forms of nonviolent resistance at all levels of society. It is important to heed Rabbi Michael Lerner's insistence that a democratically minded public, comprised of workers and activists of various stripes, needs a new language of critique and possibility, one that embraces a movement for a world of love, courage, and justice while being committed to a mode of nonviolence in which the means are as ethical as the ends sought by such struggles.[36] Such a call is as historically mindful as it is insightful, drawing upon legacies of nonviolent resistance left to us by renowned activists as diverse as Bertrand Russell, Saul Alinsky, Paulo Freire, and Martin Luther King Jr. Despite their diverse projects and methods, these voices for change all shared a commitment to a fearless collective struggle in which nonviolent strategies rejected passivity and compromise to engage in powerful expressions of opposition. To be successful, such struggles have to be coordinated, focused, and relentless. Single-issue movements will have to join with others in supporting both a comprehensive politics and a mass collective movement. We would do well to heed the words of the great abolitionist Frederick Douglass:

> It is not light that is needed, but fire; it is not the gentle shower, but thunder. We need the storm, the whirlwind, the earthquake. The feeling of the nation must be quickened; the conscience of the

nation must be roused; the propriety of the nation must be startled; the hypocrisy of the nation must be exposed; and the crimes against God and man must be proclaimed and denounced.[37]

The political repression of our times requires that we work together to redefine politics and challenge the pro-corporate two-party system. In the process, we will reclaim the struggle to produce meaningful educational visions and practices, find new ways to change individual and collective consciousness, engage in meaningful dialogue with people living at the margins of the political landscape, and overcome the factionalism of single-issue movements in order to build broad-based social movements. Proto-fascist conditions are with us again. Fortunately, Trump's arrogance as a champion of such forces is not going entirely unchecked as the great collective power of resistance to his regime deepens. Mass actions are taking place with renewed urgency every day. Facing the challenge of fascism will not be easy, but Americans are marching, protesting, and organizing in record-breaking numbers. Hopefully, mass indignation will evolve into a worldwide movement whose power will be on the side of justice not impunity, bridges not walls, dignity not disrespect, kindness not cruelty. The American nightmare is not something happening somewhere else to someone else. It's happening here, to us. The time to wake up is now. To quote James Baldwin's letter to Angela Davis:

Some of us, white and black, know how great a price has already been paid to bring into existence a new consciousness, a new people, an unprecedented nation. If we know, and do nothing, we are worse than the murderers hired in our name. If we know, then we must fight for your life as though it were our own—which it is—and render impassable with our bodies the corridor to the gas chamber. For, if they take you in the morning, they will be coming for us that night.

In the end, there is no democracy without informed citizens, no justice without a language critical of injustice, and no change without a broad-based movement of collective resistance.

NOTES

INTRODUCTION

1. On the issue of inequality, see Michael Yates, *The Great Inequality* (New York: Routledge, 2016).

2. Richard Wike, Bruce Stokes, Jacob Poushter and Jane L. Fetterolf, "U.S. Image Suffers as Publics Around World Question Trump's Leadership," *Pew Research Center* (June 26, 2017). Accessed February 12, 2018: www.pewglobal.org/2017/06/26/u-s-image-suffers-as-publics-around-world-question-trumps-leadership/

3. Cited in Thomas B. Edsall, "The Self-destruction of American Democracy," *New York Times* (November 30, 2017). Accessed February 12, 2018: www.nytimes.com/2017/11/30/opinion/trump-putin-destruction-democracy.html

4. For instance, see Andrew Spannaus, "Poverty Fuels European Extremism," *CounterPunch* (June 1, 2017). Accessed February 12, 2018: www.counterpunch.org/2017/06/01/poverty-fuels-european-extremism/

5. Gwynn Guilford, "Harvard research suggests that an entire global generation has lost faith in democracy," *Quartz Media* (November 30, 2016). Accessed February 13, 2018: qz.com/848031/harvard-research-suggests-that-an-entire-global-generation-has-lost-faith-in-democracy/

6. Roberto Stefan Foa and Yascha Mounk, "The Democratic Disconnect," *Journal of Democracy* 27:3 (July 2016). Accessed February 13, 2018: www.journalofdemocracy.org/sites/default/files/Foa%26Mounk-27-3.pdf

7. Masha Gessen, "The Autocrat's Language," *The New York Review of Books* (May 13, 2017). Accessed February 13, 2018: www.nybooks.com/daily/2017/05/13/the-autocrats-language/

8. Editorial Board, "Donald Trump Is a Unique Threat to American Democracy," *Washington Post* (July 22, 2016). Accessed February 13, 2018: www.washingtonpost.com/opinions/donald-trump-is-a-unique-threat-to-american-democracy/2016/07/22/a6d823cc-4f4f-11e6-aa14-e0c1087f7583_story.html

9. Terray Sylvester, "Suspect in fatal Portland attack yells about 'free speech' at hearing," *Reuters* (May 30, 2017). Accessed February 13, 2018: www.reuters.com/article/us-usa-muslims-portland-idUSKBN18Q11F

10. On the history of right-wing populism, see David Neiwert, *ALT-America: The Rise of the Racial Right in the Age of Trump* (London: Verso, 2017) and Steve Fraser, *The Limousine Liberal* (New York: Basic Books, 2016).

11. Masha Gessen, "Trump's Incompetence Won't Save Our Democ-

racy," *New York Times* (June 2, 2017). Accessed February 13, 2018: www.nytimes.com/2017/06/02/opinion/sunday/trumps-incompetence-wont-save-our-democracy.html

12. Ibid.

13. Brad Evans and David Theo Goldberg, "Histories of Violence: Violence to Thought," *Los Angeles Review of Books* (July 10, 2017). Accessed February 13, 2018: lareviewofbooks.org/article/histories-of-violence-violence-to-thought/#!

14. See Henry A. Giroux, *The Violence of Organized Forgetting: Thinking Beyond America's Disimagination Machine* (San Francisco: City Lights Books, 2014).

15. Cited in Ismail Khalidi, Naomi Wallace, "Trump-ocalypse Now?," *American Theater* (October 24, 2017). Accessed February 13, 2018: www.americantheatre.org/2017/10/24/trump-ocalypse-now/

16. Brad Evans, "A World Without Books Is A World Foreclosed," *The Reading List* (June 1, 2017). Accessed February 13, 2018: www.theread-inglists.com/brad-evans-reading-list/

17. Albert Camus, *The Plague* (New York: Vintage, 1991), p. 308.

18. Dan Balz and Scott Clement, "Poll: Trump's Performance Lags Behind Even Tepid Public Expectations," *Washington Post* (November 5, 2017). Accessed February 16, 2018: www.washingtonpost.com/politics/poll-trumps-performance-lags-behind-even-tepid-public-expectations/2017/11/04/35d2a912-bf4d-11e7-959c-fe2b598d8c00_story.html?utm_term=.ced811484d6d

19. Lucy P. Marcus, "Truth, Lies and Trust in the Age of Brexit and Trump," *The Guardian* (September 16, 2016). Accessed February 13, 2018: www.theguardian.com/business/2016/sep/16/truth-lies-and-trust-in-the-age-of-brexit-and-trump

20. Shaun King, "Hillary Clinton Has Been Caught Lying for a Year in Her Email Scandal," *New York Daily News* (May 26, 2016). Accessed February 13, 2018: www.nydailynews.com/news/politics/king-clinton-caught-lying-year-email-scandal-article-1.2651043

21. Matthew Yglesias, "The Bullshitter-in-Chief," *Vox* (May 30, 2017). Accessed February 13, 2018: www.vox.com/policy-and-politics/2017/5/30/15631710/trump-bullshit

22. Ibid.

23. Ibid.

24. David Leonhardt, "Lies vs. B.S." *New York Times* (May 31, 2017). Accessed February 13, 2018: www.nytimes.com/2017/05/31/opinion/lies-vs-bs.html?_r=0

25. See, for instance, the now classic Neil Postman, *Amusing Ourselves*

To Death: Public Discourse in the Age of Show Business (New York: Penguin Books, 1985, 2005); On the question of the relationship between capitalism, democracy and the media see, Robert W. McChesney, *Rich Media, Poor Democracy: Communication Politics in Dubious Times* (New York: The New Press, 2015).

26. Anne Case and Sir Angus Deaton, *Mortality and morbidity in the 21st century* (Washington, D.C.: Brookings Institute, 2017). Accessed February 13, 2018: www.brookings.edu/wp-content/uploads/2017/03/casedeaton_sp17_finaldraft.pdf

27. Roger Berkowitz, "Why Arendt Matters: Revisiting 'The Origins of Totalitarianism,'" *Los Angeles Review of Books* (March 18, 2017). Accessed February 13, 2018: lareviewofbooks.org/article/arendt-matters-revisiting-origins-totalitarianism/

28. S.M. "Crackdown: A Plan to Put More Americans in Prison," *The Economist* (May 16, 2017). Accessed February 13, 2018: www.economist.com/blogs/democracyinamerica/2017/05/crackdown

29. See, for instance, a number of insightful articles on police violence against people of color in Maya Schenwar, Joe Macare, and Alana Yu-lan Price, eds., *Who Do You Serve, Who Do You Protect?* (Chicago: Haymarket, 2016).

30. Peter Baker and David E. Sanger, "Trump Says Tillerson Is 'Wasting His Time' on North Korea," *New York Times* (October 1, 2017). Accessed February 13, 2018: www.nytimes.com/2017/10/01/us/politics/trump-tillerson-north-korea.html

31. David Smith and Lauren Gambino. "Booked! Trump, staffers who cried Wolff and a week of fire and fury," *The Guardian* (January 7, 2018). Accessed February 13, 2018: www.theguardian.com/us-news/2018/jan/07/michael-wolff-trump-book-fire-fury-reaction. See also, Robert Reich, "Seriously, How Dumb Is Trump," *Huffington Post* (January 7, 2018). Accessed February 13, 2018: www.huffingtonpost.com/entry/seriously-how-dumb-is-trump_us_5a525a1ee4b003133ec8cb66

32. Richard J. Evans, "A Warning from History," *The Nation* (February 28, 2017). Accessed February 13, 2018: www.thenation.com/article/the-ways-to-destroy-democracy/

33. Ibid.

34. Ibid.

35. Cited in Marian Wright Edelman, "Why Are Children Less Valuable than Guns in America? It Is Time to Protect Children," *Children's Defense Fund* (December 8, 2015). Accessed February 16, 2018: https://www.huffingtonpost.com/marian-wright-edelman/why-are-children-less-val_b_8842926.html

36. Editorial Board, "511 Days. 555 Mass Shootings. Zero Action From Congress," *New York Times*, November 6, 2017. Accessed February 13, 2018: www.nytimes.com/interactive/2017/10/02/opinion/editorials/mass-shootings-congress.html?action=click&pgtype=Homepage&clickSource=story-heading&module=span-abc-region&region=span-abc-region&WT.nav=span-abc-region;

Sharon LaFranier, Sarah Cohen and Richard A. Oppel Jr., "How Often Do Mass Shootings Occur? On Average, Every Day, Records Show," *New York Times* (December 2, 2015). Accessed October 2, 2016: Accessed February 13, 2018: www.nytimes.com/2015/12/03/us/how-often-do-mass-shootings-occur-on-average-every-day-records-show.html

37. Kate Murphy and Jordan Rubio, "At Least 28,000 Children and Teens Were Killed by Guns over an 11-Year-Period," *News21* (August 16, 2014). Accessed February 13, 2018: gunwars.news21.com/2014/at-least-28000-children-and-teens-were-killed-by-guns-over-an-11-year-period/

38. Gary Younge, "America's Deserving and Undeserving Dead Children," *TomDispatch* (November 1, 2001). Accessed February 13, 2018: www.tomdispatch.com/post/176201/tomgram%3A_gary_younge,_america's_deserving_and_undeserving_dead_children/

39. Natasja Sheriff, "UN Expert Slams US as Only Nation to Imprison Kids for Life without Parole," *Al Jazeera America* (March 9, 2015). Accessed February 13, 2018: america.aljazeera.com/articles/2015/3/9/un-expert-slams-us-as-only-nation-to-sentence-kids-to-life-without-parole.html

40. See Jessica Feirman with Naomi Goldstein, Emily Haney-Caron, and Jaymes Fairfax Columbo, *Debtors' Prison for Kids? The High Costs of Fines and Fees in the Juvenile Justice System* (Juvenile Law Center, 2016). Accessed February 13, 2018: debtorsprison.jlc.org/#!/map

41. John W. Whitehead, "Another Brick in the Wall: Children of the American Police State," *CounterPunch* (August 25, 2016). Accessed February 13, 2018: www.counterpunch.org/2016/08/25/another-brick-in-the-wall-children-of-the-american-police-state/

42. Juan González and Amy Goodman, "On Tyranny: Yale Historian Timothy Snyder on How the U.S. Can Avoid Sliding into Authoritarianism," *Democracy Now!* (May 30, 2017). Accessed February 13, 2018: www.democracynow.org/2017/5/30/on_tyranny_yale_historian_timothy_snyder?utm_source=Democracy+Now%21&utm_campaign=b-9c7f250d4-Daily_Digest&utm_medium=email&utm_term=0_fa2346a853-b9c7f250d4-190213053

43. Miriam Jordan, "Trump Administration Says that Nearly 200,000 Salvadorans Must Leave," *New York Times* (January 8, 2018). Accessed February 13, 2018: www.nytimes.com/2018/01/08/us/salvadorans-tps-end.

html?emc=edit_na_20180108&nl=breaking-news&nlid=15581699&ref=c-ta&_r=0

44. Alex Honneth, *Pathologies of Reason* (New York: Columbia University Press, 2009), p. 188.

45. Deepti Hajela and Michael Tarm, "Trump Travel Ban Sparks Protests, Airport Chaos," *Hamilton Spectator* (January 30, 2017), p. A6.

46. Alexander Mallin, M.L. Neste, "Controversial Trump adviser Sebastian Gorka leaves White House post," *ABC NEWS* (August 26, 2017). Accessed August 28, 2017: Accessed February 13, 2018: abcnews.go.com/Politics/controversial-trump-adviser-sebastian-gorka-leaves-white-house/story?id=49427323

47. Ta-Nehisi Coates, "The First White President," *The Atlantic* (October 2017) Accessed February 13, 2018: www.theatlantic.com/magazine/archive/2017/10/the-first-white-president-ta-nehisi-coates/537909/

48. Ibid.

49. Cornel West, "Ta-Nehisi Coates Is the Neoliberal Face of the Black Freedom Struggle," *The Guardian* (December 17, 2017). Accessed February 13, 2018: www.theguardian.com/commentisfree/2017/dec/17/ta-nehisi-coates-neoliberal-black-struggle-cornel-west

50. Ibid.

51. This issue has been brilliantly explored by Zygmunt Bauman in a number of books. See especially *Wasted Lives* (London: Polity Press, 2004) and *Identity: Conversations with Benedetto Vecchi* (London: Polity Press, 2004).

52. Marie Luise Knott, *Unlearning with Hannah Arendt*, trans. David Dollenmayer (New York: Other Press, 2011), p.17.

53. Editorial, "Donald Trump's Muslim Ban Is Cowardly and Dangerous," *New York Times* (January 28, 2017). Accessed February 13, 2018: www.nytimes.com/2017/01/28/opinion/donald-trumps-muslim-ban-is-cowardly-and-dangerous.html

54. Ibid.

55. Meara Sharma interviews Claudia Rankine, "Blackness as the Second Person," *Guernica* (November 17, 2014). Accessed February 13, 2018: www.guernicamag.com/interviews/blackness-as-the-second-person/

56. Michael M. Grynbaum, "Trump Strategist Stephen Bannon Says Media Should 'Keep Its Mouth Shut,'" *New York Times* (January 26, 2017). Accessed February 13, 2018: www.nytimes.com/2017/01/26/business/media/stephen-bannon-trump-news-media.html?_r=0

57. Naomi Klein, "Sandy's Devastation Opens Space for Action on Climate Change and Progressive Reform," *Democracy Now!* (November 15, 2012). Accessed February 13, 2018: www.democracynow.org/2012/11/15/naomi_klein_sandys_devastation_opens_space

58. Cited in Frederick Douglass, "West India Emancipation" speech at Canandaigua, New York on August 3, 1857. Accessed February 13, 2018: www.blackpast.org/1857-frederick-douglass-if-there-no-struggle-there-no-progress#sthash.8Eoaxpmo.dpuf

CHAPTER ONE

1. Byung-Chul Han, *In the Swarm: Digital Prospects*, tr. Erik Butler (Cambridge, MA: MIT Press, 2017), p. 15.

2. Les Leopold, "Why America has more prisoners than any police state," *AlterNet* (March 7, 2016). Accessed February 13, 2018: www.rawstory.com/2016/03/why-america-has-more-prisoners-than-any-police-state/

3. Robert Kuttner, "George Orwell and the Power of a Well-Placed Lie," *Bill Moyers and Company* (January 25, 2017). Accessed February 13, 2018: billmoyers.com/story/orwell-hitler-trump/

4. Hannah Arendt, "Hannah Arendt: From an Interview with Roger Errera," *New York Review of Books* (October 26, 1978). Accessed February 13, 2018: www.nybooks.com/articles/1978/10/26/hannah-arendt-from-an-interview/

5. Aaron Blake, "Kellyanne Conway Says Donald Trump's Team Has 'Alternative Facts.' Which Pretty Much Says It All," *Washington Post* (January 22, 2017). Accessed February 13, 2018: www.washingtonpost.com/news/the-fix/wp/2017/01/22/kellyanne-conway-says-donald-trumps-team-has-alternate-facts-which-pretty-much-says-it-all/?utm_term=.69ac680b5854

6. Bill Moyers, "Trump's Queen of Bull Hits a Bump in the Road," *Moyers & Company* (February 7, 2017). Accessed February 13, 2018: billmoyers.com/story/trumps-queen-of-bull-hits-a-bump-in-the-road/

7. Adam Gopnik, "Orwell's '1984' and Trump's America," *The New Yorker* (January 27, 2017). Accessed February 13, 2018: www.newyorker.com/news/daily-comment/orwells-1984-and-trumps-america

8. Viktor Frankl, *The Will to Meaning* (New York: Penguin, 1988), p. 21.

9. Masha Gessen, "Bring Back Hypocrisy! The American President and the American Way of Lying," *New York Times Sunday Review* (February 19, 2017), p. SR6.

10. Evans and Goldberg, "Histories of Violence."

11. Josh Dawsey, Isaac Arnsdorf, Nahal Toosi and Michael Crowley, "White House Nixed Holocaust Statement Naming Jews," *Politico* (February 3, 2017). Accessed February 13, 2018: readersupportednews.org/news-section2/318-66/41742-white-house-nixed-holocaust-statement-naming-jews

12. Kali Holloway, "Time Is Already Running Out on Our Democracy, Scholar Says," *AlterNet* (February 13, 2017). Ac-

cessed February 13, 2018: www.alternet.org/election-2016/
time-already-running-out-our-democracy-says-expert

13. Adam Gopnik, "Orwell's '1984' and Trump's America," *The New Yorker* (January 27, 2017). Accessed February 13, 2018: www.newyorker.com/news/daily-comment/orwells-1984-and-trumps-america

14. This term comes from Erin Ramlo in a final paper in my class titled, "Avoiding the Void: Mapping Addiction and Neoliberal Subjectivity," May 2016.

15. See, for example, Michael Wolff, *Fire and Fury: Inside the Trump White House* (New York: Harper, 2018).

16. John Wight, "Muslim Ban, White Supremacy and Fascism in Our Time," *CounterPunch* (January 31, 2017). Accessed February 13, 2018: www.counterpunch.org/2017/01/31/muslim-bans-white-supremacy-and-fascism-in-our-time/

17. See, for instance, Henry A. Giroux, *Hearts of Darkness* (New York: Routledge, 2010); Henry A. Giroux, *America's Addiction to Terrorism* (New York: Monthly Review Press, 2016).

18. This theme is taken up powerfully by a number of theorists. See C. Wright Mills, *The Sociological Imagination* (New York: Oxford University Press, 2000); Richard Sennett, *The Fall of Public Man* (New York: Norton, 1974); Zygmunt Bauman, *In Search of Politics* (Stanford, CA: Stanford University Press, 1999); and Henry A. Giroux, *Public Spaces, Private Lives* (Lanham, MD: Rowman and Littlefield, 2001).

19. Susan Dunn, "Trump's 'America First' Has Ugly Echoes from U.S. History," *CNN.Com* (April 28, 2016). Accessed February 13, 2018: www.cnn.com/2016/04/27/opinions/trump-america-first-ugly-echoes-dunn/

20. Ibid.

21. Matt Ferner, "More Bomb Threats Close Jewish Community Centers Across The Nation," *The Huffington Post* (February 20, 2017). Accessed February 13, 2018: www.huffingtonpost.com/entry/bomb-threats-jewish-community-centers_us_58ab56a5e4b0f077b3ecfec4

22. Glenn Kessler and Michelle Ye Hee Lee, "Fact-checking President Trump's Address to Congress," *Washington Post* (February 28, 2017). Accessed February 13, 2018: www.washingtonpost.com/news/fact-checker/wp/2017/02/28/fact-checking-president-trumps-address-to-congress/?utm_term=.f1cb25a601cb

23. Ibid., Adam Gopnik, "Orwell's '1984' and Trump's America."

24. Frank Bruni, "Donald Trump Will Numb You," *New York Times Sunday Review* (February 19, 2017), p. SR3.

25. Charles J. Sykes, "Why Nobody Cares the President Is Lying," *New York Times* (February 4, 2017). Accessed February 13, 2018: www.nytimes.

com/2017/02/04/opinion/sunday/why-nobody-cares-the-president-is-lying.
html

26. Glenn Kessler, "In a 30-minute interview, President Trump made
24 false or misleading claims," *Washington Post* (December 29, 2017).
Accessed February 13, 2018: www.washingtonpost.com/news/fact-checker/
wp/2017/12/29/in-a-30-minute-interview-president-trump-made-24-false-
or-misleading-claims/?utm_term=.c83cf4f97f37

27. Ned Resnikoff, "Trump's lies have a purpose. They are an assault on
democracy." *Think Progress* (November 27, 2016). Accessed February 13,
2018: thinkprogress.org/when-everything-is-a-lie-power-is-the-only-truth-
1e641751d150#.ux57mwjsz

28. Masha Gessen, "The Most Frightening Aspect of Trump's
Tax Triumph," *The New Yorker* (December 21, 2017). Accessed
February 13, 2018: www.newyorker.com/news/our-columnists/
the-most-frightening-aspect-of-trumps-tax-triumph

29. Peter Baker and Michael Tackett, "Trump Says His 'Nuclear Button'
Is 'Much Bigger' Than North Korea's," *New York Times* (January 2, 2018).
Accessed February 13, 2018: www.nytimes.com/2018/01/02/us/politics/
trump-tweet-north-korea.html?_r=0

30. See, for instance, Jeremy Scahill' s searing exposé of Mike
Pence's religious fundamentalism and the religious fanatics that he
associates with, all of whom now have access to the White House.
Jeremy Scahill, "Mike Pence Will Be the Most Powerful Christian Supremacist in U.S. History," *The Intercept* (November 15,
2016). Accessed February 13, 2018: theintercept.com/2016/11/15/
mike-pence-will-be-the-most-powerful-christian-supremacist-in-us-history/

31. This issue has been brilliantly explored by Zygmunt Bauman in a
number of books. See, especially, *Wasted Lives* (London: Polity Press, 2004)
and *Identity: Conversations with Benedetto Vecchi* (London: Polity Press, 2004).

32. Marie Louise Knott, *Unlearning With Hannah Arendt*, trans. David
Dollenmayer (New York: Other Press, 2011), p.17.

33. Juliet Eilperin, "Trump signs executive order to expand drilling off
America's coasts: 'We're opening it up,'" *Washington Post* (April 28, 2017).
Accessed February 13, 2018: www.washingtonpost.com/news/energy-en-
vironment/wp/2017/04/28/trump-signs-executive-order-to-expand-off-
shore-drilling-and-analyze-marine-sanctuaries-oil-and-gas-potential/?utm_
term=.77e549217a21

34. Matthew Rosenberg, "New C.I.A. Deputy Director, Gina Haspel,
Had Leading Role in Torture," *New York Times* (February 2, 2017). Accessed
February 13, 2018: www.nytimes.com/2017/02/02/us/politics/cia-depu-
ty-director-gina-haspel-torture-thailand.html

35. Robert L. Borosage, "Republicans in Congress Think You're an Idiot: The GOP tax bill should be toxic to everyone who is not ultra-rich," *The Nation* (November 17, 2017). Accessed February 13, 2018: www.thenation. com/article/republicans-in-congress-think-youre-an-idiot/

36. Michael M. Grynbaum, "Trump Strategist Stephen Bannon Says Media Should 'Keep Its Mouth Shut,'" *New York Times* (January 26, 2017). Accessed February 13, 2018: www.nytimes.com/2017/01/26/business/media/stephen-bannon-trump-news-media.html?_r=0

37. Ibid.

38. Joe Macare, "Real Journalism Is the Enemy of Injustice and Deceit" (February 21, 2017). Sent through personal correspondence.

39. Julie Hirschfeld Davis and Matthew Rosenberg, "With False Claims, Trump Attacks Media on Turnout and Intelligence Rift," *New York Times* (January 21, 2017). Accessed February 13, 2018: www.nytimes. com/2017/01/21/us/politics/trump-white-house-briefing-inauguration-crowd-size.html?_r=0

40. Michael M. Grynbaum, "Trump Calls the News Media the 'Enemy of the American People," *New York Times* (February 17, 2017). Accessed February 13, 2018: www.nytimes.com/2017/02/17/business/trump-calls-the-news-media-the-enemy-of-the-people.html?_r=0

41. Roger Cohen, "The Unmaking of Europe," *New York Times* (February 24, 2017). Accessed February 13, 2018: www.nytimes.com/2017/02/24/opinion/the-unmaking-of-europe.html

42. Garance Burke, "AP Exclusive: DHS Weighed Nat Guard for Immigration Roundups" *AP News* (February 18, 2017). Accessed February 13, 2018: apnews.com/5508111d59554a33be8001bdac4ef830?utm_campaign=SocialFlow&utm_source=Twitter&utm_medium=AP

43. Greg Elmer and Paula Todd, "Don't Be a Loser: Or How Trump Turned the Republican Primaries into an Episode of *The Apprentice*," *Television and News Media* 17(7), p. 660.

44. Frank Rich, "Trump's Speech Gave Us America the Ugly. Don't Let It Become Prophesy," *Reader Supported News* (January 22, 2017). Accessed February 13, 2018: readersupportednews.org/opinion2/277-75/41524-focus-trumps-speech-gave-us-america-the-ugly-dont-let-it-become-prophesy

45. Rebecca Gordon, "Tomgram: Rebecca Gordon, No 'New Normal,'" *TomDispatch.com* (November 20, 2016). Accessed February 13, 2018: www. tomdispatch.com/blog/176212/. Examples of this media response are discussed also in Neal Gabler, "And So It Begins: Normalizing the Election," *Moyers & Company* (November 23, 2016). Accessed February 13, 2018: billmoyers.com/story/media-normalizing-election/

46. See Jennifer Brett, "Oprah Panned for Saying She Feels Hope after

Trump Election," *AJC.com* (November 12, 2016). Accessed February 13, 2018: buzz.blog.ajc.com/2016/11/12/oprah-trump/

47. Nicholas Kristof, "Gritting Our Teeth and Giving President Trump a Chance," *New York Times* (November 9, 2016). Accessed February 13, 2018: www.nytimes.com/2016/11/10/opinion/gritting-our-teeth-and-giving-president-trump-a-chance.html?_r=1

48. Cited by Irish Central Staff, "Bill Gates Says Trump Could Lead America like JFK," *IrishCentral.com* (January 6, 2017). Accessed February 13, 2018: www.irishcentral.com/news/politics/bill-gates-says-trump-could-lead-america-like-jfk

49. As Robert Reich points out, while Trump's lies become more obvious, there is still a failure on the part of the established media to cut through a mountain of apologetic language when reporting on Trump and his policies. See, Robert Reich, "Straight Talk about Trump," *RobertReich.org* (January 12, 2018). Accessed February 13, 2018: robertreich.org/post/169632080345

50. Jeremy B. White, "A third of Americans think the media is the 'enemy of the people' following Trump's repeated 'fake news' attacks," *The Independent* (December 4, 2017). Accessed February 13, 2018: www.independent.co.uk/news/world/americas/us-politics/americans-media-poll-trust-trump-fake-news-attacks-a8091991.html

51. Michelle Goldberg, "Everyone in Trumpworld Knows He's an Idiot," *New York Times* (January 4, 2018). Accessed February 13, 2018: www.nytimes.com/2018/01/04/opinion/fire-fury-wolff-trump-book.html

52. Charles Blow, "Donald Trump, This Is Not Normal," *New York Times* (December 19, 2016). Accessed February 13, 2018: www.nytimes.com/2016/12/19/opinion/donald-trump-this-is-not-normal.html?_r=0

53. Bill Trott, "Bannon Role in Trump Administration Sets Off Critical Firestorm," *Reuters Business News* (November 15, 2016). Accessed February 13, 2018: www.reuters.com/article/us-usa-trump-bannon-profile-idUSKB-N13A2R1?mod=related&channelName=politicsNews

54. Discussion of Arendt can be found in: Bill Dixon, "Totalitarianism and the Sand Storm," *Hannah Arendt Center* (February 3, 2014), accessed February 13, 2018: hac.bard.edu/news/?p=12466; Marie Luise Knott, *Unlearning with Hannah Arendt*, trans. by David Dollenmayer (New York: Other Press 2011), p.17. For primary sources on this topic, see: Hannah Arendt, *The Origins of Totalitarianism* (New York: Houghton Mifflin Harcourt, 2001); Sheldon S. Wolin, *Democracy Incorporated: Managed Democracy and the Specter of Inverted Totalitarianism* (Princeton, NJ: Princeton University Press, 2008); Robert O. Paxton, *The Anatomy of Fascism* (New York: Vintage Books, 2004).

55. For a particularly excellent abridged analysis of fascism by Paxton, see Robert O. Paxton, "The Five Stages of Fascism," *The Journal of Modern History* 70:1 (March 1998), pp. 1–123.

56. Robert O. Paxton, *Anatomy of Fascism*, p. 218.

57. Ibid., pp. 41–42.

58. David Neiwert, *ALT-America: The Rise of the Racial Right in the Age of Trump* (London: Verso, 2017), pp. 355–356.

59. Juan González and Amy Goodman, "On Tyranny: Yale Historian Timothy Snyder on How the U.S. Can Avoid Sliding into Authoritarianism," *Democracy Now!* (May 30, 2017). Accessed February 13, 2018: www.democracynow.org/2017/5/30/on_tyranny_yale_historian_timothy_snyder

60. Ibid., Frank Rich, "Trump's Speech Gave Us America the Ugly. Don't Let It Become Prophesy."

61. Will Oremus, "How Fox News Described Trump's Speech: 'Muscular,' 'Masterful,' 'Completely Nonpartisan,'" *Slate* (January 20, 2017). Accessed February 13, 2018: www.slate.com/blogs/the_slatest/2017/01/20/how_fox_news_described_trump_s_inaugural_address_muscular_masterful_completely.html

62. Cited in "'It Might Not Be Good for America, But It's Good for Us': How the Media Got Rich on Trump's Rise," *Democracy Now!* (November 9, 2016). Accessed February 13, 2018: www.democracynow.org/2016/11/9/it_might_not_be_good_for

63. Jesse Druckerjan, "Kushner's Financial Ties to Israel Deepen Even With Mideast Diplomatic Role," *New York Times* (January 7, 2018). Accessed February 13, 2018: www.nytimes.com/2018/01/07/business/jared-kushner-israel.html

64. Roger Cohen, "The Banal Belligerence of Donald Trump," *New York Times* (January 24, 2017). Accessed February 13, 2018: www.nytimes.com/2017/01/24/opinion/the-banal-belligerence-of-donald-trump.html?smprod=nytcore-ipad&smid=nytcore-ipad-share&_r=1

65. Todd Gitlin, "Welcome to the Vortex," *Open Democracy* (January 7, 2017). Accessed February 13, 2018: www.commondreams.org/views/2017/01/07/welcome-vortex

66. Ted Johnson, "NPR Explains Why It Doesn't Label Some Donald Trump Statements 'Lies,'" *Variety* (January 25, 2017). Accessed February 13, 2018: variety.com/2017/biz/news/npr-donald-trump-lies-1201969581/

67. Amy Goodman, "Is the President a "Serial Fabricator"? Fired FBI Director Comey Says Trump Repeatedly Lies," *Democracy Now!* (June 9, 2017). Accessed February 13, 2018: www.democracynow.org/2017/6/9/is_the_president_a_serial_fabricator

68. James Traub, "The United States of America is Deca-

dent and Depraved," *Foreign Policy* (December 19, 2017). Accessed February 13, 2018: foreignpolicy.com/2017/12/19/the-united-states-of-america-is-decadent-and-depraved/

69. Charles J. Sykes, "Why Nobody Cares the President Is Lying," *New York Times Sunday Review* (February 4, 2017). Accessed February 13, 2018: www.nytimes.com/2017/02/04/opinion/sunday/why-nobody-cares-the-president-is-lying.html

70. David Leonhardt and Stuart A. Thompson, "Trump's Lies," *New York Times* (June 23, 2017). Accessed February 13, 2018: www.nytimes.com/interactive/2017/06/23/opinion/trumps-lies.html?_r=0. As Sonam Sheth points out, the *New York Times* printed a full page in the opinion section of the paper to reference "nearly every lie President Donald Trump had publicly told since taking office just over five months ago. The list includes contradictions by Trump on a slew of topics, like the Iraq War, NATO, the administration's travel ban, the crowd size at Trump's inauguration, and the ongoing controversy over Russia's interference in the 2016 election and the Trump campaign's possible role in it. Trump has contradicted himself on a regular basis and said many misleading statements since taking office and during the presidential campaign." Sonam Sheth, "The New York Times used a full page to print 'Trump's lies' since taking office," *SFGate* (June 25, 2017) Accessed February 13, 2018: www.sfgate.com/technology/businessinsider/article/The-New-York-Times-used-a-full-page-to-print-all-11245918.php. See also, Bill Moyer's insightful comments on the *Times* piece and the political significance of Trump's endless lying. Bill Moyers, "All of Donald Trump's Lies," *Moyers & Company* (June 26, 2017). Accessed February 13, 2018: billmoyers.com/story/donald-trumps-lies/

71. Jonathan Martin, Maggie Haberman and Alexander Burnsnov, "Why Trump Stands by Roy Moore, Even as It Fractures His Party," *New York Times* (November 25, 2017). Accessed February 13, 2018: www.nytimes.com/2017/11/25/us/politics/trump-roy-moore-mcconnell-alabama-senate.html?_r=1

72. Kelefa Sanneh, "Secret Admirers: The Conservative Intellectuals Smitten with Trump," *The New Yorker* (January 9, 2017). Accessed February 13, 2018: www.newyorker.com/magazine/2017/01/09/intellectuals-for-trump

73. For two excellent sources on the alt-right, see David Neiwert, *ALT-America: The Rise of the Racial Right in the Age of Trump* (London: Verso, 2017) and Nancy MacLean, *Democracy in Chains: The Deep History of the Radical Right's Stealth Plan for America* (New York: Viking, 2017).

74. Sanneh, "Secret Admirers."

75. Neal Gabler, "And So It Begins: Normalizing the Election," *Moyers*

& Company (November 23, 2016). Accessed February 13, 2018: billmoyers.com/story/media-normalizing-election/

76. Frank Rich, "After Trump," *New York Magazine* (November 13, 2017). Accessed February 13, 2018: nymag.com/daily/intelligencer/2017/11/frank-rich-trumpism-after-trump.html

77. George Yancy, personal correspondence with the author.

78. See, for instance, "A Handbook For Resistance" in the January 2017 issue of *In These Times*; the December 5, 2016 issue of *The Nation* on "How to Fight Back"; Anthony DiMaggio, "The Anti-Trump Uprising: Forging a Path Forward in Uncertain Times," *CounterPunch* (December 15, 2016), accessed February 13, 2018: www.counterpunch.org/2016/12/15/the-anti-trump-uprising-forging-a-path-forward-in-uncertain-times/; Robin D.G. Kelley, "After Trump," *Boston Review* (November 15, 2016), accessed February 13, 2018: bostonreview.net/forum/after-trump/robin-d-g-kelley-trump-says-go-back-we-say-fight-back; and a resistance manual launched by the Movement for Black Lives, accessed February 13, 2018: www.resistance-manual.org/Resistance_Manual_Home

CHAPTER TWO

1. See Bill Dixon's commentary on Hannah Arendt's philosophy, "Totalitarianism and the Sand Storm," *Hannah Arendt Center* (February 3, 2014). Accessed February 13, 2018: hac.bard.edu/news/?p=12466

2. Abby Martin, "Chris Hedges on Trump, Fascism and the Christian Right," *Telesur* (March 1, 2017), accessed February 16, 2018: www.telesurtv.net/english/news/Chris-Hedges-on-Trump-Fascism-and-the-Christian-Right-20170301-0002.html; Robert Reich, "Trump: The American Fascist," *Moyers & Company* (March 11, 2016), accessed February 16, 2018: www.billmoyers.com/story/trump-the-american-fascist/; Cornel West, "Donald Trump Will Unleash 'Neofascism' in US," *Telesur* (December 1, 2016), accessed February 16, 2018: www.telesurtv.net/english/news/Cornel-West-Donald-Trump-Will-Unleash-Neofascism-in-US-20161201-0033.html; Drucilla Cornell & Stephen D. Seely, "Seven Theses on Trump," *Critical Legal Thinking* (November 28, 2016), accessed February 16, 2018: www.criticallegalthinking.com/2016/11/28/seven-theses-trump/; Peter Dreier, "American Fascist," *CommonDreams* (January 20, 2017), accessed February 16, 2018: www.commondreams.org/views/2017/01/20/american-fascist; the best left analysis I have read comes from John Bellamy Foster, "Neofascism in the White House," *Monthly Review* (April 1, 2017), accessed February 16, 2018: www.monthlyreview.org/2017/04/01/neofascism-in-the-white-house/

3. See for instance the most notable of these comments by Robert Kagan, "This Is How Fascism Comes to America," *Washington Post* (May

18, 2016). Accessed February 16, 2018: www.washingtonpost.com/opinions/this-is-how-fascism-comes-to-america/2016/05/17/c4e32c58-1c47-11e6-8c7b-6931e66333e7_story.html?utm_term=.ab4f0b439dab.

4. Sarah K. Burris, "A Yale Historian Explains to Maher How Trump Resembles 1930s Fascists—and Makes the Russia Connection," *Raw Story* (March 24, 2017). Accessed February 16, 2018: www.rawstory.com/2017/03/watch-a-yale-historian-explains-to-maher-how-trump-resembles-1930s-fascists-and-makes-the-russia-connection/. See also Timothy Snyder, *On Tyranny: Twenty Lessons from the Twentieth Century* (New York: Duggan Books, 2017); Robert O. Paxton, "American Duce: Is Donald Trump a Fascist or a Plutocrat?" *Harper's Magazine* (May 2017), pp. 38–39; and Amy Goodman, "Father of Fascism Studies: Donald Trump Shows Alarming Willingness to Use Fascist Terms & Styles," *Democracy Now!* (March 15, 2016), accessed February 16, 2018: www.democracynow.org/2016/3/15/father_of_fascism_studies_donald_trump

5. Ibid., Paxton, "American Duce: Is Donald Trump a Fascist or a Plutocrat?"

6. Hannah Arendt, *The Origins of Totalitarianism* (New York: Houghton Mifflin Harcourt, 2001); Sheldon S. Wolin, *Democracy Incorporated: Managed Democracy and the Specter of Inverted Totalitarianism* (Princeton, NJ: Princeton University Press, 2008).

7. Neal Gabler, "The Sham Presidency," *Moyers & Company* (May 3, 2017). Accessed February 16, 2018: www.billmoyers.com/story/the-sham-presidency/. This is a particularly weak argument that underestimates gravely the echoes of fascism present in Trump's discourse and policies.

8. Corey Robin, "If authoritarianism is looming in the US, how come Donald Trump looks so weak?" *The Guardian* (January 13, 2018). Accessed February 16, 2018: www.theguardian.com/us-news/commentisfree/2018/jan/13/american-democracy-peril-trump-power

9. Byung-Chul Han, *The Burnout Society* (Stanford, CA: Stanford University Press, 2015), p. 51.

10. Andrew O'Hehir, "Whether Trump Is a Fascist or Is Just a Clown, He's a Threat to Democracy All the Same," *AlterNet* (May 8, 2017). Accessed February 16, 2018: www.alternet.org/right-wing/trump-really-building-fascist-regime-or-it-all-just-showmanship-either-way-threat?akid=15530.40823.ZMvjXo&rd=1&src=newsletter1076583&t=6

11. Victoria Di Grazia, "Many Call Trump a Fascist. 100 Days In, Is He Just a Reactionary Republican?" *The Guardian* (April 30, 2017). Accessed February 16, 2018: www.theguardian.com/commentisfree/2017/apr/30/donald-trump-fascist-republican-100-days

12. Cited in Richard Brody, "Pasolini's Theorem," *The New Yorker*

(April 29, 2017). Accessed February 16, 2018: www.newyorker.com/culture/richard-brody/pasolinis-theorem

13. Jacob Hamburger, "Wendy Brown: 'Who is not a Neoliberal Today?'" *Tocqueville21.com* (January 18, 2018). Accessed February 16, 2018: www.tocqueville21.com/interviews/wendy-brown-not-neoliberal-today/

14. Bess Levin, "Populist Hero Mike Pence Casts Tie-Breaking Vote to Protect Banks from Lawsuits," *Vanity Fair* (October 25, 2017). Accessed February 16, 2018: www.vanityfair.com/news/2017/10/mike-pence-arbitration-rule-vote

15. Ibid.

16. Christopher R. Browning, "Lessons from Hitler's Rise," *New York Review of Books* (April 20, 2017). Accessed February 16, 2018: www.nybooks.com/articles/2017/04/20/lessons-from-hitlers-rise/

17. Adam Gopnik, "Being Honest About Trump," *The New Yorker* (July 14, 2016). Accessed February 16, 2018: www.newyorker.com/news/daily-comment/being-honest-about-trump

18. Chauncey DeVega, "Leading Historian Believes 'It's Pretty Much Inevitable' Trump Will Try to Stage a Coup and Overthrow Democracy," *AlterNet* (May 1, 2017). Accessed February 16, 2018: www.alternet.org/news-amp-politics/leading-historian-believes-its-pretty-much-inevitable-trump-will-try-stage-coup

19. Timothy Snyder, *On Tyranny: Twenty Lessons from the Twentieth Century* (New York: Duggan Books, 2017).

20. Michael Yates, "Honor the Vietnamese, Not the Men Who Killed Them," *Monthly Review* 67:1 (2015). Accessed February 16, 2018: www.monthlyreview.org/2015/05/01/honor-the-vietnamese-not-those-who-killed-them/

21. Hannah Arendt, *The Origins of Totalitarianism*, p. 468.

22. Peter Maass, "Donald Trump's war on journalism has begun. But journalists are not his main target," *The Intercept* (May 28, 2017). Accessed February 16, 2018: www.theintercept.com/2017/05/28/donald-trumps-war-on-journalism-has-begun-but-journalists-are-not-his-main-target/

23. Ibid.

24. Robert Reich, "Trump's Rollback of Civil Rights," *Robert Reich's Blog* (May 30, 2017). Accessed February 16, 2018: www.robertreich.org/post/161257297645

25. Ibid.

26. Phillip Smith, "Why Jeff Sessions' war on weed is a futile pursuit," *Alternet* (January 10, 2018). Accessed February 16, 2018: www.salon.com/2018/01/10/why-jeff-sessions-war-on-weed-is-a-futile-pursuit_partner/

27. *New York Times* Editorial Board, "President Trump's Thing for

Thugs," *New York Times*, November 13, 2017. Accessed February 16, 2018: www.nytimes.com/2017/11/13/opinion/president-trump-authoritarianism.html

28. Jefferson Morley, "Top 5 Bad Hombres Loved by Trump," *AlterNet* (May 3, 2017). Accessed February 16, 2018: www.alternet.org/top-5-bad-hombres-loved-trump

29. Helene Fouquet and Gregory Viscusi, "Paris Exhibition on Nazi Collaboration Sheds Light on Dark Past," *Bloomberg* (December 15, 2014). Accessed February 16, 2018: www.bloomberg.com/news/articles/2014-12-15/paris-exhibition-on-nazi-collaboration-sheds-light-on-dark-past

30. Roger Cohen, "France in the End of Days: Marine le Pen's Road to Victory Is Clear Enough. Can a Pragmatist Stop the Extreme Right?" *New York Times* (April 14, 2017). Accessed February 16, 2018: www.nytimes.com/2017/04/14/opinion/sunday/france-in-the-end-of-days.html

31. Editorial Staff, "10 Popular Companies that Profited in Nazi Concentration Camps," *TopInfo Post* (January 23, 2015). Accessed February 27, 2018: en.azvision.az/news/27422/10-popular-companies-that-profited-in-nazi-concentration-camps-photos.html

32. Alexandra Rosenmann, "Noam Chomsky Unveils America's Deplorable History of Playing Footsie with Fascism," *AlterNet* (October 15, 2016). Accessed February 16, 2018: www.alternet.org/election-2016/noam-chomsky-unveils-americas-deplorable-history-playing-footsie-fascism

33. Cited in Brian Bennett, "'America First,' a Phrase with a Loaded Anti-Semitic and Isolationist History," *LA Times* (January 20, 2017). Accessed February 16, 2018: www.latimes.com/politics/la-na-pol-trump-america-first-20170120-story.html

34. Cited in John Bellamy Foster, "Neofascism in the White House," *Monthly Review* 68:11 (April 1, 2017), p. 4.

35. Michael Brenner, "How Autocracy Will Come To America," *Huffington Post* (November 30, 2016). Accessed February 16, 2018: www.huffingtonpost.com/entry/how-autocracy-will-come-to-america_us_583f559ae4b0c68e047ec72f

36. Felipe Villamor, "Rodrigo Duterte Says Donald Trump Endorses His Violent Antidrug Campaign," *New York Times* (December 3, 2016). Accessed February 16, 2018: www.nytimes.com/2016/12/03/world/asia/philippines-rodrigo-duterte-donald-trump.html

37. See: Amy Goodman "Jeremy Scahill on Trump's Embrace of Duterte's Deadly War on Drugs in the Philippines," *Democracy Now!* (May 25, 2017). Accessed February 16, 2018: www.democracynow.org/2017/5/25/jeremy_scahill_on_trumps_embrace_of

38. The transcript can be see here: www.documentcloud.org/documents/3729123-POTUS-RD-Doc.html#document/p1

39. Ibid., Felipe Villamor, "Rodrigo Duterte Says Donald Trump Endorses His Violent Antidrug Campaign."

40. Editorial, "Donald Trump Embraces Another Despot," *New York Times* (May 1, 2017). Accessed February 16, 2018: www.nytimes.com/2017/05/01/opinion/donald-trump-embraces-rodrigo-duterte.html

41. Editorial, "Accountability for Duterte," *New York Times* (March 24, 2017). Accessed February 16, 2018: www.nytimes.com/2017/03/24/opinion/accountability-for-rodrigo-duterte.html

42. Cited in Iris C. Gonzales, "Philippines' Duterte Threatens Assassination of Journalists," *New Internationalist Blog* (June 22, 2016). Accessed February 16, 2018: www.newint.org/blog/2016/06/22/philippines-duterte-threatens-assassination-of-journalists/

43. Ibid.

44. Oliver Holmes, "Trump hails 'great relationship' with Philippines' Duterte," *The Guardian* (November 13, 2017). Accessed February 16, 2018: www.theguardian.com/us-news/2017/nov/13/trump-hails-great-relationship-with-philippines-duterte

45. Richard C. Paddock, "Becoming Duterte: The Making of a Philippine Strongman," *New York Times* (March 21, 2017). Accessed February 16, 2018: https://www.nytimes.com/2017/03/21/world/asia/rodrigo-duterte-philippines-president-strongman.html

46. Bob Dreyfus, "Why Does Trump Embrace Foreign Dictators?" *Rolling Stone* (May 4, 2017). Accessed February 16, 2018: www.rollingstone.com/politics/news/why-does-trump-embrace-foreign-dictators-w480709

47. Mark Landler, "Trump Invites Rodrigo Duterte to the White House," *New York Times* (April 30, 2017). Accessed February 16, 2018: www.nytimes.com/2017/04/30/us/politics/trump-invites-rodrigo-duterte-to-the-white-house.html

48. Paddock, "Becoming Duterte: The Making of a Philippine Strongman."

49. Ibid., Felipe Villamor, "Rodrigo Duterte Says Donald Trump Endorses His Violent Antidrug Campaign."

50. Ibid., Iris C. Gonzales, "Philippines' Duterte Threatens Assassination of Journalists."

51. Cited in Jeremy Scahill, "Jeremy Scahill on Trump's Embrace of Duterte's Deadly War on Drugs in the Philippines," *Democracy Now!* (May 25. 2017). Accessed February 16, 2018: www.democracynow.org/2017/5/25/jeremy_scahill_on_trumps_embrace_of

52. Daniel Berehulak, "'They Are Slaughtering Us Like Animals,'"

New York Times (December 7, 2016). Accessed February 16, 2018: www. nytimes.com/interactive/2016/12/07/world/asia/rodrigo-duterte-philippines-drugs-killings.html

53. Judd Legum, "Why Did Trump Invite a Murderous Autocrat to the White House? Follow the Money," *Think Progress* (May 1, 2017). Accessed February 16, 2018: www.thinkprogress.org/why-did-trump-invite-a-murderous-autocrat-to-the-white-house-follow-the-money-de60bb6a88a0

54. Juan Cole, "For First Time, a US President Backs a Fascist France," *Informed Comment* (April 24, 2017). Accessed February 16, 2018: www. juancole.com/2017/04/president-fascist-france.html

55. Mark Landler, "Trump Congratulates Erdogan on Turkey Vote Cementing His Rule," *New York Times* (April 17, 2017). Accessed February 16, 2018: www.nytimes.com/2017/04/17/us/politics/trump-erdogan-turkey-referendum.html

56. Shalini Randeria, "Orbán's assault on academic freedom," *Eurozine* (April 5, 2017). Accessed February 16, 2018: www.eurozine.com/orbans-assault-on-academic-freedom/

57. Jennifer Williams and Zack Beauchamp, "Egypt's President Is a Bloodthirsty Dictator. Trump Thinks He's Done a 'Fantastic Job,'" *Vox* (April 3, 2017). Accessed February 16, 2018: www.vox.com/world/2017/4/3/15160358/trump-egypt-abdel-fattah-el-sisi-white-house

58. Joshua Hammond, "Egypt: The New Dictatorship," *The New York Review of Books* (June 8, 2017). Accessed February 16, 2018: www.nybooks.com/articles/2017/06/08/egypt-the-new-dictatorship/. See, in particular, Jack Shenker, *The Egyptians: A Radical History of Egypt's Unfinished Revolution* (New York: New Press, 2017). Also, Ibid., Jennifer Williams and Zack Beauchamp, "Egypt's President Is a Bloodthirsty Dictator."

59. Jeremy Venook, "Trump's Been Talking about His Business Interests in Russia for 30 Years," *The Atlantic* (May 10, 2017). Accessed February 16, 2018: www.theatlantic.com/business/archive/2017/05/trump-lawyers-up-conflicts-of-interest/526185/

60. Martin Pengelly, "Nikki Haley: Trump aimed to 'keep Kim on his toes' with 'nuclear button' tweet," *The Guardian* (January 7, 2018). Accessed February 20, 2018: www.theguardian.com/us-news/2018/jan/07/nikki-haley-trump-kim-nuclear-button-tweet-toes

61. Ibid., Jeremy Venook, "Trump's Been Talking about His Business Interests in Russia for 30 Years."

62. Ibid.

63. Ibid.

64. Cited in a personal correspondence (November 2016).

CHAPTER THREE

1. Jonathan Crary, *24/7: Late Capitalism and the Ends of Sleep* (Brooklyn, NY: Verso Press, 2013), pp. 14–15.

2. Zygmunt Bauman, *Liquid Fear* (London: Polity Press, 2006), pp. 135–136.

3. Zygmunt Bauman and Carlo Bordoni, *State of Crisis* (Cambridge, UK: Polity Press, 2014), pp. 14–15.

4. Ronald Aronson, "The Privatization of Hope," *Boston Review* (April 2016). Accessed February 20, 2018: bostonreview.net/editors-picks-us-books-ideas/ronald-aronson-privatization-hope. See also, Ronald Aronson, *We: Reviving Social Hope* (Chicago: University of Chicago Press, 2017).

5. I take this issue up in great detail in Henry A. Giroux, *Public Spaces, Private Lives* (New York: Routledge, 2003).

6. George Monbiot, "Neoliberalism is creating loneliness. That what's wrenching society apart," *The Guardian* (October 12, 2016). Accessed February 20, 2018: www.theguardian.com/commentisfree/2016/oct/12/neoliberalism-creating-loneliness-wrenching-society-apart

7. Rabbi Michael Lerner, "Overcoming Trump-ism: A New Strategy for Progressives," *Tikkun Magazine*, Vol. 32, No. 1, Winter 2017. Accessed February 20, 2018: www.tikkun.org/nextgen/overcoming-trump-ism-a-new-strategy-for-progressives

8. Cornelius Castoriadis, "The Destinies of Totalitarianism," *Salmagundi*, No. 60 (Spring-Summer, 1983), p. 109.

9. Judith Shulevitz, "The Lethality of Loneliness," *New Republic* (May 13, 2013). Accessed February 20, 2018: newrepublic.com/article/113176/science-loneliness-how-isolation-can-kill-you

10. Sabrina Maddeaux, "The rise of richface: why so many young women are getting cosmetic surgery," *The Globe and Mail* (Jul. 31, 2015). Accessed February 20, 2018: www.theglobeandmail.com/life/fashion-and-beauty/beauty/the-rise-of-richface-why-more-and-more-young-women-are-getting-cosmetic-surgery/article25756128/

11. Margaret Bolton, *Loneliness—the state we're in* (Oxford, UK: Age UK Oxfordshire 2012).

12. Byung-Chul Han, *In the Swarm: Digital Prospects*, tr. Erik Butler. (Cambridge, MA: MIT Press, 2017), p. 15.

13. Ibid., pp. 2, 17.

14. James Rule, "Markets, in Their Place," *Dissent* (Winter 1998), p. 31.

15. Amy Goodman, "On Tyranny: Yale Historian Timothy Snyder on How the U.S. Can Avoid Sliding into Authoritarianism," *Democracy Now!* (May 30, 2017). Accessed February 20, 2018: www.democracynow.

org/2017/5/30/on_tyranny_yale_historian_timothy_snyder?utm_source=-Democracy+Now%21&utm_campaign=b9c7f250d4-Daily_Digest&utm_medium=email&utm_term=0_fa2346a853-b9c7f250d4-190213053

16. John M. Doris, *Lack of Character: Personality and Moral Behavior* (Cambridge, UK: Cambridge University Press, 2002), p. 168.

17. David Remnick, "An American Tragedy," *The New Yorker* (November 9, 2016). Accessed February 20, 2018: www.newyorker.com/news/news-desk/an-american-tragedy-2

18. Tom Engelhardt, "Was 11/8 a New 9/11? The Election That Changed Everything and Could Prove History's Deal-Breaker," *TomDispatch.com* (December 1, 2016). Accessed February 20, 2018: www.tomdispatch.com/post/176216/tomgram%3A_engelhardt%2C_the_most_dangerous_country_on_earth/#more

19. Adam Haslett, "Donald Trump, Shamer in Chief," *The Nation* (October 4, 2016). Accessed February 20, 2018: www.thenation.com/article/donald-trump-shamer-in-chief/

20. On Trump and the discourse of shame, see Adam Haslett, "Donald Trump, Shamer in Chief."

21. On the issue of bullying as a national pastime, see Charles Derber and Yale R. Magrass, *Bully Nation: How the American Establishment Creates a Bullying Society* (Lawrence: University of Kansas, 2016).

22. Gabby Morrongiello, "Trump draws comparisons during visit to Andrew Jackson's grave," *Washington Examiner* (March 15, 2017). Accessed November 15, 2017: Accessed February 20, 2018: www.washingtonexaminer.com/trump-draws-comparisons-during-visit-to-andrew-jacksons-grave/article/2617502

23. Sophie Tatum and Dan Merica, "Trump holds event honoring Native American veterans in front of Andrew Jackson picture," *CNN*. Accessed February 20, 2018: www.cnn.com/2017/11/27/politics/donald-trump-andrew-jackson/index.html

24. I have borrowed Robinson's term from Robin D.G. Kelley, "Birth of a Nation," *Boston Review* (March 6, 2017). Accessed February 20, 2018: bostonreview.net/race-politics/robin-d-g-kelley-births-nation

25. Some of the best work on this subject has been done by Zygmunt Bauman: see *Wasted Lives* (London: Polity, 2004) and *Consuming Life* (London: Polity, 2007).

26. Katie Lobosco and Logan Whiteside, "In the Age of Trump, there's a New School Bully," *CNNMoney* (October 25, 2016). Accessed February 20, 2018: money.cnn.com/2016/10/25/news/trump-rhetoric-school-bullying/

27. W.J.T. Mitchell, "The Trolls of Academe: Making Safe Spaces into Brave Spaces," *Los Angeles Review of Books* (January 5,

2018). Accessed February 20, 2018: lareviewofbooks.org/article/
the-trolls-of-academe-making-safe-spaces-into-brave-spaces/

28. Brad Evans and Julien Reid, "The Promise of Violence in the Age of Catastrophe," *Truthout* (January 5,
2014). Accessed February 20, 2018: truth-out.org/opinion/
item/20977-the-promise-of-violence-in-the-age-of-catastrophe

29. Neal Gabler, "How the Media Enabled Donald Trump
by Destroying Politics First," *Moyers & Company* (March 4,
2016). Accessed February 20, 2018: billmoyers.com/story/
how-the-media-enabled-donald-trump-by-destroying-politics-first/

30. Charles Derber and Yale R. Magrass, *Bully Nation*, p. 153.

31. Jessica Lustig, "From 'Hamilton' to Donald Trump: Are All
'Grievances' Created Equal?" *New York Times Magazine* (October 25, 2016).
Accessed February 20, 2018: www.nytimes.com/2016/10/30/magazine/
from-hamilton-to-donald-trump-are-all-grievances-created-equal.htm-
l?rref=collection%2Fsectioncollection%2Fmagazine&action=click&con-
tentCollection=magazine&region=rank&module=package&version=high-
lights&contentPlacement=6&pgtype=sectionfront

32. For an excellent analysis and critique of the right-wing trolling universe, see Andrew Marantz, "Trolls for Trump," *The New Yorker*
(October 30, 2016). Accessed February 20, 2018: www.newyorker.com/
magazine/2016/10/31/trolls-for-trump

33. Jared Keller, "Trump's Grand Troll Campaign Is Just Getting Started," *The Village Voice* (October 26, 2016). Accessed February 20, 2018: www.
villagevoice.com/news/trumps-grand-troll-campaign-is-just-getting-started-
9264778?utm_source=Newsletters&utm_medium=email

34. Andrew Marantz, "Trolls for Trump," *The New Yorker.*

35. Mark Danner, "The Magic of Donald Trump," *The New York Review
of Books* (May 26, 2016). Accessed February 20, 2018: www.nybooks.com/
articles/2016/05/26/the-magic-of-donald-trump/

CHAPTER FOUR

1. Marian Wright Edelman, "Why America May
Go to Hell," *Huffington Post* (November 17, 2017). Accessed February 20, 2018: www.huffingtonpost.com/entry/
why-america-may-go-to-hell_us_5a0f4dd4e4b023121e0e9281

2. Ibid.

3. Tara Culp-Ressler, "The Oklahoma Republican Party's Deeply
Offensive Facebook Post," *ThinkProgress* (July 14, 2015). Accessed February
20, 2018: thinkprogress.org/the-oklahoma-republican-partys-deeply-offen-
sive-facebook-post-e4516db63598/

4. Ibid. Tara Culp-Ressler.

5. Paul Krugman, "Republicans Simply Want to Hurt People," *AlterNet* (January 12, 2018). Accessed February 20, 2018: www.alternet.org/news-amp-politics/paul-krugman-republicans-simply-want-hurt-people

6. Greg Jericho, "Flogging the dead horse of neoliberalism isn't going to improve the economy," *The Guardian* (April 2, 2017). Accessed February 20, 2018: www.theguardian.com/business/grogonomics/2017/apr/02/flogging-the-dead-horse-of-neoliberalism-isnt-going-to-improve-the-economy; for a rebuttal to this position, see Colin Crouch, *The Strange Non-death of Neo-liberalism* (London: Polity, 2011).

7. Ariel Dorfman, Ariel Dorfman, "Trump's War on Knowledge," *The New York Review of Books* (October 12, 2017). Accessed February 20, 2018: www.nybooks.com/daily/2017/10/12/trumps-war-on-knowledge/

8. Ibid.

9. Jean Franco, *Cruel Modernity* (Durham, NC: Duke University, 2013), p. 2.

10. Christopher Ingraham, "Fringe Groups Revel as Protests Turn Violent," *New York Times* (June 2, 2017). Accessed February 20, 2018: www.nytimes.com/2017/06/02/us/politics/white-nationalists-alt-knights-protests-colleges.html?_r=0

11. See for instance, the incident in which a white nationalist, 35-year-old Jeremy Christian, accused two young women, one of whom was wearing a hijab, "of terrorism, tax evasion and general un-Americanness. When three men stepped up to intervene in the assault, Christian was ready with a knife, stabbing each one, successively, in the jugular and killing two of them. See Shane Burley, "As the 'alt-right' moves to violence, community responses matter," *Wagingnonviolence* (June 1, 2017). Accessed February 20, 2018: wagingnonviolence.org/feature/alt-right-violence-portland-community-response/

12. See the following detailed sources on this issue: Lisa Marie Cacho, *Social Death: Racialized Rightlessness and the Criminalization of the Unprotected* (New York: New York University Press, 2012); Saskia Sassen, *Expulsions: Brutality and Complexity in the Global economy* (Cambridge, MA: Harvard University Press, 2014); Brad Evans and Henry A. Giroux, *Disposable Futures: The Seduction of Violence in the Age of Spectacle* (San Francisco: City Lights 2015).

13. Jordan Weissmann, "Trump's Budget Director Has a Breathtakingly Cynical Excuse for Cutting Aid to the Poor," *Slate* (March 16, 2017). Accessed February 20, 2018: www.slate.com/blogs/moneybox/2017/03/16/mulvaney_says_cutting_aid_to_the_poor_is_compassionate.html

14. Ibid.

15. Nancy Gertner and Chiraag Bains, "Mandatory minimum sentences are cruel and ineffective. Sessions wants them back," *Washington Post* (May 15, 2017). Accessed February 20, 2018: www.washingtonpost.com/posteverything/wp/2017/05/15/mandatory-minimum-sentences-are-cruel-and-ineffective-sessions-wants-them-back/?utm_term=.a7027b1209ea.

16. Ibid. Gertner and Bains, "Mandatory minimum sentences are cruel and ineffective. Sessions Wants them Back." There are a number of excellent books on prison reform, including the following: Elizabeth Hinton, *From the War on Poverty to the War on Crime: The Making of Mass Incarceration in America* (Cambridge, MA: Harvard University Press, 2016); Nell Bernstein, *Burning Down the House: The End of Juvenile Prison* (New York: The New Press, 2016); Maya Schenwar, *Locked Down, Locked Out: Why Prison Doesn't Work and How We Can Do Better* (San Francisco: Berrett-Koehler Publishers, Inc. 2014); Michelle Alexander, *The New Jim Crow* (New York: The New Press, 2010).

17. Brad Evans, "Humans in Dark Times," *New York Times* (February 23, 2017). Accessed February 20, 2018: www.nytimes.com/2017/02/23/opinion/humans-in-dark-times.html?_r=0

18. Elizabeth Grossman, "This Is What the Brutal Consequences of Trump's Proposed Budget Slash for the Labor Dept. Would Look Like," *AlterNet* (March 19, 2017). Accessed February 20, 2018: www.alternet.org/what-slashing-labor-department-budget-21-percent-would-mean

19. Paul Krugman, "The Scammers, the Scammed and America's Fate," *New York Times* (March 24, 2017). Accessed February 20, 2018: www.nytimes.com/2017/03/24/opinion/the-scammers-the-scammed-and-americas-fate.html

20. Matthew Goldstein, "As C.E.O. Pay Packages Grow, Top Executives Have the President's Ear," *New York Times* (May 28, 2017). Accessed February 20, 2018: www.nytimes.com/2017/05/26/business/ceo-compensation-pay-president-donald-trump.html

21. Tom Engelhardt, "Little Big Man: Into the Whirlwind," *TomDispatch.com* (May 28, 2017). Accessed February 20, 2018: www.tomdispatch.com/post/176288/tomgram%3A_engelhardt%2C_thank_you%2C_donald/#more

22. Jeff Pegues, "Man captures video of 'patient dumping' outside Baltimore hospital," *CBS NEWS* (January 10, 2018, 7:04 PM). Accessed February 20, 2018: www.cbsnews.com/news/man-captures-video-of-patient-dumping-outside-baltimore-hospital/

23. Richard J. Evans, "A Warning from History," *The Nation* (February 28, 2017). Accessed February 20, 2018: www.thenation.com/article/the-ways-to-destroy-democracy/

24. Ibid.

25. Jonathan Schell, "Cruel America," *The Nation* (September 28, 2011). Accessed February 20, 2018: www.thenation.com/article/163690/cruel-america

26. Kim Soffen and Denise Lu, "What Trump Cut in His Budget," *Washington Post* (March 16, 2017). Accessed February 20, 2018: www.washingtonpost.com/graphics/politics/trump-presidential-budget-2018-proposal/?tid=a_inl&utm_term=.489231e7a326

27. Robert Reich, "4 Reasons the Trump Administration Is Unspeakably Cruel," *AlterNet* (March 17, 2017). Accessed February 20, 2018: www.alternet.org/news-amp-politics/robert-reich-4-reasons-trump-administration-unspeakably-cruel

28. Ibid.

29. Marian Wright Edelman, "President Trump's War on Children," *Children's Defense Fund* (May 26, 2017). Accessed February 20, 2018: cdf.childrensdefense.org/site/MessageViewer?dlv_id=47996&em_id=47006.0

30. Julie Hirschfield Davis, "Trump's Budget Cuts Deeply into Medicaid and Anti-Poverty Efforts," *New York Times* (May 22, 2017). Accessed February 20, 2018: www.nytimes.com/2017/05/22/us/politics/trump-budget-cuts.html?_r=0

31. Dan Rather, "We Must Be Steady as the Winds of Our Age Swirl and Rattle at our Souls," *Reader Supported News* (May 28, 2017). Accessed February 20, 2018: readersupportednews.org/opinion2/277-75/43817-focus-we-must-be-steady-as-the-winds-of-our-age-swirl-and-rattle-at-our-souls

32. Paul Baskin, "What Trump's Budget Outline Would Mean for Higher Ed," *The Chronicle of Higher Education* (March 16, 2017). Accessed February 20, 2018: www.chronicle.com/article/What-Trump-s-Budget-Outline/239511?cid=pm&utm_source=pm&utm_medium=en&elqTrackId=b7079d71a014fb6910f188d2d5753ac&elq=70dd649a3da84960b-d6012a5ceb0aee2&elqaid=12999&elqat=1&elqCampaignId=5365

33. Steven Rosenfeld, "Trump's Budget Vision Would Transform America into War-Obsessed, Survival-of-the-Fittest Dystopia," *AlterNet* (March 16, 2017). Accessed February 20, 2018: www.alternet.org/election-2016/trumps-budget-vision-would-transform-america-war-obsessed-survival-fittest-dystopia?akid=15308.40823.d8Ix8e&rd=1&src=newsletter1073980&t=2

34. Julie Hirschfeld Davis and Patricia Cohen, "Trump Tax Plan Would Shift Trillions From U.S. Coffers to the Richest," *New York Times* (April 27, 2017). Accessed February 20, 2018: www.nytimes.com/2017/04/27/us/politics/individual-business-tax-wealth.html

35. Ibid. Marian Wright Edelman, "President Trump's War on

Children."

36. Jessica Tayler, Danielle Kurtzblen, and Scott Horsley, "Trump Unveils 'Hard Power' Budget that Boosts Military Spending," *National Public Radio* (March 16, 2017). Accessed February 20, 2018: www.npr.org/2017/03/16/520305293/trump-to-unveil-hard-power-budget-that-boosts-military-spending

37. Ibid. Marian Wright Edelman," President Trump's War on Children."

38. Cited in Deirdre Fulton, "'Morally Obscene' Trump Budget Proposal Stands to Make America Cruel Again," *CommonDreams* (March 16, 2017). Accessed February 20, 2018: www.commondreams.org/news/2017/03/16/morally-obscene-trump-budget-proposal-stands-make-america-cruel-again

39. Aaron Rupar, "Fox News Host Argues Stripping Coverage from Millions is no biggie since 'we're all going to die'" *ThinkProgress* (June 28, 2017). Accessed February 20, 2018: thinkprogress.org/kennedy-fox-news-trumpcare-we-are-all-going-to-die-50d86cbd9bb5

40. Robert Reich, "Trumpcare isn't about health. It's a tax cut for the 1%," *The Guardian* (June 26, 2017). Accessed February 20, 2018: www.theguardian.com/commentisfree/2017/jun/26/trumpcare-health-tax-cut-1-percent

41. Laila Lalami, "The Senate Health-Care Bill Is Morally Indefensible," *The Nation* (June 27, 2017). Accessed February 20, 2018: www.thenation.com/article/the-senate-healthcare-bill-is-morally-indefensible/

42. Ibid.

43. Dahr Jamail, "The GOP's Health Care Legislation Is Cruel and Punitive, Doctors Say," *Truthout* (July 10, 2017). Accessed February 20, 2018: www.truth-out.org/news/item/41213-the-gop-s-health-care-legislation-is-cruel-and-punitive-doctors-say

44. Katherine Gallagher Robbins and Rachel West, "Trump's Medicaid Work Requirements Could Put At Least 6.3 Million Americans at Risk of Losing Health Care," *Center for American Progress* (January 12, 2018). Accessed February 20, 2018: www.americanprogress.org/issues/poverty/news/2018/01/12/444953/trumps-medicaid-work-requirements-put-least-6-3-million-americans-risk-losing-health-care/?utm_source=newsletter&utm_medium=email&utm_campaign=progReport

45. Claire Snell-Rood & Cathleen Willging, "GOP health care bill would make rural America's distress much worse," *The Conversation* (June 26, 2017). Accessed February 20, 2018: theconversation.com/gop-health-care-bill-would-make-rural-americas-distress-much-worse-78018gop-health-care-bill-would-make-rural-americas-distress-much-worse-78018

46. Cited in Amy Goodman, "Senate GOP Healthcare Bill Estimated to

Kill 28,600 More in U.S. Each Year & Drop 22M from Insurance," *Democracy Now!* (June 27, 2017). Accessed February 20, 2018: www.democracy-now.org/2017/6/27/senate_gop_healthcare_bill_estimated_to

47. David Cecere, "New study finds 45,000 deaths annually linked to lack of health coverage," *Harvard Gazette* (September 17, 2009). Accessed February 20, 2018: news.harvard.edu/gazette/story/2009/09/new-study-finds-45000-deaths-annually-linked-to-lack-of-health-coverage/

48. Slavoj Žižek, *Demanding the Impossible* (New York: Indigo, 2013), p. 63

49. Zygmunt Bauman, *Identity—Conversations with Benedetto Vecchi* (London: Polity Press, 2004), p. 40.

50. Ibid. p. 72.

51. Peter Baker, "'Very Frustrated' Trump Becomes Top Critic of Law Enforcement," *New York Times* (November 3, 2017). Accessed February 20, 2018: www.nytimes.com/2017/11/03/us/politics/trump-says-justice-dept-and-fbi-must-do-what-is-right-and-investigate-democrats.html?hp&action=click&pgtype=Homepage&clickSource=story-heading&module=-first-column-region&region=top-news&WT.nav=top-news

52. Timothy Shenk, "Booked: The Origins of the Carceral State," *Dissent* (August 30, 2016). Accessed February 20, 2018: www.dissentmagazine.org/blog/booked-origins-carceral-state-elizabeth-hinton

53. Richard A. Friedman, "What Cookies and Meth Have in Common," *New York Times* (July 2, 2017). Accessed February 20, 2018: www.nytimes.com/2017/06/30/opinion/sunday/what-cookies-and-meth-have-in-common.html?_r=0

54. Zygmunt Bauman and Leonidas Donskis. *Liquid Evil* (Polity Press, 2016: Cambridge, UK), p. 8.

CHAPTER FIVE

1. Oxfam, "An Economy for the 99 percent," *Oxfam Briefing Paper* (January 2017). Accessed February 20, 2018: www.oxfam.org/sites/www.oxfam.org/files/file_attachments/bp-economy-for-99-percent-160117-en.pdf

2. This is a play on Henry A. Kissinger's comment in describing Lenin's approach to politics, which was politics as a continuation of war by other means, thus turning Clausewitz's argument "on its head." See: Christopher Bassford, *Clausewitz in English: The Reception of Clausewitz in Britain and America, 1815–1945* (New York: Oxford University Press, 1994), p.198.

3. João Biehl, *Vita: Life in A Zone of Social Abandonment* (Los Angeles, CA: University of California Press, 2005), p. 20.

4. See, for instance, Judith Butler, *Precarious Life: The Powers of Mourning and Violence* (London: Verso Press, 2004).

5. Zygmunt Bauman, *Liquid Times* (London: Polity Press, 2007), p.11

6. Ibid., Butler, pp. 34, 33.

7. Julia Conley, "'People Are Dying' But Trump Gives Himself Perfect '10' for Puerto Rico Response," *CommonDreams* (October 19, 2017). Accessed February 20, 2018: www.commondreams.org/news/2017/10/19/people-are-dying-trump-gives-himself-perfect-10-puerto-rico-response

8. Ibid.

9. Ibid.

10. Michael Melia, "Puerto Rico investigating possible post-hurricane disease outbreak after 4 deaths," *The Associated Press* (October 11, 2017). Accessed February 20, 2018: globalnews.ca/news/3797040/puerto-rico-hurricane-disease-outbreak-deaths

11. Aaron Blake, "Trump doesn't get it on Puerto Rico. He just proved it by lashing out at San Juan's mayor." *Washington Post* (September 30, 2017). Accessed February 20, 2018: www.washingtonpost.com/news/the-fix/wp/2017/09/30/trump-doesnt-get-it-on-puerto-rico-he-just-proved-it-by-lashing-out-at-san-juans-mayor/?utm_term=.174cba31d3c6

12. Jon Lee Anderson, "The Mayor of San Juan on Trump's 'Big Mouth' and What Puerto Rico Needs," *The New Yorker* (October 12, 2017). Accessed February 20, 2018: www.newyorker.com/news/news-desk/the-mayor-of-san-juan-on-trumps-big-mouth-and-what-puerto-rico-needs

13. Ibid.

14. Frances Robles, "Puerto Rico's Health Care Is in Dire Condition, Three Weeks after Maria," *New York Times* (October 10, 2017). Accessed February 20, 2018: www.nytimes.com/2017/10/10/us/puerto-rico-power-hospitals.html

15. Ibid.

16. Lauren Berlant, "Slow Death (Sovereignty, Obesity, Lateral Agency)," *Critical Inquiry*, 33 (The University of Chicago, Summer 2007). Accessed February 20, 2018: users.clas.ufl.edu/burt/%20Tempest%20Drown%20before%20reading/lauren%20Berlant%20slow%20death.pdf

17. Cited in ibid., Frances Robles, "Puerto Rico's Health Care Is in Dire Condition, Three Weeks after Maria."

18. Mark Hand, "Trump's second-class response to Hurricane Maria deepens the divide with Puerto Rico," *Think-Progress* (October 17, 2017). Accessed February 20, 2018: thinkprogress.org/puerto-rico-and-mainland-america-fb2911337deb/

19. Stan Cox, Paul Cox, "Before Maria, Forcing Puerto Rico to Pay It's Debt Was Odious. Now It's Pure Cruelty," *CounterPunch* (October 3, 2017). Accessed February 20, 2018: www.commondreams.org/views/2017/10/03/maria-forcing-puerto-rico-pay-its-debt-was-odious-now-its-pure-cruelty

20. Amy Davidson Sorkin, "Disasters Will Happen," *The New Yorker*

(October 16, 2017), p. 21.

21. Paul Krugman, "Let them eat paper towels," *New York Times* (October 12, 2017). Accessed February 20, 2018: www.nytimes.com/2017/10/12/opinion/trump-tweets-puerto-rico.html?_r=0

22. Ibid., Jon Lee Anderson, "The Mayor of San Juan on Trump's 'Big Mouth' and What Puerto Rico Needs."

23. Alexia Fernández Campbell, "Trump to Puerto Rico: your hurricane isn't a 'real catastrophe' like Katrina" *Vox* (October 3, 2017). Accessed February 20, 2018: www.vox.com/2017/10/3/16411488/trump-remarks-puerto-rico

24. Jeffrey St. Clair, "The Resident Evil," *CounterPunch* (October 6, 2017). Accessed February 20, 2018: www.counterpunch.org/2017/10/06/the-resident-evil/

25. Sonali Kolhatkar, "Trump's Cruel Indifference to Puerto Rico," *Truthdig* (September 28, 2017). Accessed February 20, 2018: www.truthdig.com/articles/trumps-cruel-indifference-puerto-rico/

26. Ta-Nehisi Coates, "The First White President," *The Atlantic* (October 2017). Accessed February 20, 2018: www.theatlantic.com/magazine/archive/2017/10/the-first-white-president-ta-nehisi-coates/537909/

27. Ryan Teague Beckwith, "'We Cannot Admit Everyone.' Read a Transcript of Jeff Sessions' Remarks on Ending the DACA," *Time* (September 05, 2017). Accessed February 20, 2018: time.com/4927426/daca-dreamers-jeff-sessions-transcript/

28. Juan Cole, "Deporting Dreamers Would Cost U.S. $460 Billion," *Truthdig* (September 6, 2017). Accessed February 20, 2018: www.truthdig.com/articles/deporting-dreamers-will-cost-u-s-400-billion-10-years

29. William Finnegan, "Is Ending DACA the Worst Decision Trump Has Made?" *The New Yorker* (September 18, 2017). Accessed February 20, 2018: www.newyorker.com/magazine/2017/09/18/is-ending-daca-the-worst-decision-trump-has-made

30. Ibid.

31. Mark Joseph Stern, "Jeff Sessions Spews Nativist Lies While Explaining Why Trump Is Killing DACA," *Bill Moyers and Company* (September 5, 2017). Accessed February 20, 2018: www.slate.com/blogs/the_slatest/2017/09/05/sessions_daca_speech_was_full_of_nativist_lies.html

32. For a brilliant analysis of Trump's rise to power as part of a broader history of American conservatism, see Lawrence Grossberg, *Under the Cover of Chaos: Trump and the Battle for the American Right* (London: Pluto Press, 2018).

33. Alexander Bolton, "Negotiating with Trump like negotiating with Jell-O," *The Hill* (January 20, 2018). Ac-

cessed February 20, 2018: thehill.com/homenews/
senate/369929-schumer-working-with-trump-like-negotiating-with-jello

34. Eileen Sullivan, "'Outrageous,' White House Says of DACA
Ruling, as Trump Calls Court System 'Broken,'" *New York Times* (January
10, 2018). Accessed February 20, 2018: www.nytimes.com/2018/01/10/
us/politics/outrageous-white-house-says-of-judges-daca-ruling.
html?emc=edit_nn_20180111&nl=morning-briefing&nlid=51563793&te=1

35. Michael D. Shearjan, "Trump Must Keep DACA Protections for
Now, Judge Says," *New York Times* (January 9, 2018). Accessed February 20,
2018: www.nytimes.com/2018/01/09/us/trump-daca-improper.html

36. Jeffrey St. Clair, "The Resident Evil," *CounterPunch* (October 6,
2017). Accessed February 20, 2018: www.counterpunch.org/2017/10/06/
the-resident-evil/

37. Ibid.

38. Ibid.

39. John W. Whitehead, "Mass Shootings: The Military-Enter-
tainment Complex's Culture of Violence Turns Deadly," *The Ruth-
erford Institute* (October 3, 2017). Accessed February 20, 2018: www.
rutherford.org/publications_resources/john_whiteheads_commentary/
mass_shootings_the_military_entertainment_complexs_culture_of_violence

40. Ibid.

41. Ibid.

42. Cornelius Castoriadis, *The Rising Tide of Insignificancy: The Big Sleep*
(New York: Not Bored, 2003), p. 4.

43. Wendy Brown, "Apocalyptic Populism," *Eurozine* (September 5, 2017). Accessed February 20, 2018: www.eurozine.com/
apocalyptic-populism/

44. Ariel Dorfman, "Trump's War on Knowledge," *The New York Review
of Books* (October 12, 2017). Accessed February 20, 2018: www.nybooks.
com/daily/2017/10/12/trumps-war-on-knowledge/

45. Paul Street, "The NRA's Latest Terrorist Attack on U.S. Soil,"
CounterPunch (October 4, 2017). Accessed February 20, 2018: www.counter-
punch.org/2017/10/04/the-nras-latest-terrorist-attack-on-u-s-soil/

46. Chris Hedges, "America's 'Death Instinct' Spreads Misery Across the
World," *AlterNet* (September 30, 2014). Accessed February 20, 2018: www.
alternet.org/world/americas-death-instinct-spreads-misery-across-world

47. Josep R. Llobera, "The Origins of Nazi Ideology," *The Making of
Totalitarian Thought* (New York, Berg: 2003), p. 135.

48. Weismann interviewed on CBS Nightly News on October 20, 2017. Accessed February 20, 2018: www.cbsnews.com/
videos/1020-cbs-evening-news/

49. Eric Lipton, "Why Has the E.P.A. Shifted on Toxic Chemicals? An Industry Insider Helps Call the Shots," *New York Times* (October 21, 2017). Accessed February 20, 2018: www.nytimes.com/2017/10/21/us/trump-epa-chemicals-regulations.html?hp&action=click&pgtype=Homepage&clickSource=story-heading&module=first-column-region&region=top-news&WT.nav=top-news

50. Chris Hedges, "America's Addiction to Violence – From War to Vigilante Mobs – Is a Conservative Legacy," *AlterNet* (June 25, 2015). Accessed February 20, 2018: www.alternet.org/books/chris-hedges-americas-addiction-violence-war-vigilante-mobs-conservative-legacy

51. Robert O. Paxton, "The Five Stages of Fascism," *The Journal of Modern History* 70:1 (March 1998), p. 12.

CHAPTER SIX

1. Denver Nicks, "The U.S. Is Still No.1 at Selling Arms to the World," *Time Magazine* (December 26, 2015). Accessed February 20, 2018: time.com/4161613/us-arms-sales-exports-weapons/. See also Andrew J. Bacevich, *Washington Rules: America's Path to Permanent War* (New York: Metropolitan Books, 2010).

2. Trump's address to a joint session of Congress can be found in: "Here Are 4,826 Words Donald Trump Included in His Speech," *Mother Jones* (February 28, 2017). Accessed February 20, 2018: www.motherjones.com/politics/2017/02/read-full-text-donald-trumps-speech-congress

3. Michael S. Schmidt, "Dismayed by Trump, Head of Drug Enforcement Administration to Leave," *New York Times* (September 26, 2017). Accessed November 14, 2017: Accessed February 20, 2018: www.nytimes.com/2017/09/26/us/politics/chuck-rosenberg-dea-resigns.html

4. Kim Soffen, "Yes, Violence in America Has Suddenly Increased. But That's Far from the Whole Story," *Washington Post* (July 8, 2016). Accessed February 20, 2018: www.washingtonpost.com/news/wonk/wp/2016/07/08/why-america-feels-so-violent-right-now/?utm_term=.2be7b2d502ce

5. David Leonhardt, "The Lawless Presidency," *New York Times* (June 6, 2017). Accessed February 20, 2018: www.nytimes.com/2017/06/06/opinion/the-lawless-presidency.html

6. Jennifer Rubin, "Why Trump and Sessions are now in a heap of legal trouble," *Washington Post* (January 5, 2018). Accessed February 20, 2018: www.washingtonpost.com/blogs/right-turn/wp/2018/01/05/a-heap-of-legal-trouble-for-trump-and-sessions/?utm_term=.1a0db8900a19

7. Peter Baker, Michael S. Schmidt, and Maggie Haberman, "Citing Recusal, Trump Says He Wouldn't Have Hired Session," *New York Times* (July 19, 2017). Accessed February 20, 2018: mobile.nytimes.

com/2017/07/19/us/politics/trump-interview-sessions-russia.html

8. Jeffrey Tobin, "Donald Trump and the Rule of Law," *The New Yorker* (January 6, 2018). Accessed February 20, 2018: www.newyorker.com/news/daily-comment/donald-trump-and-the-rule-of-law

9. Ibid. David Leonhardt, "The Lawless Presidency."

10. Marjorie Cohn, "Donald Trump vs. The Rule of Law," *Truthout* (August 02, 2017). Accessed February 20, 2018: www.truth-out.org/news/item/41480-donald-trump-vs-the-rule-of-law

11. Amy Goodman, "Cornel West on Donald Trump: This Is What Neo-Fascism Looks Like," *Democracy Now!* (December 1, 2016). Accessed February 20, 2018: www.democracynow.org/2016/12/1/cornel_west_on_donald_trump_this

12. John Cassidy, "A Racist in the Oval Office," *The New Yorker* (January 12, 2017). Accessed February 20, 2018: www.newyorker.com/news/our-columnists/trump-shithole-comment-racist-in-the-oval-office?mbid=nl_Daily%20011218%20Nonsubs&CNDID=42733863&sp-MailingID=12736804&spUserID=MTM4NzE1OTE4NjE5S0&spJo-bID=1321138695&spReportId=MTMyMTEzODY5NQS2

13. Michael D. Shear and Julie Hirschfeld Davis, "Stoking Fears, Trump Defied Bureaucracy to Advance Immigration Agenda," *New York Times* (December 23, 2017). Accessed February 20, 2018: www.nytimes.com/2017/12/23/us/politics/trump-immigration.html?_r=1

14. Dahlia Lithwick, "Trump Lays Down His Law," *Slate* (January 20, 2017). Accessed February 20, 2018: www.slate.com/articles/news_and_politics/jurisprudence/2017/01/trump_s_inaugural_address_was_terrifying.html

15. Chauncey DeVega, "Trump's Election Has Created 'Safe Spaces' for Racists: Southern Poverty Law Center's Heidi Beirich on the Wave of Hate Crimes," *Salon* (March 8, 2017). Accessed February 20, 2018: www.salon.com/2017/03/08/trumps-election-has-created-safe-spaces-for-racists-southern-poverty-law-centers-heidi-beirich-on-the-wave-of-hate-crimes/

16. Cited in ibid., Chauncey DeVega, "Trump's Election Has Created 'Safe Spaces' for Racists."

17. Sasha Bruce, "NARAL Statement on Nomination of Tom Price as Secretary of HHS," *NARAL Pro-Choice America* (November 16, 2016). Accessible February 27, 2018: www.prochoiceamerica.org/2016/11/29/naral-statement-nomination-tom-price-secretary-hhs/

18. Ari Berman, "Jeff Sessions, Trump's Pick for Attorney General, Is a Fierce Opponent of Civil Rights," *The Nation* (November 18, 2016). Accessed February 20, 2018: www.thenation.com/article/jeff-sessions-trumps-pick-for-attorney-general-is-a-fierce-opponent-of-civil-rights/

19. Carimah Townes, "Despite his racist past, Jeff Sessions confirmed as

attorney general," *ThinkProgress* (February 3, 2017). Accessed February 20, 2018: thinkprogress.org/despite-racist-past-jeff-sessions-confirmed-as-attorney-general-46f70e02eec2

20. Emily Bazelon, "Department of Justification," *New York Times* (February 28, 2017). Accessed February 20, 2018: www.nytimes.com/2017/02/28/magazine/jeff-sessions-stephen-bannon-justice-department.html

21. Miranda Blue, "12 Reasons Jeff Sessions Should Never Be Attorney General," *Right Wing Watch* (November 18, 2016). Accessed February 20, 2018: www.rightwingwatch.org/post/12-reasons-jeff-sessions-should-never-be-attorney-general/

22. Andrew Kaczynski, "Sen. Sessions: Central Park Five Ad Shows Trump Has Always Believed In Law And Order," *BuzzFeed News* (August 18, 2016). Accessed February 20, 2018: www.buzzfeed.com/andrewkaczynski/sen-sessions-central-park-five-ad-shows-trump-has-always-bel?utm_term=.ym71O7vMP#.fuqqeGk90

23. Ibid.

24. Amy Goodman, "A White Nationalist & Anti-Semite in the Oval Office: Trump Taps Breitbart's Bannon as Top Aide," *Democracy Now!* (November 14, 2016). Accessed February 20, 2018: www.democracynow.org/2016/11/14/a_white_nationalist_anti_semite_in

25. Associated Press, "Conservative Flame-Thrower to Get Key White House Position," *New York Times* (November 14, 2016). Accessed February 27, 2018: apnews.com/dc5d25fc3c5e4c8fb35022d9917ad44d

26. Amy Goodman, "A White Nationalist & Anti-Semite."

27. Rebecca Gould, "Regime Change Abroad, Fascism at Home: How US Interventions Paved the Way for Trump," *CounterPunch* (November 29, 2016). Accessed February 20, 2018: www.counterpunch.org/2016/11/29/regime-change-abroad-fascism-at-home-how-us-interventions-paved-the-way-for-trump/

28. Loren Thompson, "For the Defense Industry, Trump's Win Means Happy Days Are Here Again," *Forbes* (November 9, 2016). Accessed February 20, 2018: www.forbes.com/sites/lorenthompson/2016/11/09/for-the-defense-industry-trumps-win-means-happy-days-are-here-again/#90fe95652f02

29. William D. Hartung, "A Pentagon Rising: Is a Trump Presidency Good News for the Military-Industrial Complex?" *TomDispatch* (November 22, 2016). Accessed February 20, 2018: www.tomdispatch.com/blog/176213/tomgram%3A_william_hartung%2C_trump_for_the_defense/

30. Robbie Martin, "Trump's Dark Web of Far Right Militarists Who Want to Attack Iran," *The Real News* (November 28,

2016). Accessed February 20, 2018: therealnews.com/t2/index.
php?option=com_content&task=view&id=31&Itemid=74&jumival=17662

31. Melvin A. Goodman, "Trump's Campaign of Militarization," *CounterPunch* (November 23, 2016). Accessed February 20, 2018: www.counterpunch.org/2016/11/23/trumps-campaign-of-militarization/

32. Matthew Rosenberg and Maggie Haberman, "Michael Flynn, Anti-Islamist Ex-General, Offered Security Post, Trump Aide Says," *New York Times* (November 17, 2006). Accessed February 20, 2018: www.nytimes.com/2016/11/18/us/politics/michael-flynn-national-security-adviser-donald-trump.html

33. Ibid.

34. Lawrence Douglas, "Lying Got Michael Flynn Fired. But that's What the Trump White House Does Best," *The Guardian* (February 15, 2017). Accessed February 20, 2018: www.theguardian.com/commentisfree/2017/feb/15/lying-got-michael-flynn-fired-trump-white-house

35. Andrew Bacevich, "Trump Loves to Do It, but American Generals Have Forgotten How," *Tom Dispatch* (November 29, 2016). Accessed February 20, 2018: www.tomdispatch.com/post/176215/tomgram%3A_andrew_bacevich,_the_swamp_of_war/

36. Hugh Handeyside, "Does What Happened to this Journalist at the US-Canada Border Herald a Darker Trend?" *CommonDreams* (November 30, 2016). Accessed February 20, 2018: www.commondreams.org/views/2016/11/30/does-what-happened-journalist-us-canada-border-herald-darker-trend

37. Grace Guarnieri, "4 Hair-Raising Facts About Trump's Potential Homeland Security Pick," *Salon* (November 29, 2016). Accessed February 20, 2018: www.alternet.org/election-2016/4-hair-raising-facts-about-trumps-potential-homeland-security-pick?akid=14939.40823.PgLddF&rd=1&src=newsletter1068046&t=6

38. Michael D. Shear, "Trump as Cyberbully in Chief? Twitter Attack on Union Boss Draws Fire," *New York Times* (December 8, 2016). Accessed February 20, 2018: mobile.nytimes.com/2016/12/08/us/politics/donald-trump-twitter-carrier-chuck-jones.html

39. Madeline Farber, "Union Leader Says He's Getting Threats after Donald Trump Attacked Him on Twitter," *Fortune* (December 9, 2016). Accessed February 20, 2018: fortune.com/2016/12/08/carrier-union-leader-threats-donald-trump/

40. Jenna Johnson, "Trump often condemns Democrats, defends Republicans on harassment allegations," *Washington Post* (November 17, 2017). Accessed February 20, 2018: www.washingtonpost.com/politics/

trump-often-condemns-democrats-defends-republicans-on-harassment-al-legations/2017/11/17/a3d890fc-cbb9-11e7-aa96-54417592cf72_story.html?undefined=&utm_term=.13dcdb35f3d5

41. Ashley Parker and John Wagner, "Trump retweets inflammatory and unverified anti-Muslim videos," *Washington Post* (November 29, 2017). Accessed February 20, 2018: www.washingtonpost.com/news/post-politics/wp/2017/11/29/trump-retweets-inflammatory-and-unverified-anti-mus-lim-videos/?utm_term=.68e8d8c43c84

42. Ibid.

43. Peter Baker and Eileen Sullivan, "Trump Shares Inflammatory Anti-Muslim Videos, and Britain's Leader Condemns Them," *New York Times* (November 29, 2017). Accessed February 20, 2018: www.nytimes.com/2017/11/29/us/politics/trump-anti-muslim-videos-jayda-fransen.html

44. Charles Blow, "Trump, Proxy of Racism," *New York Times* (November 30, 2017). Accessed February 20, 2018: www.nytimes.com/2017/11/30/opinion/trump-racism-white-supremacy.html

45. Ibid. Peter Baker and Eileen Sullivan.

46. Ibid. Ashley Parker and John Wagner.

47. Terry Gross, "Megyn Kelly on Trump and the Media: 'We're in a Dangerous Phase Right Now,'" *Fresh Air* (December 7, 2016). Accessed February 20, 2018: www.npr.org/2016/12/07/504622630/megyn-kelly-on-trump-and-the-media-were-in-a-dangerous-phase-right-now. See Chris Hedge's informative commentary on this interview at Chris Hedges, "Demagogue-in-Chief," *TruthDig* (December 11, 2016). Accessed February 20, 2018: www.truthdig.com/report/item/demagogue-in-chief_20161211

48. Angela Nagle, *Kill All Normies: Online Culture Wars from 4chan and Tumblr to Trump and the Alt-Right* (London: Zero Books, 2017).

49. Frank Rich, "Don't Be Fooled: Donald Trump Will Never Walk Away From His Businesses," *New York Magazine* (November 30, 2016). Accessed February 20, 2018: nymag.com/daily/intelligencer/2016/11/donald-trump-will-never-walk-away-from-his-businesses.html

50. Ibid.

51. John Nichols, "Wilbur Ross Is a Disgrace to Himself and His Country," *The Nation* (May 23, 2017). Accessed February 20, 2018: www.thenation.com/article/wilbur-ross-disgrace-country/

52. Ibid. Nichols.

53. Will Worley, "Saudi Arabia to Behead Disabled Man 'For Taking Part in Protests' after 'Forced Confession," *The Independent* (May 26, 2017). Accessed February 20, 2018: www.independent.co.uk/news/world/mid-dle-east/saudi-arabia-behead-disabled-man-munir-adam-protests-forced-confession-torture-death-sentence-court-a7758041.html

54. Amy Goodman, "Retired Police Detective: Trump's Comments Endorsing Police Brutality are 'Treasonous'," *Democracy Now!* (July 31, 2017). Accessed February 20, 2018: www.democracynow.org/2017/7/31/retired_police_detective_trumps_comments_endorsing?utm_source=Democracy+Now%21&utm_campaign=2d339108f9-Daily_Digest&utm_medium=email&utm_term=0_fa2346a853-2d339108f9-190213053

55. Ibid.

56. For two excellent sources analyzing both police violence and the extortion imposed on poor Blacks, see Keenaga-Yamahtta Taylor, "The Double Standard of Justice," *From #BlackLivesMatter to Black Liberation* (Chicago: Haymarket, 2016) and Truthout Collective, *Who Do You Serve, Who Do You Protect?* (Chicago: Haymarket, 2016).

CHAPTER SEVEN

1. Editorial Board, "The Hate He Dares Not Speak Of," *New York Times* (August 13, 2017). Accessed February 20, 2018: www.nytimes.com/2017/08/13/opinion/trump-charlottesville-hate-stormer.html?ref=opinion&_r=0

2. Jelani Cobb, "The Battle of Charlottesville," *The New Yorker* (August 13, 2017). Accessed February 20, 2018: www.newyorker.com/news/daily-comment/the-battle-of-charlottesville?mbid=nl_TNY%20Template%20-%20With%20Photo%20(198)&CNDID=42733863&sp-MailingID=11688178&spUserID=MTM4NzE1OTE4N-jE5S0&spJobID=1221185809&spReportId=MTIyMTE4NTgwOQS2

3. Glenn Thrush, "New Outcry as Trump Rebukes Charlottesville Racists 2 Days Later," *New York Times* (August 14, 2017). Accessed February 27, 2018: www.nytimes.com/2017/08/14/us/politics/trump-charlottesville-protest.html?hp&action=click&pgtype=Homepage&clickSource=story-heading&module=a-lede-package-region&region=top-news&WT.nav=top-news

4. Michael D. Shear and Maggie Habermanaug, "Trump Defends Initial Remarks on Charlottesville; Again Blames 'Both Sides,'" *New York Times* (August 15, 2017). Accessed February 20, 2018: www.nytimes.com/2017/08/15/us/politics/trump-press-conference-charlottesville.html?hp&action=click&pgtype=Homepage&clickSource=story-heading&module=a-lede-package-region&region=top-news&WT.nav=top-news&_r=0

5. Jeffrey St Clair, "To See or to Nazi: Trump's Moral Blindspot is America's" *CounterPunch* (August 18, 2017). Accessed February 20, 2018: www.counterpunch.org/2017/08/18/to-see-or-to-nazi-trumps-moral-blindspot-is-americas/

6. Adam Shatz, "Trump set them free." *London Review of Books* (August

15, 2017). Accessed February 20, 2018: www.lrb.co.uk/blog/2017/08/15/adam-shatz/trump-set-them-free/

7. Adam Goldman, "Trump Reverses Restrictions on Military Hardware for Police," *New York Times* (August 28, 2017). Accessed February 20, 2018: www.nytimes.com/2017/08/28/us/politics/trump-police-military-surplus-equipment.html?mcubz=3&_r=0

8. Marjorie Cohn, "Trump's Arpaio Pardon Signals to White Supremacists: 'I've Got Your Back.'" *Truth Dig* (August 28, 2017). Accessed February 20, 2018: www.truth-out.org/news/item/41753-trump-s-arpaio-pardon-signals-to-white-supremacists-i-ve-got-your-back

9. Jake Johnson, "Since Trump's Election, 20 States Have Moved to Criminalize Dissent." *CommonDreams* (June 20, 2017), accessed February 20, 2018: www.commondreams.org/news/2017/06/20/trumps-election-20-states-have-moved-criminalize-dissent; Ariel Malka and Yphtach Lelkes, "In a new poll, half of Republicans say they would support postponing the 2020 election if Trump proposed it," *Washington Post* (August 10, 2017), accessed February 20, 2018: www.washingtonpost.com/news/monkey-cage/wp/2017/08/10/in-a-new-poll-half-of-republicans-say-they-would-support-postponing-the-2020-election-if-trump-proposed-it/?utm_term=.72f-915936b5c

10. Juan González, "On Tyranny: Yale Historian Timothy Snyder on How the U.S. Can Avoid Sliding into Authoritarianism," *Democracy Now!* (May 30, 2017). Accessed February 20, 2018: www.democracynow.org/2017/5/30/on_tyranny_yale_historian_timothy_snyder

11. Antonio Gramsci, *Prison Notebooks*, ed. & trans. Quintin Hoare & Geoffrey Nowell Smith (New York: International Publishers, 1971), p. 275–76.

12. See, for instance, James K. Galbraith, *Welcome to the Poisoned Chalice: The Destruction of Greece and the Future of Europe* (New Haven, CT: Yale University Press, 2016).

13. Zygmunt Bauman, "Symptoms in search of an object and name," *The Great Regression*, ed. Heinrich Geiselberger (Cambridge, UK: Polity Press, 2017), pp. 13, 25.

14. Ibid., p. 14.

15. "Full text of Viktor Orbán's speech at Bile Tusnad (Tusnádfürd) of 26 July 2014," *The Budapest Beacon* (July 29, 2014). Accessed February 20, 2018: budapestbeacon.com/public-policy/full-text-of-viktor-orbans-speech-at-baile-tusnad-tusnadfurdo-of-26-july-2014/10592

16. Pankaj Mishra, "Politics in the age of resentment: the dark legacy of the Enlightenment," in *The Great Regression*, ed. Heinrich Geiselberger (Cambridge, UK: Polity Press, 2017), p. 105.

17. Heinrich Geiselberger, ed., *The Great Regression* (London: Polity Press, 2017).

18. Arjun Appadurai, "Democracy Fatigue," in Heinrich Geiselberger, ed., *The Great Regression* (London: Polity Press, 2017), pp. 1–2.

19. Paul Mason, "Trump could be out of office within a year—but the US's problems would be just beginning," *The Guardian* (August 7, 2017). Accessed February 20, 2018: www.theguardian.com/commentisfree/2017/aug/07/trump-out-in-year-usa-problems-just-beginning-paul-mason?CMP=fb_gu

20. See, for instance, his attack on affirmative action in favor of White nationalist views of themselves as aggrieved victims of racist discrimination. Christopher Ingraham, "White Trump voters think they face more discrimination than blacks. The Trump administration is listening," *Washington Post* (August 2, 2017). Accessed February 20, 2018: www.washingtonpost.com/news/wonk/wp/2017/08/02/white-trump-voters-think-they-face-more-discrimination-than-blacks-the-trump-administration-is-listening/?utm_term=.614098d6ef86

21. Carol Anderson, "The Politics of White Resentment," *New York Times* (August 5, 2017). Accessed February 20, 2018: www.nytimes.com/2017/08/05/opinion/sunday/white-resentment-affirmative-action.html?_r=0

22. Arjun Appadurai, "Democracy Fatigue," in Heinrich Geiselberger, ed., *The Great Regression* (London: Polity Press, 2017), pp. 8–9.

23. Mike Lofgren, "Maybe This Is How Democracy Ends." *AlterNet* (January 11, 2017). Accessed February 20, 2018: www.alternet.org/election-2016/how-democracy-ends

24. Jessical Silver-Greenberg, "Consumer Bureau Loses Fight to Allow More Class-Action Suit," *New York Times*, October 25, 2017. Accessed February 20, 2018: www.nytimes.com/2017/10/24/business/senate-vote-wall-street-regulation.html?rref=collection%2Fbyline%2Fjessica-silver-greenberg&action=click&contentCollection=undefined&region=stream&module=stream_unit&version=latest&contentPlacement=2&pgtype=collection

25. John Nichols, "Trump's Base of Support is Collapsing," *The Nation* (August 4, 2017). Accessed February 20, 2018: www.thenation.com/article/trumps-base-of-support-has-almost-entirely-collapsed/

26. David Horowitz, *The Art of Political War for Tea Parties* (Dallas, TX: Spence Publishing, 2000).

27. The Data Team, "Daily Chart Attitudes Towards the Mainstream Media Take an Unconstitutional Turn," *The Economist* (Au-

gust 2017). Accessed February 20, 2018: www.economist.com/blogs/graphicdetail/2017/08/daily-chart-0

28. Ariel Malka and Yphtach Lelkes, "In a new poll, half of Republicans say they would support postponing the 2020 election if Trump proposed it," *Washington Post* (August 10, 2017). Accessed February 20, 2018: www.washingtonpost.com/news/monkey-cage/wp/2017/08/10/in-a-new-poll-half-of-republicans-say-they-would-support-postponing-the-2020-election-if-trump-proposed-it/?utm_term=.dd228da2cd10

29. Bess Levin, "Mike Pence Spent Nearly $250,000 to Walk Out of a Football Game," *Vanity Fair* (October 9, 2017). Accessed February 20, 2018: www.vanityfair.com/news/2017/10/mike-pence-colts-game

CHAPTER EIGHT

1. David Broder, "Being Anti-Trump Isn't Enough," *Jacobin*, No. 24 (Winter 2017). Accessed February 20, 2018: www.jacobinmag.com/2017/02/being-anti-trump-isnt-enough

2. For an informative analysis of the merging of neoliberalism and right-wing populism, see Wendy Brown, "Apocalyptic Populism," *Eurozine* (September 5, 2017). Accessed February 20, 2018: www.eurozine.com/apocalyptic-populism/

3. Nancy Fraser, "Progressive neoliberalism versus reactionary populism: a Hobson's choice," *The Great Regression*, ed. Heinrich Geiselberger (Cambridge, UK: Polity Press, 2017), pp. 41–42.

4. David Graeber, *The Democracy Project: A History, A Crisis, A Movement* (New York: Random House, 2013), pp. 281–282.

5. Chris Hedges, "Donald Trump's Greatest Allies Are the Liberal Elites," *Truthdig* (March 7, 2017). Accessed February 20, 2018: www.truthdig.com/report/item/donald_trumps_greatest_allies_are_the_liberal_elites_20170305

6. Katie Anders, "Have Democrats lost 900 seats in state legislatures since Obama has been president?" *Punditfact* (January 25, 2015). Accessed February 20, 2018: www.politifact.com/punditfact/statements/2015/jan/25/cokie-roberts/have-democrats-lost-900-seats-state-legislatures-o/

7. See, for instance, Chuck Schumer, "A Better Deal for American Workers," *New York Times* (July 24, 2017). Accessed February 20, 2018: www.nytimes.com/2017/07/24/opinion/chuck-schumer-employment-democrats.html?_r=0

8. Anthony DiMaggio, "'A Better Deal'? Dissecting the Democrats' 'Populist' Turn in Rhetoric and Reality," *CounterPunch* (July 28, 2017). Accessed February 20, 2018: www.counterpunch.org/2017/07/28/a-better-deal-dissecting-the-democrats-populist-turn-in-rhetoric-and-reality/

9. Eric Cheyfitz, "A 'Better Deal' for American Workers?" *Counter-Punch* (August 1, 2017). Accessed February 20, 2018: www.counterpunch. org/2017/08/01/a-better-deal-for-american-workers/

10. Andrew J. Bacevich, "Slouching Toward Mar-a-Lago: The Post-Cold-War Consensus Collapses Tuesday," *Truthout* (August 08, 2017). Accessed February 20, 2018: www.truth-out.org/opinion/item/41541-slouch-ing-toward-mar-a-lago-the-post-cold-war-consensus-collapses

11. Mark Penn and Andrew Stein, "Back to the Center, Democrats." *New York Times* (July 6, 2017). Accessed February 20, 2018: www.nytimes. com/2017/07/06/opinion/center-democrats-identity-politics.html?_r=0

12. Ibid. Mark Penn and Andrew Stein.

13. Leonard Steinhorn, "How Did Democrats Be-come the Party of Elites?" *Bill Moyers and Company* (July 12, 2017). Accessed February 20, 2018: billmoyers.com/story/ how-did-democrats-become-the-party-of-elites/

14. Jonathan Chait, "How 'Neoliberalism' Became the Left's Favorite Insult of Liberals," *New York Magazine* (July 16, 2017). Accessed February 20, 2018: nymag.com/daily/intelligencer/2017/07/how-neoliberalism-be-came-the-lefts-favorite-insult.html. This position has been definitively criticized in Thomas Frank, *Listen, Liberal: Or, What Ever Happened to the Party of the People?* (New York: Picador, 2017).

15. Leah Hunt-Hendrix, "The Wrong Way to Rebuild the Dem-ocratic Party," *Politico Magazine* (February 24, 2017). Accessed February 20, 2018: www.politico.com/magazine/story/2017/02/ democrats-progressives-new-leaders-david-brock-third-way-214811

16. For a rebuttal of Chait's argument, see Mike Kon-czal, "'Neoliberalism' isn't an empty epithet. It's a real, pow-erful set of ideas," *Vox* (July 18, 2017). Accessed February 20, 2018: www.vox.com/the-big-idea/2017/7/18/15992226/ neoliberalism-chait-austerity-democratic-party-sanders-clinton

17. See, for instance, Thomas Frank, "How Dems Created 'Liberalism of the Rich.'" *Bill Moyers and Company* (March 29, 2016). Accessed February 20, 2018: billmoyers.com/story/the-blue-state-model/

18. Ian Swanson, "Obama says he'd be seen as moderate Republican in the 1980s," *The Hill* (December 14, 2012). Accessed February 20, 2018: thehill.com/policy/finance/272957-obama-says-his-economic-policies-so-mainstream-hed-be-seen-as-moderate-republican-in-1980s

19. Ibid., Jonathan Chait, "How 'Neoliberalism' Became the Left's Favorite Insult of Liberals."

20. Ibid.

21. Michael Corcoran, "Thousands of Bernies? Progressive Groups

Aim to Build a Majority From the Bottom Up," *Truthout* (August 6, 2017). Accessed February 20, 2018: www.truth-out.org/news/item/41518-thousands-of-bernies-progressive-groups-aim-to-build-a-majority-from-the-bottom-up

22. See, for instance, Les Leopold, "6 Reasons Why Resisting Trump Is Not Enough: Here's How We Might Be Able to Save Our Democracy," *AlterNet* (January 1, 2017). Accessed February 20, 2018: www.alternet.org/election-2016/challenge-our-hands-save-democracy-lot-bigger-trump

23. Nancy Fraser, "Progressive neoliberalism versus reactionary populism: a Hobson's choice," *The Great Regression*, ed. Heinrich Geiselberger. (Cambridge, UK: Polity Press, 2017), p. 46.

24. Ibid. Fraser, p. 44.

25. Michelle Alexander, Naomi Klein and Keeanga-Yamahtta Taylor, "Trying to Build in the Rubble of Neoliberalism" *TruthOut* (July 6, 2017). Accessed February 20, 2018: www.truth-out.org/opinion/item/41175-trying-to-build-in-the-rubble-of-neoliberalism-michelle-alexander-and-naomi-klein-on-bringing-movements-together-in-the-trump-era

26. Rabbi Michael Lerner, "Overcoming Trump-ism: A New Strategy for Progressives," *Tikkun Magazine*, Vol. 32, No. 1 (Winter 2017). Accessed February 20, 2018: www.tikkun.org/nextgen/overcoming-trump-ism-a-new-strategy-for-progressives

27. Zygmunt Bauman and Leonidas Donskis. *Liquid Evil* (Cambridge,: Polity Press, 2016), p. 88

28. William J. Barber, II, "We are witnessing the birth pangs of a Third Reconstruction: We need a moral movement to create change," *Think Progress* (December 15, 2016). Accessed February 20, 2018: thinkprogress.org/rev-barber-moral-change-1ad2776df7c#.4h0jv9rzt

29. David Harvey, "Neoliberalism Is a Political Project," *Jacobin* (July 23, 2016). Accessed February 20, 2018: www.jacobinmag.com/2016/07/david-harvey-neoliberalism-capitalism-labor-crisis-resistance/

30. Katrina Forrester, "Libidinal Politics," *Harper's Magazine* (February 2017). Accessed February 20, 2018: harpers.org/archive/2017/02/trump-a-resisters-guide/5/

31. For a brilliant analysis of the merging of identity politics and a broader struggle for a radical democracy, see Robin D.G. Kelley, "After Trump," *Boston Review* (November 15, 2016), accessed February 20, 2018: bostonreview.net/forum/after-trump/robin-d-g-kelley-trump-says-go-back-we-say-fight-back; Robin D.G. Kelley, "Births of a Nation," *Boston Review* (March 6, 2017), accessed February 20, 2018: bostonreview.net/race-politics/robin-d-g-kelley-births-nation

CHAPTER NIINE

1. Rev. Martin Luther King Jr., "Beyond Vietnam: A Time to Break Silence," *American Rhetoric*, n.d. Accessed February 27, 2018: www.americanrhetoric.com/speeches/mlkatimetobreaksilence.htm

2. Bobby Seale, *Power to the People: The World of the Black Panthers* (New York: Harry N. Abrams Publisher, 2016); Joshua Bloom and Waldo E. Martin Jr., *Black against Empire: The History and Politics of the Black Panther Party* (Berkeley: University of California Press, 2016).

3. Keenaga-Yamahtta Taylor, "The Double Standard of Justice," *From #BlackLivesMatter to Black Liberation* (Chicago: Haymarket, 2016).

4. See, for instance, Joan Pedro-Carañana and Simona Rentea, "Glimpse into a Key Party Debate: Deciding the Future of Podemos," *Open Democracy* (February 5, 2017). Accessed February 27, 2018: www.opendemocracy.net/can-europe-make-it/joan-pedro-cara-ana-simona-rentea/glimpse-into-key-party-debate-deciding-future-o

5. Lacino Hamilton, "This Is Going to Hurt," *The New Inquiry* (April 12, 2017). Accessed February 27, 2018: thenewinquiry.com/this-is-going-to-hurt/

6. Les Leopold, "Wanted: A Massive Education, Organizing Drive and Progressive Vision to Vanquish Trump," *CommonDreams* (June 3, 2017). Accessed February 27, 2018: www.commondreams.org/views/2017/06/03/wanted-massive-education-organizing-drive-and-progressive-vision-vanquish-trump

7. See, for instance, Dr. Martin Luther King Jr., *Where Do We Go from Here: Chaos or Community?* (New York: King Legacy, 2010); John J. Ansbro, Martin Luther King Jr.: *Nonviolent Strategies and Tactics for Social Change* (New York: Madison Books, 2000); Vaclav Havel, et al., *The Power of the Powerless* (New York: Routledge, 1985); Joshua Bloom and Waldo E. Martin Jr., *Black against Empire: The History and Politics of the Black Panther Party* (Berkeley: University of California Press, 2016); Gene Sharp, *From Dictatorship to Democracy* (New York: The New Press, 2012).

8. One commentary on this issue can be found in Ira Chermus, "Trump, a Symptom of What? A Radical Message from a Half-Century Ago," *Truthout* (April 17, 2017). Accessed February 27, 2018: www.truthout.org/opinion/item/40239-trump-a-symptom-of-what-a-radical-message-from-a-half-century-ago

9. Gregg LaGambina interviews Javier Marías, "The World Is Never Just Politics: A Conversation with Javier Marías," *Los Angeles Review of Books* (February 9, 2017). Accessed February 27, 2018: lareviewofbooks.org/article/conversation-javier-marias/

10. On DeVos's incompetence and racist understanding of history, see

Anthony DiMaggio, "DeVos and the 'Free Lunch' Flimflam: Orwell, Neo-feudalism, and the Destruction of the Welfare State," *CounterPunch* (March 7, 2017). Accessed February 27, 2018: www.counterpunch.org/2017/03/07/devos-and-the-free-lunch-flimflam-orwell-neofeudalism-and-the-destruction-of-the-welfare-state/

11. Jelani Cobb, "Ben Carson, Donald Trump, and the Misuse of American History," *The New Yorker* (March 8, 2017). Accessed February 27, 2018: www.newyorker.com/news/daily-comment/ben-carson-donald-trump-and-the-misuse-of-american-history

12. Ibid.

13. Paul Gilroy, *Against Race: Imagining Political Culture beyond the Color Line* (Cambridge: The Belknap Press of Harvard University Press, 2000), pp. 145–146.

14. João Biehl, *Vita: Life in a Zone of Social Abandonment* (Los Angeles: University of California Press, 2005), p. 10.

15. Cited in Hélène Cixous and Catherine Clément, *The Newly Born Woman*, trans. Betsy Wing, Theory and History of Literature Series, Volume 24 (Minneapolis: University of Minnesota Press, 1986), p. ix.

16. Samantha Rose Hill, "American Politics and the Crystallization of Totalitarian Practices," *Medium* (December 16, 2016). Accessed February 27, 2018: medium.com/quote-of-the-week/american-politics-and-the-crystallization-of-totalitarian-practices-464e1f02f514#.fyuncour9

17. Jeffrey St. Clair, "Fools on the Hill: Trump and Congress," *CounterPunch* (March 3, 2017). Accessed February 27, 2018: www.counterpunch.org/2017/03/03/fools-on-the-hill-trump-and-congress/

18. The classic commentary on politics as show business can be found in Neil Postman, *Amusing Ourselves to Death: Public Discourse in the Age of Show Business* (New York: Penguin Books, 1985, 2005).

19. Robin D.G. Kelley, "After Trump," *Boston Review* (November 15, 2016). Accessed February 27, 2018: bostonreview.net/forum/after-trump/robin-d-g-kelley-trump-says-go-back-we-say-fight-back

20. Ballotpedia, "State Legislatures Project" (January 2018). Accessed February 27, 2018: ballotpedia.org/State_legislative_special_elections,_2017

21. Michael Lerner, *The Left Hand of God: Taking Back our Country from the Religious Right* (New York: HarperOne, 2007).

22. On this issue, see "Introduction," in Peter A. Hall and Michele Lamont, eds., *Successful Societies: How Institutions and Culture affect Health* (New York: Cambridge University Press, 2009), pp. 1–22.

23. Jennifer Silva, *Coming Up Short: Working-Class Adulthood in an Age of Uncertainty* (New York: Oxford University Press, 2013), p. 16.

24. This issue is taken up in great detail in Michael Lerner, "Over-

coming Trump-ism: A New Strategy for Progressives," *Tikkun* (January 31, 2017). Accessed February 27, 2018: www.tikkun.org/nextgen/overcoming-trump-ism-a-new-strategy-for-progressives.

25. Lerner, "Overcoming Trump-ism"

CONCLUSION

1. Some of the more recent books on resistance include: Timothy Snyder, *On Tyranny: Twenty Lessons* (New York: Tim Duggan Books, 2017); Charles Derber, *Welcome to the Revolution: Universalizing Resistance for Social Justice and Democracy in Perilous Times* (New York: Routledge, 2017); Henry A. Giroux, *The Public in Peril: Trump and the Menace of American Authoritarianism* (New York: Routledge, 2017); Naomi Klein, *No Is Not Enough: Resisting Trump's Shock Politics and Winning the World We Need* (Chicago: Haymarket Press, 2017); Bill Ayers, *Demand the Impossible!: A Radical Manifesto* (Chicago: Haymarket Press, 2016); Keeanga-Yamahtta Taylor, *From #BlackLivesMatter to Black Liberation* (Chicago: Haymarket Press, 2016).

2. Judith Shulevitz, "Year One: Resistance Research," *The New York Review of Books* (November 9, 2017). Accessed February 27, 2018: www.nybooks.com/daily/2017/11/09/year-one-resistance-research/

3. Brad Evans, "Humans in Dark Times," *New York Times* (February 23, 2017). Accessed February 27, 2018: www.nytimes.com/2017/02/23/opinion/humans-in-dark-times.html

4. Jon Wells, "Steeltown Sanctuary: Hamilton Is among the Few 'Sanctuary Cities' in Canada," *The Hamilton Spectator* (February 24, 2017). Accessed February 27, 2018: www.thespec.com/news-story/7158445-steeltown-sanctuary-hamilton-is-among-the-few-sanctuary-cities-in-canada/

5. Brit McCandless, "Seeking sanctuary in the face of deportation," *CBSNews.com* (May 21, 2017). Accessed February 27, 2018: www.cbsnews.com/news/seeking-sanctuary-in-the-face-of-deportation/

6. Theo Anderson, "Cities Go Rogue Against Trump and the Radical Right," *In These Times* (February 23, 2016). Accessed February 27, 2018: inthesetimes.com/article/19895/sanctuary-cities-resistance-trump

7. See, for instance, David Rosen, "Popular Insurgencies: Reshaping the Political Landscape," *CounterPunch* (March 21, 2017). Accessed February 27, 2018: www.counterpunch.org/2017/03/21/popular-insurgencies-reshaping-the-political-landscape/. For an important liberal analysis of the rise in power of cities to challenge the excesses of neoliberal capitalism, see Benjamin J. Barber, *If Mayors Ruled the World: Dysfunctional Nations, Rising Cities* (New Haven, CT: Yale University Press, 2014).

8. Cited in Ibid. Theo Anderson, "Cities Go Rogue Against Trump and the Radical Right."

9. Allen Colbern, "Sanctuaries for 'Illegals' have historically been good for American Democracy," *Politics of Color* (September 21, 2015). Accessed February 27, 2018: politicsofcolor.com/sanctuaries-for-illegals-have-histori-cally-been-good-for-american-democracy/

10. Václav Benda. "The Parallel 'Polis,'" in *Civic Freedom in Central Europe: Voices from Czechoslovakia* (Palgrave Macmillan, 1991: Cambridge, UK), pp 35–41.

11. See Barbara Falk, "Between past and future," *Eurozine* (May 26, 2011). Accessed February 27, 2018: www.eurozine.com/between-past-and-future/

12. The Shutdown Collective, "To Halt the Slide into Authoritarianism, We Need a General Strike," *Truthout* (February 11, 2017). Accessed February 27, 2018: www.truth-out.org/news/item/39449-to-halt-the-slide-into-authoritarianism-we-need-a-general-strike

13. Salvador Hernandez and Adolfo Flores, "Churches Are Readying Homes and Underground Railroads to Hide Immigrants from Deportation under Trump," *BuzzFeed News* (February 25, 2017). Accessed February 27, 2018: www.buzzfeed.com/salvadorhernandez/sanctuary-church-es-v-trump-deportation-mandate?utm_term=.ouDAy5Rgq#.dvbXM8Dzb

14. Theo Anderson, "How the Left's Long March Back Will Begin in the States," *In These Times* (February 6, 2017), accessed February 27, 2018: inthesetimes.com/article/19867/how-the-lefts-long-march-back-will-begin-in-the-states; Katie Klabusich, "States and Cities Push Back on Reproductive Health Attacks Saturday," *Truthout* (March 04, 2017), accessed February 27, 2018: www.truth-out.org/news/item/39710-states-and-cities-push-back-on-reproductive-health-attacks

15. Juan González, "Immigrants Fighting for Sanctuary Cities and Campuses to Protect Millions from Trump Deportation Push," *Democracy Now!* (November 22, 2016). Accessed February 27, 2018: www.democracynow.org/2016/11/22/immigrants_lead_push_for_sanctuary_cities

16. Sara M. Evans and Harry C. Boyte, *Free Spaces: The Sources of Democratic Change in America* (New York: Harper and Row, 1986). See also Harry C. Boyte, "Free Spaces Can Help Us Fight Trumpism," *The Nation* (December 5, 2016). Accessed February 27, 2018: www.thenation.com/ar-ticle/free-spaces-can-help-us-fight-trumpism/. Also, see Francesca Polletta, "'Free Spaces' in Collective Action," *Theory and Society* Vol. 38. (1999), pp. 1–38.

17. Robin D.G. Kelley, "Black Study, Black Struggle," *Boston Review* (March 7, 2016). Accessed February 27, 2018: bostonreview.net/forum/robin-d-g-kelley-black-study-black-struggle

18. Ibid. Timothy Snyder, *On Tyranny*.

19. On Lerner's Global Marshall Plan, see: Rabbi Michael Lerner, Benedictine Sister Joan Chittister, and Cornel West, "The Global Marshall Plan," (Berkley: Network of Spiritual Progressives, 3107), accessed February 27, 2018: www.spiritualprogressives.org/wp-content/uploads/2017/01/Global-Marshall-Plan-1.pdf; also, see Rabbi Michael Lerner, "Overcoming Trump-ism: A New Strategy for Progressives," *Tikkun* (Winter 2017), accessed February 27, 2018: www.tikkun.org/nextgen/overcoming-trump-ism-a-new-strategy-for-progressives.

20. George Lakoff, "Ten Points for Democracy Activists," *George Lakoff Blog* (February 10, 2017). Accessed February 27, 2018: georgelakoff.com/2017/02/10/ten-points-for-democracy-activists/

21. Bill Quigley, "Ten Examples of Direct Resistance to Stop Government Raids," *CounterPunch* (February 22, 2017). Accessed February 27, 2018: www.commondreams.org/views/2017/02/22/ten-examples-direct-resistance-stop-government-raids

22. William J. Barber, II, "We are witnessing the birth pangs of a Third Reconstruction: We need a moral movement to create change," *Think Progress* (December 15, 2016), accessed February 27, 2018: thinkprogress.org/rev-barber-moral-change-1ad2776df7c#.4h0jv9rzt; Laurie Goodstein, "Religious Liberals Sat Out of Politics for 40 Years. Now They Want in the Game," *New York Times* (June 10, 2017), accessed February 27, 2018: www.nytimes.com/2017/06/10/us/politics/politics-religion-liberal-william-barber.html?_r=0

23. Theo Anderson, "How the Left's Long March back will begin in the States," *In These times* (February 6, 2017). Accessed February 27, 2018: inthesetimes.com/article/19867/how-the-lefts-long-march-back-will-begin-in-the-states

24. See, for instance, the brilliant: Robin D.G. Kelley, "Black Study, Black Struggle," *Boston Review* (March 7, 2016). Accessed February 27, 2018: bostonreview.net/forum/robin-d-g-kelley-black-study-black-struggle

25. Forum, "Trump: A Resister's Guide," *Harper's Magazine* (February 2017). Accessed February 27, 2018: harpers.org/archive/2017/02/trump-a-resisters-guide/

26. See, for instance, Henry A. Giroux, *Neoliberalism's War on Higher Education* (Chicago: Haymarket, 2014); Henry Heller, *The Capitalist University* (London: Pluto Press, 2016).

27. See, for instance, ibid., Henry A. Giroux.

28. Harvey J. Kaye, "Who Says It Can't Happen Here?" *Bill Moyers* (February 27, 2017). Accessed February 27, 2018: billmoyers.com/story/says-cant-happen/

29. Chris Hedges, "Donald Trump's Greatest Al-

lies Are the Liberal Elites," *Truthdig* (March 7, 2017). Accessed February 27, 2018: www.truthdig.com/report/item/donald_trumps_greatest_allies_are_the_liberal_elites_20170305

30. Stanley Aronowitz, "Where Is the Outrage?" *Situations* 5:2 (2014), p. 33.

31. Charles Derber, private correspondence with the author, January 29, 2014.

32. Chris Hedges, "Make America Ungovernable," *Truthdig* (February 6, 2017). Accessed February 27, 2018: www.truthdig.com/report/item/make_america_ungovernable_20170205

33. Chris Mooney and Juliet Eilperin, "Trump Transition Says Request for Names of Climate Scientists Was 'Not Authorized,'" *Washington Post* (December 14, 2016). Accessed February 27, 2018: www.washingtonpost.com/news/energy-environment/wp/2016/12/14/trump-transition-says-request-for-names-of-climate-scientists-was-not-authorized/?utm_term=.76189cb20ebe

34. See, for instance Charles Derber, *Welcome to the Revolution: Universalizing Resistance for Social Justice and Democracy in Perilous Times* (New York: Routledge, 2017).

35. Dana Nuccitelli, "This Is Not Normal—Climate Researchers Take to the Streets to Protect Science," *The Guardian* (December 16, 2016). Accessed February 27, 2018: www.theguardian.com/environment/climate-consensus-97-per-cent/2016/dec/16/this-is-not-normal-climate-research-ers-take-to-the-streets-to-protect-science

36. See Rabbi Michael Lerner, "Overcoming Trump-ism: A New Strategy for Progressives," *Tikkun* (Winter 2017), pp. 4–9; Rabbi Michael Lerner, "Yearning for a World of Love and Justice: An Introduction to the Ideas of *Tikkun* and the Network of Spiritual Progressives (NSP)," *Tikkun* (April 30, 2015). Accessed February 27, 2018: www.tikkun.org/nextgen/yearning-for-a-world-of-love-and-justice-the-worldview-of-tikkun-and-our-network-of-spiritual-progressives

37. Frederick Douglass, "The Meaning of July Fourth for the Negro," *History as a Weapon* (speech given at Rochester, New York, July 5, 1852). Accessed February 27, 2018: www.historyisaweapon.com/defcon1/douglass-july4.html

INDEX

ACKNOWLEDGMENTS

Susan Searls Giroux provided invaluable support and help throughout the writing of this manuscript. Her creativity and insights appear throughout this book and for that I am enormously grateful. Maya Sabados, my assistant, was an invaluable resource in helping me gather the research, edit the work, and think through a number of drafts. I am particularly grateful to Alana Price, Maya Schenwar, and Britney Schultz, who have continually supported my writing at *Truthout* where ideas for some of the chapters in this book first appeared. Their commentaries and editing always improved my work. I am also grateful to Emma Niles at *Truthdig* and Jeffrey St. Clair at *Counterpunch*, who have given me an opportunity to publish my work. I am both fortunate and grateful for being able to work with City Lights, and with Greg Ruggiero, my editor, who graciously believes in and supports my work and is the best editor with whom I have ever worked. My students at McMaster have always been a source of inspiration for me and I am grateful for being able to work with them. I am enormously grateful to Vivian Lewis, the McMaster University Librarian, for her support and the pleasure of being able to work with and learn from her. I am also grateful for the institutional support provided by my dean, Ken Cruikshank. I am very fortunate to have been able to work at McMaster University since 2004. The upper levels of administration have provided me with encouragement and invaluable support in allowing me to do my work. I am grateful for my long relationship with Zygmunt Bauman, who read much of this manuscript before he died. He was a giant among intellectuals. I will miss him. George Yancy is a new friend and a brilliant writer. I am honored that he agreed to write the foreword for this book.

ABOUT THE AUTHOR

Henry A. Giroux is a world-renowned educator, author, and public intellectual. He currently holds the Professorship for Scholarship in the Public Interest and The Paulo Freire Distinguished Scholar Chair in Critical Pedagogy. His most recent books include *The Violence of Organized Forgetting* (City Lights, 2014); *Neoliberalism's War on Higher Education* (Haymarket, 2014); *Disposable Futures* (City Lights, 2015); *Dangerous Thinking* (Routledge, 2015); *America's Addiction to Terrorism* (Monthly Review Press, 2016), and *America at War with Itself* (City Lights, 2017). A prolific writer and political commentator, he has appeared in a wide range of media, including *Truthout*, *Salon*, *CounterPunch*, the *New York Times* and *Bill Moyers & Company*. He currently lives in Hamilton, Ontario, Canada, with his wife, Dr. Susan Searls Giroux.